The
Trillion Dollar Enterprise

The Trillion-Dollar Enterprise

**How the Alliance Revolution
Will Transform Global Business**

Cyrus Freidheim

PERSEUS BOOKS

Reading, Massachusetts

ISBN 0-7382-0004-2

Library of Congress Catalog Card Number: 98–86416

Perseus Books is a member of the Perseus Books Group

Jacket design by Andrew Newman
Text design by Joyce C. Weston
Set in 11-point Sabon by Carlisle Communications, Inc.

1 2 3 4 5 6 7 8 9–DOH–0201009998
First printing, September 1998

Perseus Books are available at special discounts for bulk purchases in the U.S. by corporations, institutions, and other organizations. For more information, please contact the Special Markets Department at HarperCollins Publishers, 10 East 53rd Street, New York, NY 10022, or call 212-207-7528.

Find us on the World Wide Web at
http://www.aw.com/gb/

To Mitzi, Lynn, Stephen, and Scott

Contents

— ❖ —

Preface

HOW THIS CONCEPT CAME ABOUT: AN INTRODUCTION

A few years ago, at our Booz·Allen Advisory Board meeting in Paris, we were discussing how the global corporation would evolve over the next decade. It was clear that most companies had long been thinking in international terms, and we were trying to determine what their next steps should be.

In preparation for the meeting, Booz·Allen & Hamilton had done a lot of research. We had talked extensively to our clients and reviewed internal research projects on alliances and on the extended enterprise, which is a way of looking at a company and all its suppliers as one unit. As a result of this spade work, we thought we had a good idea of how companies should act during the coming decade in the increasingly competitive international arena. We presented our ideas—brilliantly, I thought.

THE LIGHT SWITCHED ON

We were wrong. Bob Galvin, chairman of Motorola, didn't hesitate to tell us so. "You're not asking the right questions," he said, after we gave our tentative conclusions. "And you are short-sighted." Galvin said in no uncertain terms that we should be thinking forty and fifty years out, not ten, and we should be asking how corporations can shape the environment in which they live and compete, not merely react to it.

"You should be thinking about what having trillion-dollar entities will mean."

The room fell hushed. Corporate titans such as Peter Wallenberg (who controls most of Sweden's industry), Dick Rosenberg (CEO of BankAmerica), Yoh Kurosawa (CEO of Industrial Bank of Japan), John Prescott (CEO of Broken Hill Proprietary Company), and the six Booz·Allen partners (myself among them, I'm afraid), felt spanked for our nearsightedness.

Larry Fuller, chairman of Amoco, saved us by asking, "Don't we have trillion-dollar enterprises today?" He went on to describe the network of alliances and relationships that take on the development and exploration of oil around the world. These independent companies act as a unit, or a single enterprise, as they undertake huge, multiyear, bet-the-ranch efforts. Frequently, the venture continues for decades. "If we add the combined sales of all the companies involved in such an exercise," Fuller said, "we must be approaching $1 trillion in total revenues. The management challenge far exceeds the running of 'mere' $50 billion corporations."

Fuller was right, of course. These new enterprises are becoming the rule, rather than the exception, as customers, suppliers, unrelated companies, and even competitors join together to accomplish big, expensive, and risky jobs in the oil industry as well as in telecommunications, aerospace, and elsewhere.

"Given this, trillion-dollar enterprises may very well become commonplace . . . and soon," Fuller said.

That brief interchange helped bring together trends, ideas, and research that we at Booz·Allen had been batting around for some time. We had realized that companies were struggling to deal with a business world that was irreversibly globalizing, just as nations were forming blocs and protecting their borders. The development of huge enterprises linking independent companies together was the solution developed by business—in the main unwittingly—to deal with these two incompatible forces.

We can see the results all around us. We are experiencing the turbulent consolidation of the global telecom industry into two or three giant networks of companies—one centered on British Telecom and AT&T (with partners Cie Generale des Eaux, Telefonica de España, and Mannesman AG) and the other with France Telecom and Deutsche Telekom (with Sprint). These are giant networks indeed, and each is adding new partners across the world.

We have watched the global aerospace industry head toward two competitive groups—Boeing and Airbus—each managed as a single enterprise that is developing and producing new commercial aircraft through a network of alliances. The merger of Boeing and McDonnell Douglas solidified the power of the Boeing group. Both Boeing and Airbus have over ten major, and one hundred smaller, partners in their respective enterprises.

What follows is a discussion of the way in which we believe trillion-dollar enterprises will develop and how they will affect corporations, the people who work for them, governments, and businesses that choose to remain independent.

THE TRILLION-DOLLAR ENTERPRISE STARTED HERE

I introduced the concept of the *trillion-dollar enterprise* in a speech at the World Economic Forum in Davos, Switzerland, in 1993. The audience reaction was divided into two camps: those who didn't believe the world would evolve this way, and those who thought I was a babbling academic. Neither was encouraging. Since then, the concept has been tested and molded through discussions with corporate executives worldwide, presented to forums for debate and critique, and exposed to wider audiences through several articles in the United States and abroad. Since then, the world has marched briskly in this direction.

Since the Davos meeting, the response from chief executives and senior managers has shifted from disbelief to concern about the impact these economic giants will have on people and nations. For example, the students and faculty of several Dutch universities reacted with outrage to my speech at their annual Veerstichting Conference, held in the magnificent thirteenth-century cathedral of Pieterskirk at the University of Leiden (a short carriage ride from Amsterdam). The conference is sponsored by the leading corporations in the Netherlands (e.g., Royal Dutch Shell, ABN, KLM, Unilever), with half the audience from the executive ranks of those corporations and half selected from the best in the Dutch universities. The annual conference is a dialogue between students and business on the big issues affecting their lives. The students at the conference appeared to be of one mind when it came to the possibility of trillion-dollar enterprises—kill the beast. "Giant commercial enterprises would again threaten to engulf the freedoms of people and nations." Shades of Servan

Schreiver's *American Challenge;* the trillion-dollar enterprise was seen as another form of U.S. imperialism invading Europe.

Questions such as "Will it happen?" and "Will we have trillion-dollar businesses?" have been replaced by "Are they good or bad?" and "What should we do to prepare for or prevent it?" Comments such as "This has nothing to do with me," which we heard just a couple of years ago, have given way to "How am I going to deal with this thing?"

STRUCTURE OF THE BOOK

This book is aimed at answering just that question: How am I going to deal with the evolution of networks of companies acting as huge, single, powerful enterprises?

The first section describes why consolidation, globalization, and nationalism lead naturally to the trillion-dollar enterprise and why the global corporation is disadvantaged in the competitive world of the future.

The sharp rise in alliances is the precursor to the trillion-dollar enterprise. Alliances are, on careful inspection, an attractive vehicle for expansion and consolidation. They can be very profitable and can avoid much of the baggage that comes with acquisitions.

This section describes the trillion-dollar enterprise and its evolution and lays the groundwork for understanding what the new world will be like. It ends with a discussion of which industries will be first in line to form *relationship* or trillion-dollar enterprises. The relationship enterprise and its giant offspring, the trillion-dollar enterprise, are networks of independent corporations from around the world, joined by alliances, that operate as a single entity against a common objective.

The message in the second section is: The world is changing and anyone (from independent entrepreneurs to CEOs of trillion-dollar enterprises) who plans to win in that world needs to understand the requirements for success and how to prepare themselves. This section explores in detail how these new economic giants will affect business leaders, directors, and managers at all levels. As part of this section, best practices are defined by how Booz·Allen's experience and research see them today and as we project them into the future.

Managers will need new leadership skills—such as arbitration, diplomacy, and compromise—to succeed in this new world. This section concludes with a chapter on governance, explaining what changes will be required of boards of directors in the era ahead.

The third section explores the trillion-dollar enterprise issue from a public policy perspective: Is the trillion-dollar enterprise good or bad? Two scenarios demonstrate how trillion-dollar enterprises might evolve into major players on the world scene with governments, unions, competitors, and world organizations. The section discusses the options available at various levels of government—national, regional, and global—to protect against the potential dark side of the trillion-dollar enterprise and what governments can do to foster the development of the trillion-dollar enterprise if they think it is a good thing. The potential power of a trillion-dollar enterprise to sidestep laws, create cartels, dominate industries, and overrun sovereign nations is great. Its size and economic power could easily translate into political power, but could also spur massive economic development. The possibility of a new form of cultural imperialism is clear, as consumers across the world buy and adapt to products, media, and entertainment from these global giants.

This book is intended to be a road map for future business managers and leaders and entrepreneurs as they take on the fresh challenges of the twenty-first century. Just as our ancestors confronted the challenges of the twentieth century one hundred years ago, we, too, face an uncertain future, but one with even greater opportunities.

The
Trillion-Dollar Enterprise

— ❖ —

Why the Trillion-Dollar Enterprise Is Inevitable

"Virtually every industry is consolidating," Paul O'Neill, CEO of ALCOA, said as we stood on the veranda of Skibo Castle in the highlands of Scotland. "While there will always be room for small, highly creative firms, there will be giants that rule the earth," he continued, as he sipped his Glenmorangie. "We haven't begun to understand their potential size and scope. They will be built by the same mix of vision and genius and risk taking that made Andrew Carnegie [in whose castle we were standing] the greatest tycoon of his age."

The giants he was talking about will be the product of acquisitions, joint ventures, alliances of all kinds. They will not be the conglomerates of the 1970s and '80s that attempted to gain stability by diversifying risk, spreading their investments over separate businesses. Rather, these new enterprises will focus all their resources on dominating one, or a few, fields. They will restructure whole industries, change their economics, and turn the basis of competition upside down. They will, collectively, have all the capabilities necessary to win in a tough, competitive, global marketplace.

In preceding decades, mergers and acquisitions have been the primary vehicles for this kind of consolidation. Today and into the next century, alliances will play a major role in the consolidation of industries, in part because of the shortcomings of the global corporation.

Consolidation on a global scale is very expensive, and often the global corporation must make major compromises in the selection of acquisition partners because of cost or national restrictions (e.g., on making purchases in the airlines, defense, and oil industries). Hence, many of the best prizes are simply unavailable. The relationship enterprise slides by these limitations and goes directly to the best in any country with an offer to form an alliance with its crown jewel; no size problems, no national restrictions, no antitrust, no funding limitations, just a strong relationship with the prime cut of the best company.

The relationship enterprise is a network of such alliances that operates as a single company in selected key areas. It is consolidation without huge investment, battles over ownership, postmerger headaches, and regrets. The investment dollars can go into building market positions, new products, capacity, and capabilities for the enterprise rather than for shares of an acquired company. The relationship enterprise is a natural evolution, a consequence of the political and economic forces of our times.

As consolidation through these networks of alliances occurs and the networks increase in focus and size, eventually crossing the trillion- dollar mark, we will see the new *Tyrannosaurus rex* of the economic world, the trillion-dollar enterprise. It will be huge and powerful; it will move economics and technology ahead dramatically; it will serve customers everywhere; it will dominate its industries globally; it will help some nations and threaten others.

This evolution is a natural product of industrial globalization and political polarization. It stems from the need to capture the economies of scale and the scope of consolidation without the baggage and limitations of acquisitions and mergers. It stems from the historic drive of corporate leaders to overcome whatever obstacles lay in the way of their growth and progress.

Don't be lulled into complacency, however. Although the concept of the relationship enterprise is powerful and many companies are moving in this direction, the management challenges are considerable. We'll get back to those in a subsequent section.

First, why is the trillion-dollar enterprise inevitable?

Why Not the Global Corporation?

CHAPTER

1

When Bob Burt, CEO of FMC Corporation, one of the world leaders in industrial products and specialty chemicals, heard me introduce the concept of the trillion-dollar enterprise in my 1993 speech, "The Global Corporation: Obsolete So Soon," at the World Economic Forum in Davos, Switzerland, he joked, "I've just reorganized my firm to become a global corporation, and you tell me it is obsolete already! Just when I think I have the answer, someone changes the question."

GLOBAL, GLOBAL, GLOBAL

The most trumpeted development in corporate organization and strategy in the 1980s and early '90s has been the global corporation. Over one hundred books and ten times that many articles and seminars have been devoted to the advent of this newest form of enterprise: its purpose, its challenges, its necessity, its structure, its strategy, its organization; how to build it, how to manage it, how to compete through it, and what it takes to be successful in it.

The word *global* has become an integral part of the business vocabulary. In recent years, if a strategy or organization or human resource plan didn't have a global perspective, it just wouldn't fly. Try to find an annual report that doesn't have the word *global* in it or doesn't extol the company's global outlook.

The product of all this is global marketplace, global economy, global managers, and global citizens—and we all talk about the global village. Such words as *international, multinational, world, worldwide,* and *foreign* have all been replaced by *global.* So the global corporation, whether the cause or the result of this movement, was crowned as the obvious solution to this cosmic change in how we think about commerce and industry.

Whoops! Are we a little too quick in declaring victory to a corporate form that we don't yet understand, that might not be the best, and that certainly is not the *only* solution for meeting the challenge of an integrating world economy?

I'm not suggesting a requiem for the global corporation. Rather, I feel it is early for a coronation. Companies will and should continue to expand internationally. They will and should develop global perspectives and global strategies and global managers. They will and should continue to make cross-border acquisitions. Companies that follow this strategy will grow and be major players in the world's economy of the twenty-first century. But they also will be limited in scope, in geographic spread, in the ability to be world leaders in their industries. Those limitations will contain their competitiveness and will give rise to another form of organization, the relationship enterprise.

Let's look more closely at what has been happening. As corporations got bigger, they simply outgrew their native countries. To oversimplify, there is just so much hot cocoa mix that Nestlé can sell in Switzerland. Even companies that were perfectly content to sell only domestically were forced to expand when foreign-based companies began invading their turf. Beginning in the 1970s, and certainly by the early 1980s, it was clear that no market was safe from foreign competition. The enablers are well known: instant telecommunications link people anywhere on earth; many capitals are a few hours or at most a day away by plane; liberalized trade offers goods to anyone who can pay; media leap borders and tell everyone of the possibilities of the good life. The list is almost endless.

So the concept of the global corporation, which sources products with great efficiency worldwide and whose executives are citizens of the world, was born. The problem is, corporations are not now—nor were they ever—nearly as global as we think.

While the number of global products is growing rapidly—Coke, TV, Levi's, computers, cell phones, airplanes, and so on—the vast majority of what any country consumes is produced within its borders; the world average is over 90 percent. Just a decade ago, Ford launched its first global car, but the European and U.S. versions had only one part in common, a water-pump seal. Alex Trotman, Ford's CEO, concluded that the only way to achieve a global car was to reorganize the company with one product development department.

Management is certainly not global. A few nonnationals have found their way into executive suites of even the most global corporations, but only a handful of corporations, for example, ABB, the energy equipment giant with split headquarters in Sweden and Switzerland, have broken the 10 percent level. The CEO slot is almost universally reserved for a national. Ford Motor Company, Coca-Cola, and Heinz were refreshing exceptions in the United States in the 1990s.

Despite a large share of assets and sales outside the home country, boards are overwhelmingly national in composition. About 10 percent of board seats of public U.S. corporations are held by non-U.S. citizens, according to 1997 Conference Board studies. Change is coming, however. One in five boards of large U.S. corporations include a non-U.S. citizen, up from less than one in ten in the mid 1980s. Not until the late 1980s did a public Japanese company, Sony, name a foreigner to its board; few have followed suit. Foreign board members in Asia are as rare as British sumo wrestlers. Most nonnational board members in the United States and Europe are from closely related countries (e.g., over half the non-U.K. citizens on U.K. boards are from the Commonwealth countries, and 40 percent of non-U.S. citizens on U.S. boards are Canadian or British).

CONSTRAINTS ON THE GLOBAL CORPORATION

The home country bias is natural—and pervasive. Key decisions are made at headquarters; R&D, product design, and engineering are kept at home. Probably the only common denominator in executive suites of global corporations across the world is that they are populated by nationals. But more than a home country bias keeps a damper on a company's efforts to become a truly global corporation; there are serious structural problems as well.

Global corporations face four major constraints:

1. Capital
2. Ownership
3. Need for bureaucracy
4. Aspirations of the best people

Let's run through them quickly.

Capital

No matter what business you are in and no matter how big you are, capital is a limitation. Capital is the lifeblood of growth. Capital is necessary to fund all of the wonderful investment opportunities that surface to the CEO's desk. Allocation of capital is virtually always a game of scarce resources. The more creative a corporation, the larger the demand for high opportunity investments.

Acquisitions require capital—in the form of cash, debt, and equity. Large acquisitions require huge amounts of capital, the same capital for which other investments stand in line. Alliances require significantly less capital.

The tremendous cost of developing untapped markets and staying technologically competitive strains even the healthiest and wealthiest companies. Industry leadership is always capital intensive. The commercial aerospace industry calculates that a new super-jumbo jet will cost $15 to $20 billion to develop, excluding supporting infrastructure—not even Boeing can swallow that elephant. Similarly, the cost of installation of a transpacific fiber-optic cable network will exceed $5 billion—many times what any one competitor is willing to risk. Even mature industries, such as auto and diesel engine companies, choke on the cost of meeting environmental standards without pooling industry investment.

The crucial requirement to compete effectively on a global scale is to marshall world class capabilities, and that takes money. The

situation is especially tough because capital is raised predominantly at home, even for companies that do the majority of their
business elsewhere. For example, 60 percent of Honda's sales occur outside Japan, but less than 10 percent of its stock is owned by
foreign investors.

These data might be surprising, because we have had an explosion of cross-border funding. But closer inspection shows that *over
half* the flow of capital is in government obligations. U.S. portfo-
lios are concentrated on U.S. stocks. The largest mutual funds, pension funds, and asset managers—e.g., Fidelity, Bankers Trust, Wells
Fargo, TIAA–CREF, and CALPers, which have almost $1.5 trillion
under management—invest less than 10 percent overseas. Cross-
border funding of private corporations is growing and will receive
a major boost from the introduction of the EMU (European common currency) particularly across Europe

Martin Feldstein said that although capital is free to move across
borders in search of the highest returns, it doesn't. A company may
move its capital to seek greater returns—for example, to build a new
plant in Brazil or invest in a subsidiary in Singapore—but a country's
capital (pension funds, mutual funds, banks and insurance companies, capital markets) stays home. Otherwise, as Feldstein pointed
out, the level of investment in France would depend only on the profitability of investment in France, and not on the available savings in
France. And that's not how it works! In fact, increased savings in a
country correlates one for one with increased investment. Hence,
Feldstein concluded, despite substantial cross-border capital flows
(which can be attributed predominantly to government securities
and intracorporate funding), different rates of return among countries persist and are not arbitraged by private capital moving to
higher-return countries.

Alliances require significantly less capital than acquisitions. If you
want to tap into a country's capital market, you need to be home
owned.

Ownership

The second major constraint faced by global corporations is ownership, the very basis of the corporate structure. If the capabilities
needed to succeed globally don't exist within the corporation, they

need to be acquired or built. If acquisition is the chosen route (because building is too expensive, takes too long, is too risky, is impractical, or for some other reason), corporations choose among companies that are available, affordable, and permissible—not necessarily the ones that are the best. This can be a huge compromise. There are multiple obstacles to acquiring the best company in a country. Who, after all, has the $100 billion needed to buy Ford even if the family would sell? You can't even think about buying Deutsche Telekom, and the British government owns a "golden" share of privatized British Aerospace, which keeps it in British hands. Government regulation stops foreign majority in a wide range of industries, including commercial aviation, oil, banking, insurance, telecommunications, utilities, and auditing. Even in the decade of privatization, the restrictions are tough.

Equally important, if you acquire a company for its capabilities in Asian distribution, for example, you get the obsolete plants, corporate deadwood, and executive air force along with it. If you want to reengineer your new acquisition in Europe, think hard. The employment laws in Europe make downsizing the workforce a very expensive, very lengthy, and often court-bound process. Irving Kristol noted recently in the *New York Times* that the primary mission of European government is not economic growth or security or competitiveness; it is preserving the social welfare system. The model seems to be Sweden, but France and Belgium are not far behind.

Ownership also hauls in the antitrust brigade. When British Airways acquired TAP of France, they had to divest segments. (An alliance, of course, would have brought no action.) The European Community almost stopped Boeing from acquiring McDonnell Douglas and extracted heavy conditions (e.g., Boeing had to rescind its exclusive contracts with its customers) for their eventual agreement. The FCC commissioner blasted the potential AT&T merger with SBC (one of the regional Bell telephone companies), derailing the talks. In the telecommunications industry, giants routinely form alliances with one another.

Conclusion: Ownership has serious downsides in building a global business.

Need for Bureaucracy

Ownership breeds the third major constraint, the need for bureaucracy and structure. Ownership means accountability to shareholders, and that accountability creates a need for controls. If your alliance partner in Singapore violates financial and trading laws and blows $1 billion, it's nothing more than a shame (as long as they didn't blow *your* billion!) and you get another partner. If your Singapore subsidiary does it, your whole company goes down the tube (as happened in the case of the old-line British investment bank, Barings). If you are a U.S. company and own a subsidiary anywhere in the world, you are subject to all U.S. laws, and, consequently, you establish controls to ensure that no one steps out of line. You file taxes in the host country, worry about U.S. foreign tax credits, audit the subsidiary's operations, and set policies on everything from compensation to the environment and safety, to accounting practices, and to ethical standards. If the subsidiary has financial problems, you must explain them to Wall Street. If the managers don't measure up, you must replace them. Often, companies build complex, bureaucratic, costly corporate systems and require subsidiaries to use them. Those costs, although buried, are very real.

With controls comes bureaucracy. I'll bet that Barings (which lost a billion dollars through an errant trader in its Singapore office), Daiwa (whose employee in New York reported huge profits on fraudulent trades for over five years and which lost its banking license in the United States for not reporting the fraud when it was uncovered), and Sumitomo (for which fraudulent actions in the copper markets by a trader in New York resulted in huge losses and fines) wish they had had more bureaucracy. The embarrassment of your French subsidiary's offering "incentives" to purchasing agents in the Middle East is unacceptable. But the dark side of bureaucratic controls, particularly in a multinational context, is the brakes they put on creativity and flexibility. You have the unhappy confluence of decision makers distant from the market, controls honed in that distant culture, and the blurring of responsibility and accountability. Few people would accuse our largest global corporations of being nimble.

The need to own assets is the Achilles' heel of the global corporation. The current movement toward empowering decentralized businesses is a response to this problem, but it's a partial solution at best. The fundamental decisions about the allocation of resources almost always remain centralized, no matter how many decisions are pushed out into the field. Advice on almost anything from headquarters typically lacks cultural awareness, customer understanding, urgency . . . you get the point.

Conclusion: If you want the freedom to live without cross-border handcuffs, alliances beat ownership hands down.

Aspirations of the Best People

The final, and possibly the most compelling disadvantage of the global corporation is that people, no matter where they live, don't want foreigners controlling their destinies.

Have you ever known a company whose management wanted to be acquired by a foreign corporation? I can think of only two situations in which this might happen: first, if the alternative was bankruptcy, and second, if the payout to the principals was extraordinary. A takeover by another national corporation strikes fear in the heart of any executive; but the fear is for jobs, not the concern of being a division of another company. Not so in the case of a foreign owner.

The manager's first reaction is, "This won't work. They won't understand what's going on here and will make me do things that are wrong in the market or with my people. I won't understand their systems, their language, their way of thinking." Nationalistic feelings come popping into the minds of the local management team. Nationalism strikes home when a foreign flag flies over a previously independent local company.

If the best of the management team have alternatives, they will seriously consider them. After all, they'll conclude, "I want to run a company one day, to be a CEO, and that just won't happen with my German [or Japanese or Brazilian or American] parent." The statistics strongly support that concern. The one hundred largest companies in Japan, Germany, the United States, and Brazil can count the number of nonnational CEOs on one hand.

Real stars want to run their own show, and that usually (with 97% probability) means a company of the same nationality. Top people (who have bright futures and alternatives) almost invariably leave after a foreign takeover. Jerre Stead is a typical example. Stead, at age forty-eight, joined Square D, an industrial electrical and electronics firm, in 1988, to turn the company around—which he did very well. In 1992, Schneider (France) acquired Square D, and Stead left immediately. He went to AT&T and ran two of their largest businesses. After three years and one intermediate stop, Stead became head of Ingram Micro, a computer reseller and wholesaler, which he took public in less than a year. Although his career is far from over, Stead has made more millions than he ever dreamed he would, and he has a superior track record of management success. But he'd probably still be running Square D, had it not been acquired by a foreign corporation.

The situation is much different for an in-country acquisition. Many heads of acquired companies remain on the job, and several become CEOs of the acquirer. Current examples include Pat Ryan, CEO of Aon and John Bryan, CEO of Sara Lee.

The downside is clear: the best people leave, and the rest stick around with the wrong attitude. In the optimistic scenario, managers wait to see what the new bosses want and how they will be treated. The burden of dealing with these fears and attitudes, which must be filtered through a different culture, lies with the global corporation. A terrible burden.

It is wonderful to speak of their managers as global citizens, but all corporations and managers are bound to a culture, affected by local political interests, and unable to remain unbiased in the face of other-than-obvious trade-offs. Corporations will have a home country—and a home culture—whose interests they reflect even as they operate around the world. And this includes the companies they acquire in other countries. The cultural transition from French corporation to French subsidiary of a U.S. company can be subtle, but is always real. The Brazilian manager of the Japanese subsidiary in São Paulo will never achieve the status of her Japanese counterparts at the Tokyo headquarters, and the likelihood of her becoming a top executive in Tokyo is almost zero.

Culturally attuned corporations are aware of this issue and take extraordinary measures to retain the local nature of their acquired foreign corporations. Nationals typically head the foreign subsidiaries. ABB is at the forefront. ABB implemented a strong geographic–product-line matrix organization to balance local autonomy of foreign subsidiaries with the scale and efficiency of a global product line. ABB's top management includes executives from several countries. English is ABB's common language even though its headquarters are in Switzerland and Sweden. Yet despite the best corporate leadership, a sound organizational concept, and extraordinary cultural awareness, ABB cannot escape the constraints on global corporations of capital, ownership, control, and people. Allocation of funds is determined centrally, and the expected battles between global product managers and country managers rage on. More than three thousand profit centers is monitored in Zurich. Off-budget performance merits a visit from headquarters. Recently, ABB abolished the geographic layer of management in the name of cost aid efficiency.

Conclusion: The best people want a shot at the top jobs. If you want the best people, they must believe they can make it to the top.

A WORD IN FAVOR OF OWNERSHIP

Before we consider hammering nails in the global corporation's coffin, we should recognize the considerable advantages of ownership. Ownership (i.e., acquisition or merger) is the best way to build an enterprise under several important circumstances. For example, if value can be created by reducing costs through consolidation of redundant operations, departments, or activities, ownership is usually the most efficient and effective means to achieve this end. When Chase and Chemical Bank merged, they didn't need two branches on every corner or two accounting departments or two demand deposit systems or two credit cards. By getting rid of duplicate activities and moving well down the cost-scale curve, Chase Bank reduced costs by $1.7 billion, or 20 percent of the combined premerger total, and became a significantly stronger competitor in its markets (according to published accounts and discussions with executives involved).

If the value of the combination derives from an integration and restructuring of core activities, ownership is your best vehicle. For example, the merger of Boeing and McDonnell Douglas moved Boeing from a second-tier defense player to a leader and provided Boeing access to substantial government research, which will benefit its commercial aerospace business. Integration of some engineering and development activities will make the combination a more powerful and lower-cost competitor. Alliance could not have achieved these benefits for Boeing. Airbus should recognize that it also would become a significantly stronger competitor if it merged the commercial aerospace partners into one corporation. Coordination of procurement, elimination of duplicate activities, and true integration of product development and engineering would save Airbus billions of dollars.

In-country industry consolidations can best be accomplished by mergers, whether to fill out a product line, expand into a new geographic area, or strengthen capabilities. A merger or acquisition is easier to negotiate and quicker to implement, and with it, change can be mandated. If the consolidation task is clear, the economics are attractive, and there are no cultural or legal barriers, acquisition is the answer. Alliances take time to negotiate, and you may never stop negotiating. Kraft has made a number of acquisitions of branded products in recent years, among them Churny Cheese, Lender's bagels, Frusen Gladje ice cream, Tombstone pizza, POLLY-O cheese, and Budget Gourmet dinners. With Kraft's scale, manufacturing footprint, and dominant distribution capability, it can add a product using few of the people from the acquired company and without incurring other costs normally associated with selling and distributing a product, with the possible exception of advertising. Just add it to the truck and put it on the shelf.

Cross-border consolidations through mergers are tougher to pull off. Still, some conditions favor acquisition over alliance. For example, a food company (e.g., Unilever) might buy a foreign company for its product line. Value would be unlocked by doing away with administrative, marketing, and distribution organizations and costs and, possibly, with manufacturing and product development. The parent company would absorb these activities, adding little or no cost, and would give the product line substantially greater distribution, preferred shelf space, cooperative advertising, and promotions. Few of these advantages are available through an alliance.

Acquisitions have several other advantages over alliances. Acquisitions are easier to negotiate. Once an acquirer believes that the strategic logic and business economics make sense, price is the dominant variable, particularly with public companies. Other factors such as who will be boss are important, but are usually subordinate to price in negotiations. Alliances require careful, partnerlike negotiation of a range of complex variables—valuation, ownership shares, mutual obligations, authorities, sharing the profits, transfer pricing, people, organization, systems, reporting, compensation, and so on. Typically, these factors are less important in merger or acquisition negotiations.

Acquisitions are easier to manage. No partners need be convinced of a change in personnel, of an investment, of a new marketing strategy, or, frankly, of any changes in the acquired business, including its sale. Ownership has rights, and acquisition buys those rights. But be careful not to confuse *easier* with *better*.

Acquisitions may be easier to exit. Many variables are at work in a divestiture, the most important of which is finding interested buyers. If there are interested buyers and if the entanglements with the parent are not complex and serious, then divestiture can be smooth. Companies sell off businesses by the carload every day. Exiting an alliance depends on the prenuptial arrangements and the continued goodwill of the partners. Without those two conditions, exiting can be a nightmare, but with proper conditions in place, the process is likely to be smooth. Witness the dissolving of Elenco, the biotech joint venture between Eli Lilly and Dow Chemical; Dow simply took over the alliance based on pre-agreed conditions.

Choosing between acquisition and alliance depends on the circumstances and options. Neither is better in every situation. Let's look at the changing environment that is tipping the scales toward alliances, particularly for cross-border deals.

WHILE BUSINESS IS GLOBALIZING . . .

We all know that business is globalizing, but let us step back in history to understand the trends that give us insight into globalization in the decades ahead. The drivers of industries globalization are the spread of practicies that improve standards of living, trade, and conquest or accquistion. Improvements in real standards of living did not begin for the human race until the nineteenth century. Only then did cumulative GNP growth begin to exceed population growth. Up to that point, the primary fact of life was the population's need to feed itself. When the production of food exceeded the population's need, population grew. When famine or overpopulation resulted in an inadequate supply of food, the population flattened or declined. The eighteenth-century economist Thomas Malthus articulated the theory that fit these hard-core facts.

In his seminal book, *Vital Dust,* Nobel laureate Christian de Duve notes, "In the space of a few millennia (after more than 1 million years of hunting and gathering), virtually the whole of mankind had adopted the agrarian mode of life and vast areas of forests had given way to farmland. At the same time, the growth of technology, the birth of modern science, the burgeoning of industry made further attacks on the biosphere . . . the final blow (to nature) was inflicted by the advances of medicine and sanitation, which increasingly saved human lives that would have been eliminated in the past by poor hygiene, malnutrition and disease. Thanks to these advances, the curtailment of the human population by natural selection was thwarted, resulting in the demographic explosion of the last 150 years." That demographic explosion lead to the greatest migration of people in history.

The primary factor driving increasing standards of living has been industrialization, the leverage that machines gave humans to produce more per capita and thus to accumulate wealth. Communications alerted virtually all peoples of the world to the wonders and comforts that were being enjoyed in industrializing countries—and they wanted some too!

International trade—beyond neighboring nation-states—began centuries ago. Various parts of the world discovered one another as they sought new trade routes. On the darker side, the empires of Cyrus the Great, and Alexander and the Caesars were driven by the desire to own resources not available in their home countries. The acquisition game was a rough business in those days, particularly for the acquired. The golden parachute is a significant advance from being dragged through the city of the conquering tribe behind the leader's chariot.

The history of international trade follows the histories of Eastern and Western civilizations fairly closely. In the nineteenth century, international trade exploded, as the Industrial Revolution spread across Europe, the United States, the Commonwealth countries, and to a few Asian nations. The first half of the twentieth century saw a regression. Two world wars clearly demonstrated that the traditional way of expanding trade—conquest—no longer worked. Political enablers stepped in, such as the United Nations to keep peace, and GATT (the General Agreement on Tariffs and Trade) to set some common rules. The Marshall Plan set a new standard of international cooperation through trade that enabled rapid reconstruction of a flattened Europe. Similarly, enlightened U.S. policies enabled Japan to rebuild its industrial base. The post–World War II boom gave a huge boost to international trade.

Rising international trade has many implications. It provides new or better or cheaper goods to the importing country. It provides new markets for countries' exports, resulting in employment and rising living standards. But it also is a threat to those companies and employees with whom imports compete. Protection of local employment through trade barriers is as old as the Roman Empire.

Setting up shop in another country is a centuries-old practice as well. Acquisition of a business or company in another country (through purchase rather than conquest), on the other hand, is a relatively new phenomenon—within the past 150 years. And major cross-border acquisition activity didn't begin until after World War II, just a half century ago.

Assets owned by foreign companies have grown substantially in the past thirty years. Viewed from a historical perspective, economic conquest as opposed to military conquest is relatively recent. Still, governments and their people don't like the idea of being taken over, even if the takeover is only economic. So most nations put certain crown jewels out of bounds to foreign investors. You can own a tire plant in my backyard, but you cannot own my oil field. You can buy a supermarket chain but not my banks. Although these restrictions are looser now than they were ten years ago, most restrictions didn't even exist a century ago because no one was buying. For our purposes here, suffice to say that restrictions on trade and acquiring assets across borders are very real and a major block to the globalization freight train.

Nevertheless, the tidal waves of international trade and the Hollywood–Madison Avenue dream machine have created huge demand in every corner of the world. Technology and communications are making it easier to do business worldwide. Corporations have been scrambling to capture a share of this demand.

As companies have expanded, they have found that tastes around the globe are similar. Just about anywhere in the world, you can find a teenager with a Walkman on her head, a Coke in her hand, and Levi's on her hips. U.S. movies and music influence the cultures of all but those who prohibit their entry. Few countries have roadways free of Fiats or Fords or Toyotas.

Through the middle 1980s, this international growth was achieved predominantly by exporting, setting up shop, licensing, or acquiring local companies. Although these forms of international commerce continue to expand rapidly, they face major obstacles.

In less than three decades, international business has been transformed from predominantly exporting to global sourcing and production, global marketing and distribution, and even global research and product development. Only a decade ago, Lucent Technologies, the former manufacturing arm of AT&T, had just a few thousand employees outside the United States. Today, that number is over thirty thousand.

Internal sourcing of components between companies related by ownership or alliance represents the fastest growing segment of international trade. Companies now view the world not only as a market, but also as a source of low-cost and high-quality suppliers. Toy companies and clothing manufacturers have set up shop in Asia to produce goods that are sold in the United States and Europe. India has become an outsourcing capital for the computer software industry. The largest part of the trade deficit between the United States and Japan (over half the total 1997 trade deficit of $60 billion) is in automotive parts shipped from Japan to U.S. and Japanese auto plants in the United States.

The key point is that the nature of international business has changed. The management task is fundamentally different and far more complex than it was only twenty years ago. As Didier Pineau-Valencienne, CEO of the global electrical and electronic Schneider Group based in Paris, stated to me at one of our Booz·Allen advisory board meetings, "We need to know the best practices not only of our thirty plants across the world, but of every plant anywhere that does something similar to ours so that we can keep abreast of competition and at least have a chance to be a leader. Innovation that can transform my business can come from any industry in any country at any time. There are great opportunities in this new global economy, but it is filled with great risks as well."

The impact of rising international trade on a business and on industry is clear. It starts with the consumer. If you, as a consumer, have a choice among competing products, you will select the one that most suits your requirements and budget. Price usually breaks ties. International trade increases choice. Hence, each business must compete at home against all products offered to its customers, including those from other countries. Since products can come from anywhere (unless protectionist barriers block them), the standards that products must meet become global standards.

Countries that have open trade policies expose their industries to the toughest competition, which either makes local businesses very competitive or sinks them. As a result, countries are becoming very strong in industries in which they are able to operate at the best international level and are outsourcing (to other countries) those industries or tasks in which they are not competitive. This creates a difficult situation, particularly when the industries whose products or services are on the potential outsourcing list are large employers. Textile workers in industrialized countries have fought hammer and tongs for protection against "unfair" low-cost foreign competition. They have been losing this battle for years, as labor rates and productivity cannot keep pace with those of Asian textile workers. Japan has worried about the hollowing of its manufacturing industries as companies move more and more labor-intensive tasks offshore.

Over the past fifty years, another profound change has taken place in international trade. For centuries, trade had been in goods—natural resources (e.g., coal, timber, oil, minerals) and products made in one country that had markets in others. Only two centuries ago international trade was predominantly barter— my glass beads for your tobacco. (I don't count the coercive trade of the conquistadores as trade, but as plunder.)

Since World War II, knowledge has become a driver of world trade. A sound argument can be made that for most international trade other than that in natural resources and agricultural products, knowledge is the dominant driver. If two countries produce cars, one imports the cars of the other not because there are no cars available locally, but because the other country has figured out how to produce a car better suited to the buyer—knowledge. The same is true for most products. Hence, knowledge and its principal off-spring, technology, have propelled trade to record levels and will continue to do so for decades to come.

As a result, great companies are driven to global standards in every element of their business—research, production, marketing, personnel, sourcing, product development, financing, intellectual capital, information—lest they become competitively disadvantaged. It is the relentless pursuit of knowledge (a.k.a. technology, productivity, creativity, capabilities) that is driving globalization, not the flight to low wages. As Dani Rodrik noted in "Sense and Nonsense in the Globalization Debate," "If [the flight to low wages were the principal driver of outsourcing], the world's most formidable exporters would be Bangladesh and a smattering of African countries."

And as companies consider how to become (and remain) the best in each area of business, they must look globally for capabilities. Acquiring a low-cost plant in Mexico may be attractive in the short term, but unless that plant keeps up with, or exceeds, world standards in cost, quality, reliability, and customer service, the parent company's advantage will be short-lived. Owning assets can be attractive if the company has the will and resources to maintain world standards, as does Motorola. Most companies have neither the will nor the resources and should be (and are) considering alternative ways of acquiring important capabilities and knowledge, such as through strategic alliances.

... NATIONS ARE TURNING INWARD

Globalization is a megatrend that, short of a world war, will continue for decades—probably for the whole of the twenty-first century. All thinking companies are devising strategies to compete, win, or at least survive in that world. A factor that makes operating globally complex and difficult is that the forces of protectionism, nationalism, and isolationism are rising again.

It is hard to find a moment in history when nations did not try to protect their borders and economies, with varying results. The ancient Persians, Romans, Huns, and Mongols proved that strong nations can sweep away the defenses of the weak. This fact was amply demonstrated in our century as well; the Maginot Line was easily circumvented. Nevertheless, the desire of nations to protect their cultures, the well-being of their citizens, and a stable social order leads them to act in their own self-interests. The governments of Singapore and China may seem oppressive through Western eyes, but in relation to their value systems, these governments are acting in the interests of their societies. They measure progress over long periods and recognize the perils of unrest that history has taught in these regions.

Self-interest drives countries to regulate trade to their advantage and to accept only investments that are supportive of their parochial national interests. Japan was allowed to play by different rules in international trade as it rebuilt after the war. Now that it has one of the most powerful economies in the world, other nations are looking to Japan to revise its practices to conform with the international trade standards for strong nations. Japan, however, has clearly demonstrated what we all should expect—it is operating in its own self-interest and will not change unless its self-interest will be served by that change.

The United States and, to some degree, the countries of Europe believe that a freer system of international commerce is in their self-interest, that is, that they will win if the playing field is level. Hence it is not surprising that the United States and Europe are the strongest advocates for lower trade and investment barriers. We should note that even in these enlightened societies, the political forces for protecting jobs are vocal and gaining influence. A higher-than-historic unemployment rate can get any politician bounced out of office. Recall the French elections of 1997, when President Chirac called for a confirmation of his austerity program in the face of chronic, double-digit unemployment. His party's loss was devastating, and a Socialist government was formed with a pledge to protect jobs at any cost—even, it seems, at the cost of France's future.

We cannot expect any of the emerging economies to be advocates of free trade and investment unless they specifically benefit and their cultures remain intact. As companies determine how best to acquire the capabilities and compete in new markets, they must keep these indisputable facts in mind.

Little difference exists in the attitudes and behavior of nations in the nineteenth century, in this century, and in this decade. Nor should we expect a change in the next decade or century. Union leaders don't get elected to dissipate jobs, nor do presidents and prime ministers.

Globalization is exacerbating the problem big time. In most countries, there is a social contract between the citizens and the state. The specific nature of the contract is different in virtually every country and has roots in the culture that has been shaped by the events, circumstances, the media, protestors, and leaders of the country over decades or even centuries.

Historically in Eastern cultures, the family was the principal safety net for old or infirm individuals. As industrialization swept Japan, the corporation took over at least some of this role for workers and their families, providing the security of lifetime employment, medical care, pensions, subsidized housing, even family support. The government was expected to maintain order, but not to be the primary supplier of social benefits.

In Western countries, the government has provided social benefits and has legislated that additional benefits and working conditions be provided by employers. Most of Western society finds its philosophical and social roots in Rousseau and Jefferson; the society has an obligation to its citizens, and the citizens have an obligation to their society. In order for the government to supply benefits, it needs taxes, which citizens agree to pay, and laws, which citizens agree to obey.

Globalization is directly or indirectly altering these social contracts. "Employers can move abroad, but (most) employees cannot," says Rodrik. Capital can move, but labor can't. The debate rages about the evils (in social terms) and the benefits (in economic terms) of globalization. The meeting in mid-1997 of European heads of state in Amsterdam to hammer out the common currency for the EU (European Union) was stormed by the unemployed masses in Europe. Their demand: put jobs now at the top of the EU priorities, not all those long-term dreams of European unity, a common currency, balanced social policies, and competitiveness with the rest of the world.

People want to control their own economic destiny. Consider the popularity of the far right—LePen in France, Zhirinovski in Russia, Buchanan in the United States—who focus on fear of foreigners, fear of trade, and fear of lost jobs. Draped in patriotism, the message of these ultranationalists is clear and to many, compelling: If you open your borders, you will lose your jobs and your standard of living. Coal miners in the United Kingdom and rice farmers in Japan have enormous influence. Late in 1997, the U.S. Congress refused to give President Clinton fast-track authority to negotiate a free-trade agreement with South America—a major setback for free trade by the forces of isolationism. At the end of the day, political interests demand that governments create domestic jobs and work for domestic interests.

Carlos Fuentes, former Mexican ambassador to France, captured this sentiment well in an article syndicated by the *Herald Tribune* in June 1997: "For all the talk of globalization, politics is above all a local matter. Globalization without localization is little more than a phantom. It is a danger that places societies at the mercy of a minority of multinational corporations and of a fleeting abundance of investments that, like the swallows, are here today and gone tomorrow."

Recently, Tom Friedman wrote of politics in the age of NAFTA (the North American Free Trade Agreement) in the *New York Times*. He cited the Australian election in which John Howard "charged that Australians were losing their national icons, indeed their very sovereignty, to the global market." Howard beat incumbent Paul Keating by a landslide.

Friedman continued, "People everywhere are struggling to find a balance between NAFTA and neighborhood, between their desire to preserve a sense of national identity and control over their own lives in a world where they can only survive economically if they link up to distant soulless global institutions and manufactured markets—from APEC to EU which don't have any identity at all."

In Michael Sandel's book, *Democracy's Discovery*, the Harvard professor of political theory argues that modern democracies will not be able to sustain themselves unless they can find ways of contending with the global economy while also giving expression to their people's distinctive identities and their aspirations.

William Greider makes a case that global expansion is undermining social structures and leading us toward a major economic and social crisis. In his book, *One World, Ready or Not,* he argues that global business transfers low-cost work, weakening social safety nets in developed economies and promoting the repression of political rights in developing economies. His solution? Slow or regulate globalization.

The hard fact is that economic forces are compelling corporations to expand and compete globally at exactly the same time that the tides of nationalism are rising worldwide.

We will revisit the policy issues in the final section of the book. If globalization is raising such an uproar, imagine the impact the trillion-dollar enterprise could have.

GLOBALIZATION AND NATIONALISM

Individually, these two forces—globalization of business and nationalism—are understandable and predictable. Every CEO of a company that operates beyond a neighborhood knows that competition can come from anywhere in the world and understands that the market for his company's products and services knows no national boundaries. Motorola's Bob Galvin recently said that corporations need to think of their geographic markets in terms of consumers (i.e., population) rather than GNP. On that basis, the United States is only 5 percent of the world market. Motorola is heeding that advice, as its sales excede 70 percent outside its home country, compared with 25 percent a decade ago.

Throughout history, business owners and managers have figured out how to survive and prosper in the world they faced. Over the past two centuries, businesses have been challenged to deal with extraordinary change in the rules of combat, in the means of combat, in the places of combat. Imagine yourself as the head of a business in 1865 just after the Civil War in the United States. Much of the land has been devastated, the stagecoach is being replaced by the railroad, the economic conditions are horrible, most production is suited for armaments, many of the young men that businesses rely on are dead or maimed. Who would have known that the United States and Europe were on the edge of the greatest industrial revolution in history?

This century has seen massive swings in economic fortunes. At the end of World War II, the productive capacity of Germany and Japan was annihilated, a total of a million young men were dead, the United States was exhausted from the Depression and the war, and no one had any money. The technological revolution that followed in massive waves raised the standards of living in the industrialized world beyond anything even the most optimistic seers had prophesied.

At each moment in history, business leaders have had to understand the forces that were shaping their world and to work those forces to their advantage through profound and fundamental changes. Why should we think that 2000 is any different from 1865, or 1900, or 1945? To the contrary, the tides of economic and political change through which business must maneuver are clear on the horizon. This is why the emergence of new forms of business enterprises is inevitable.

Neither globalization nor nationalism can be ignored. Both are real and very important to business in the coming decades. These are two of the most important forces that will define the economic playing fields of the twenty-first century.

Jim Hoge, editor of *Foreign Affairs,* said it well in his introduction to a recent issue:

> As I wrote in my first issue as editor of *Foreign Affairs,* we want to provide our readers with a perspective that stretches beyond the frameworks traditionally used to think about international affairs. The old approaches, whereby nation-states were the most important actors and military force and diplomacy were the main instruments of action, no longer suffice. Nowadays, the far-reaching influence of financiers, media moguls, executives, and heads of nongovernmental organizations can be the envy of presidents and generals; the ability to promote cooperation is becoming as important to national survival as the ability to prevail in armed conflict; and instantaneous, widespread and cheaper forms of international communications are redefining diplomacy.

An international strategy that relies exclusively on exports, setting up shop in other countries, and acquiring local companies is seriously flawed. Countries are carefully erecting barriers to protect their self-interests. Businesses cannot grow as they have in the past.

Remember that business is about the productive use of capabilities and assets (people, capital, natural resources) to grow and make money. Politics and national aspirations can get in the way. Politics is about creating environments conducive to social stability and raising the welfare of citizens. Business, although essential, often gets in the way.

The companies that will play best in the coming decades will craft strategies that recognize these conflicting trends and take advantage of them. The business must be global—in outlook, in markets, in sourcing, in technology, in culture and people. But the business also must be at home in many countries, an advantage where governments are protecting local industry, and are tapped into local talent, resources, and funding.

Economic forces are compelling corporations to expand and compete globally at exactly the same time that the tides of nationalism are rising worldwide. To deal with these contradictory forces, companies that have battled fiercely with one another are coming together. They have no choice. These are the conditions that make the twenty-first century the age of collaboration and the breeding ground for the trillion-dollar enterprise.

A Natural Evolution

The conflict between nationalism and globalization may well be a breeding ground for the trillion-dollar enterprise, but where is the evidence that business is moving in that direction?

Not only is there strong evidence, but I believe that the evolution toward relationship enterprises and, eventually, the trillion-dollar enterprise is both natural and inevitable. As we saw in the last chapter, all other things being equal, ownership is the preferred form of consolidation. But, of course, all things are not equal. Ownership has major drawbacks, particularly with cross-border consolidation.

It is very difficult to acquire the best firm in any country. The global corporation must deal directly with multiple cultures, national employment practices, local laws and regulations, and uneven playing fields for their foreign-owned subsidiaries. In addition, mergers or acquisitions come with the odd business that can't be unloaded easily. The best and brightest in a country typically want to work for a company headquartered at home. They know the stats on how many foreigners populate top management in global firms and prefer to play on the favorable side of those odds.

Consciously or unconsciously, many companies are addressing the dilemma of globalizing in a parochial world by reducing their reliance on acquisitions and increasing their involvement in alliances. Alliances have been exploding in the 1990s.

In this chapter we will explore the question, Why alliances? particularly with their considerable challenges that will be discussed in the next section. Alliances represent a natural—and profitable—evolution, as consolidation moves truly globally. Alliances form the foundation of the next stage of evolution in the structure of a business enterprise. Alliances are profitable; they enable companies to add capabilities without major investment; they are becoming central to the strategies of growing corporations; and networks of alliances are beginning to form. The evolution from the global corporation to the relationship enterprise is taking place today.

CONSOLIDATION MARCHES ON

The trend toward increased size is not at all new. Over the past fifty years, the average size in real U.S. dollars has grown dramatically for corporations (in sales) and financial institutions (in assets). The assets of the ten largest banks in the world have doubled every five years for the past thirty years—more than twice the growth rate of the banking industry over that period. Every bank in the top ten is the product of at least one major merger, as are most of the banks in the top twenty-five.

Revenues for the top ten industrial companies have also been growing at twice the average rate of GNP for the major countries. In almost every major industry, the top five competitors have a larger share of industry revenues in every five-year period. The consolidation rage is, if anything, accelerating. In 1997, according to Securities Data Company, U.S. companies were involved in mergers with a market value of over $1 trillion—50 percent higher than in 1996, which set the previous record by a good margin, and more than double the value in 1988, the peak year in the wild 1980s. Europe and even beleaguered Asia are experiencing similar explosions of consolidation. Although cross-border mergers are growing, the lion's share of the boom involves companies from the same country.

Exhibit 2-1 ❖ **ALLIANCES GROWING AS A SOURCE OF REVENUE**

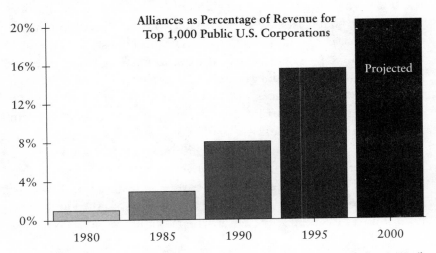

Alliances as Percentage of Revenue for Top 1,000 Public U.S. Corporations

Source: Columbia University; European Trade Commission; studies by Booz·Allen & Hamilton, 1983–1987, 1988–1992, 1994–1995. Projection by author.

These figures don't tell the whole story, however. Most alliances don't hit the revenue or asset lines of companies' financial statements, and we don't know how to value alliances as we do mergers. For example, Corning reports sales of $6 billion, but if we count the sales of its fifty alliances, the number is close to $12 billion. Archer-Daniels-Midland has reported sales of $13 billion, but that figure is doubled if we include their network of international alliances with Toepfer (Germany), CIP (France), and Kuok (China). Alliances have become a major part of virtually all large commercial organizations.

Even though most alliances don't hit the revenue line of the income statement, alliances are growing dramatically in importance as a source of reported revenue for companies. Based on Booz·Allen's 1997 survey, 18 percent of the revenue generated by the top one thousand U.S. firms comes from alliances—up from about 1 percent just fifteen years ago—and that figure should exceed 20 percent by 2000. (see Exhibit 2-1.)

To understand why the present explosion in alliances is a natural bridge between the world of ownership and a world of collaboration, between the global corporation and the relationship enterprise, alliances merit a closer look.

WHAT ARE ALLIANCES?

Alliances have been around forever. Countries have formed alliances with neighbors to protect themselves or to conquer another country since the beginning of time. Just think about the Romans and Goths creating the early European empires, or Sun Tsu's comments on alliances 2,500 years ago in *The Art of War*. Alliances made international trading possible as early as the fifteenth century. The core of Machiavelli's recommendations to the prince was to create beneficial alliances. The Rothschilds, Morgans, and other great financiers of the nineteenth century knew the value of alliances well.

During the Industrial Revolution of the late nineteenth and the twentieth centuries, merger and acquisition became the dominant methods of consolidation. And appropriately so. The Industrial Revolution was about newly invented machinery and equipment and plants and productive capacity rather than intellectual capital or capabilities. The economic driver was scale and efficiency of production. In this new environment, the primary objective was to control assets, and the best way to control assets was to own them. This remains true today. Merger or acquisition enables the surviving entity to combine assets and activities, substantially lower costs, and become a stronger competitor.

Nothing in this book should lead you to conclude that the age of mergers is over. To the contrary, mergers, supermergers (Chase and Chemical banks and Monsanto and American Home Products), and megamergers (Ciba Geigy/Santos, BP Amoco, and Travelers/Citicorp) will take place whenever integration of assets favorably changes the economics of companies and industries. Banks merge and close branches; credit companies merge and move down the scale-economies curve; hospitals merge and use beds and equipment more efficiently; manufacturing companies merge to combine facilities, increase scale economies, and spread the cost of R&D over more volume; agribusiness companies merge to improve the economics of the supply chain. In all cases, integration of physical assets is central to achieving the economic objectives of the combination.

Alliances are different. Alliances combine capabilities. Alliances allow targeted combinations of the parts of your partner you want. Alliances do not give the same level and type of control as majority ownership. For example, the Roman Empire was based on conquest

Exhibit 2-2 ❖ EXTENDED ENTERPRISE SEGMENTATION

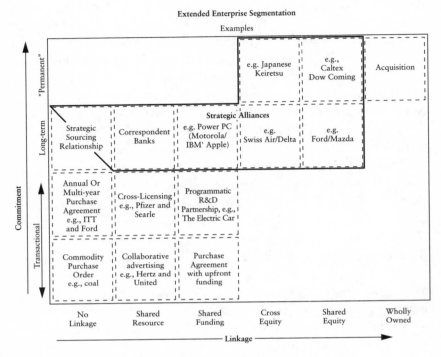

Extended Enterprise Segmentation

Examples

Source: Booz·Allen & Hamilton Analysis, 1995–1998.

(ownership), which gave the Romans access to the resources and wealth of vassal nations. The alliance between the United States and the United Kingdom in World War II only promised mutual defense and support; neither could order the other to do anything.

TYPES OF ALLIANCES

Before we go further, let's consider how alliances work in today's business world, paying particular attention to strategic alliances. We distinguish between transactional and strategic alliances on the bases of commitment (short term vs. long term) and linkage (from none to shared equity). The ultimate form of commitment (permanent) and linkage (wholly owned) is an acquisition.

As Exhibit 2-2 shows, many types of alliances exist. The exhibit arrays alliances along the two defining dimensions: length and nature of the commitment (the vertical axis) and degree and nature of linkage (the horizontal axis).

Transactional Alliances

The section in the lower left quadrant lists alliances of a transactional nature. These alliances are established for a specific purpose, typically to improve each company's ability to conduct its business. Cross-licensing is a good example as with Searle's Cox II drug through Pfizer's sales force. Licenses can be very important. In the pharmaceutical industry, for example, 70 percent of Marion, Merrill, Dow's revenue is derived from licenses, and 50 percent of Bristol-Myers Squibb comes from licensed products. The average for the top twenty pharmaceutical companies is in the 25 to 35 percent range. Even the most self-reliant companies, such as Eli Lilly, receive 5 to 10 percent of revenues from licenses, according to a study done in 1996 by Booz·Allen. But the arrangements are contractual and typically involve little interaction between the firms other than the right to use a product or technology under defined conditions.

An open-ended purchase order is a form of transactional alliance that facilitates smooth and efficient relations between a supplier and a buyer. For example, a supplier (e.g., ITT Automotive) will win a contract to supply all the brakes on the Ford Taurus. The car may be in production for several years with volumes going up and down. It's an important contract, but both firms continue to operate their businesses independently.

Strategic Sourcing

Strategic sourcing involves a longer-term commitment. At its core, strategic sourcing is a partnership between buyer and seller that goes beyond the arm's-length contracts of old. The alliance partners can reduce the cost and friction between supplier and buyer by sharing product-development plans and responsibilities, by jointly programming production, by sharing considerable information (even confidential information), and, overall, by working much more closely together than do typical suppliers and customers. Strategic sourcing is on the border between transactional and strategic alliances. The degree of sharing determines the side of the line for an alliance.

The concept of strategic sourcing has swept through many industries. Companies that purchase by sending out specs, getting a handful of bids, and choosing the cheapest one, are now viewed as being in the Stone Age. Bob Lutz, vice chairman of Chrysler, put it well when he told me, "We used to get three bids and hammer our suppliers on cost and wind up with an $11 price per part. We now choose a partner and work together to reduce cost and improve quality and efficiency and obtain a $6 price—and we both make more money."

Under the banner of strategic sourcing, companies have dramatically reduced the number of suppliers (e.g., Ford has reduced the number of its suppliers by 70% in the past ten years and continues to reduce). The degree of cooperation and interaction has also deepened. If you want to dig deeper into strategic sourcing, you should read the recently published *Balanced Sourcing* by Tim Lassiter.

Strategic Alliances

Moving to the right and up on Exhibit 2-2, the level and nature of commitment and sharing increase. The relationships referred to as strategic alliances are outlined. These are the alliances I mean when I speak of trillion-dollar enterprises.

Strategic alliances begin with a long-term commitment and shared resources. Correspondent relationships in banking have been prevalent for decades. For example, First Chicago NBD, now Banc One, has established an alliance with Barclays Bank in England to serve its customers in the United Kingdom. The U.K. subsidiary of Sara Lee Corporation, which banks with First Chicago NBD, can use Barclays for letters of credit, foreign exchange, and cash management. The alliance allows First Chicago NBD to provide services to its customers far from headquarters without the expense of maintaining branches and employees everywhere.

Shared Funding

In shared-funding alliances, partners pool financial resources typically to develop new technologies or products. That's what Motorola, Apple, and IBM did to create the Power PC (see Exhibit 2-3); the three companies pooled research programs and made financial commitments to develop a new generation of engine for personal computers.

Exhibit 2-3 ❖ CASE STUDY: SHARED FUNDING OF THE POWER PC

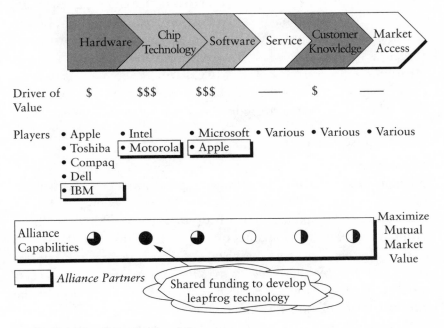

Source: Booz·Allen & Hamilton analysis.

Shared funding is common in the oil industry. British Petroleum, now BP Amoco, and Statoil jointly explore, produce, and market in frontier regions. A group of ten partners is developing the major on-shore (Azeri, Chirag) and offshore (Guneshli fields in the Caspian Sea) reserves together with SOCAR, the state oil company of Azer-baijan. The foreign partners include BP Amoco, Pennzoil, Lukoil (Russia), Statoil (Norway), McDermott, Aramco, Turkish Petro-leum, and Delta Nimar. The North Sea was developed by a cross-word puzzle of alliances. Partners commit to supplying the engineers, construction personnel, equipment, and whatever else is necessary to explore and produce oil in isolated or difficult locations. Planning and decision making are joint, and the spoils are shared.

The ill-fated Microelectronics and Computing Technology Com-pany (MCC), originally headed by Admiral Bobby Inman, was a shared-funding alliance created in 1982 by Control Data and DEC with several U.S. high-tech companies to keep the United States ahead of Japan in the chip world and develop the next generation of software. None of the companies had the resources to go it alone, so they created an alliance funded by all to produce chips that all would use. Intel, Motorola, and Texas Instruments beat MCC to the punch, and the MCC venture never achieved its promise. We must never forget that alliances can fail, however compelling the logic for their creation. In this case, few of the MCC partners had a viable base for competing and winning in the computer and semiconductor business. Many have exited the industry as independent players.

Cross-Equity Alliances

In cross-equity alliances, two or more partners own pieces of each other, as in the Japanese *keiretsu* arrangements of cross-ownership of minority stakes. For example, Mitsubishi Bank owns 5 to 10 percent of fifteen companies that constitute the core of the Mitsubishi group. In turn, these companies own shares of Mitsubishi Bank and of several other companies in the group. These ownership positions carry tacit but real agreements that the companies will have preferred business relationships with one another. In the case of the *keiretsu*, these relationships can be very deep and include joint planning, research, engineering, and manufacturing. It may be difficult to determine the boundaries between companies in a *keiretsu*.

In the last several years, the world's airlines have begun to establish cross-equity alliances. Swissair, Singapore Air, and Delta formed the Global Excellence Alliance in 1989. They cemented their relationship with cross-equity purchases. Singapore International Air (SIA) purchased 4.6 percent of Delta's equity and a 2.8 percent stake in Swissair. Delta acquired 2.7 percent of SIA shares, and Swissair bought a 0.6 percent interest in SIA. Although none of these stakes represents even close to a controlling interest, they do act as a tangible bond among the partners. The three airlines now link schedules, market together, and combine their frequent-flyer programs. In 1995, they formed DSS (Delta, Swiss, Singapore) World Sourcing, equally owned by the three partners of the Global Excellence Alliance, to find quality sources of products and services at cost savings to the three partners. British Airways bought a stake in U.S. Airways as the underpinning to a transatlantic alliance. Now British Airways has divested its U.S. Airways equity and alliance to make way for an alliance with American Airlines.

Exhibit 2-4 ❖ CASE STUDY: CALTEX

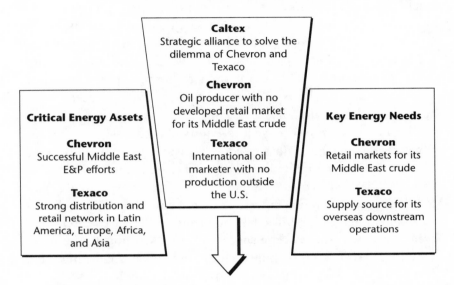

Source: Booz·Allen & Hamilton analysis.

Shared-Equity Alliances

Shared-equity alliances usually entail the formation of a new business, commonly referred to as a joint venture. A classic example from the energy industry was the creation of Caltex by Chevron and Texaco in the 1930s. As shown in Exhibit 2-4, going into the alliance, Chevron was successful in exploration and production in the Middle East and Texaco had a strong distribution and retail network in Latin America, Europe, Africa, and Asia. Chevron needed retail markets for its Middle East crude; Texaco needed a supply source for its overseas downstream operations. Caltex was formed as a shared-equity venture to solve the dilemma for both companies. The results have been excellent.

Uno-Ven was an alliance created by PDVSA (the state-owned oil company of Venezuela) and Unocal to sell refined Venezuelan crude in the United States. Star Enterprises was formed by Texaco and Saudi Aramco to build a strong marketing arm in the eastern United States with Saudi money and oil and Texaco's market presence. Texaco and Saudi Aramco are owners of Star, an independent refining and marketing company. Star and Texaco have now formed another shared-equity alliance with Shell. The three parents—Royal Dutch Shell, Texaco, and Saudi Aramco—will own shares in the consolidated U.S. refining and marketing assets that were contributed by the three firms. The move toward consolidation of the downstream oil industry is gaining momentum in both Europe and the United States as oil companies look for ways to improve profitability and growth on a large chunk of their assets that have produced low returns for at least a decade.

Corning has set up fifty shared-equity alliances—Dow Corning, Owens Corning Fiberglass, Siecor, Samsung Corning, Eurokera, Optical Fibers, and Pittsburgh Corning, to mention a few. Although the specifics of each alliance vary to suit the particular market, partner, and circumstances, all have a common root; each partner contributed capabilities that enabled the alliance to enter (often create) a new business. The success ratio of Corning's alliances is very high. According to James Houghton, former Corning CEO, forty-one of the fifty alliances are successful; only nine have failed. The contribution of its alliances to Corning's bottom line now exceeds $500 million annually.

Strategic Alliances: Commitment

There are many types of alliances, but commitment is what makes alliances strategic. Companies enter a number of more transactional relationships through licensing, joint programs, and sourcing arrangements. Whereas all those are important, they are not considered strategic alliances.

Alliances are about growth. Alliances are about capabilities. Alliances are about consolidation. Combining our technology with your distribution gives big advantages to both of us—without either of us losing our independence. And if we work this way, neither one of us has to deal with all the other parts of each other's business that we don't understand or need.

Capabilities are widely recognized as the key competitive differentiators among corporations. But few companies are the world's best at more than a handful of capabilities, and rarely on a global scale. One of the most important challenges for growth is to be able to deploy world-class capabilities wherever you conduct your business. So the best companies are searching to obtain capabilities from whatever means available—acquisition, internal development, hiring, and various forms of partnerships and alliances.

WHAT'S GOING ON?

Although alliances have been around for centuries, accurate data on alliances was rare until recently. During the 1970s, about 750 new commercial strategic alliances were recorded. Possibly, more existed. The alliance movement gained steam in the 1980s as the difficulties with transnational mergers became apparent in a rapidly globalizing economy. The annual rate of strategic-alliance formation grew from around 100 to about 2,000 over the decade of the 1980s. The United States trailed Asia and Europe in the 1970s and '80s, both in numbers of alliances and in percentage of transnational alliances. In the United States, less than half the alliances involved other countries, whereas outside the United States, 75 percent did.

When history is finally written, the 1990s will be known as the dawn of the age of collaboration. By mid-decade, the average annual rate of alliance formation had exceeded 10,000 worldwide. It is anticipated that the rate will more than double by the turn of the century. That's a tenfold increase since 1990 and a hundredfold increase since 1980.

Alliances are redefining corporate boundaries. We are moving from highly parochial, well-guarded, impermeable, turf-conscious castles to collegial, sharing, permeable, flexible, moving areas of influence and responsibility.

The nature of strategic alliances has shifted from issues peripheral to the core business of the partners to issues squarely in the crosshairs of the firms' strategy. Take the auto industry as an example. The major U.S. automakers began cooperating in the 1970s and early 1980s by cofunding research to solve environmental problems—first with catalytic converters and later with the development of the electric car. Although important, these alliances were not focused on sensitive and competitive core issues, such as product development, proprietary manufacturing, and marketing.

All that has changed in the past ten years. For example, GM formed an alliance with Toyota, known as New United Motor Manufacturing, Incorporated (NUMMI), to build a plant in Fremont,

California. The plant is jointly owned and managed by GM and Toyota. Designs are principally Japanese, and the vehicles are marketed through GM and Toyota dealers across the United States.

NUMMI is a good example of the basic change in alliances from peripheral to fundamental. Partners on both sides are attempting to solve fundamental strategic problems in their core businesses through alliances. In GM's case, that means obtaining a high-quality, low-cost car for their U.S. dealers. For Toyota, it means solving a tough political problem in the U.S. market. The auto industry has been in the center of the balance-of-trade argument between the United States and Japan. The trade imbalance ballooned in the 1980s when Japanese cars flooded the United States market. Toyota found the GM deal attractive because it helped them with two serious problems. First, the political issue was about to turn ugly, with import restrictions (then informal, but threatening to become more stringent). Second, with large sales in U.S. dollars of products whose manufacture was paid for in yen, Toyota was exposed to serious losses if the yen strengthened against the dollar. And the yen increased threefold, from 250 yen to the U.S. dollar in 1982 to near 80 yen to the U.S. dollar in 1995. Although the yen softened to 120 to 145 yen to the U.S. dollar in 1997 and 1998, it remains much stronger than it was in the days of Japan's auto-export boom. The world changed in the decade from 1986 to 1996. According to the Department of Commerce, Japanese car exports to the United States were 3.5 million in 1986 and only 1.1 million in 1996; Japanese vehicles produced in the United States on the other hand grew from 600,000 to 2.4 million over that same period.

There are many more examples. The key point is that companies are now seeking to solve tough strategic problems that are central to their business through alliances. Except in a relatively few cases, this approach is new to the United States, although it is business as usual in Japan and much of the rest of Asia.

Alliances Are Profitable

The conventional wisdom in U.S. management circles through the 1980s was that alliances were difficult to manage, didn't last very long, lost money as often as not, and were an all-around headache for anyone but the Japanese.

The Japanese, so the myth continued, formed alliances with U.S. companies to steal their secrets and then steal their markets. Like all conventional wisdom and myths, there were plenty of incidents to back up the beliefs. Little real research was done to find out how alliances fared statistically. Peter Pekar's research has moved us well into the realm of reality on the financial performance of alliances.

Regrettably, the research doesn't go much farther back than the middle 1980s. So we can't debunk the old myths with facts. We can only set the current record straight and wonder if the past was really so different.

Fact 1: Alliances are more profitable on average than are the regular operations of companies. In his study of 2,500 U.S. alliances from 1988 to 1992, Pekar found that the average return on investment for alliances was 17 percent, compared with the 11.5 percent average return for U.S. industry during that same period (see Exhibit 2-5).

Booz·Allen and Pekar ran another study for 1988 to 1996 of 5,000 U.S. and global alliances and found that the average return for strategic alliances exceeded 16 percent, a full 4 percent higher than the average ROI (return on investment) experienced by the participating corporations on their own.

Alliance Analyst's 1995 study showed that the twenty-five most alliance-active U.S. companies in the *Fortune* 500 averaged just over 17 percent return on equity, compared with the overall *Fortune* 500 average return of 12 percent and a dismal 10 percent for the twenty-five least alliance-active companies. As in the first study, the results were favorable compared with average industry ROIs in almost every industry included in the study (see Exhibit 2-6).

Let's get more data out before we probe the whys. Harbison and Pekar dug deeper and found **fact 2: The average return on investment for alliances rose significantly as companies gained experience (i.e., formed more alliances)** (see Exhibit 2-7).

As Exhibit 2-7 shows, there is a strong learning effect. This occurs in the United States as well as around the world. Experienced firms earn twice the ROI that inexperienced firms earn on their alliances. This relationship between ROI and alliance experience is

Exhibit 2-5 ❖ **COMPARISON OF RETURN ON INVESTMENT**

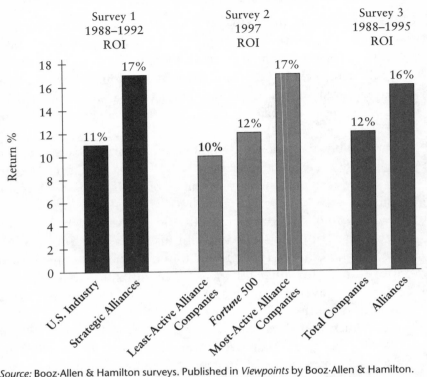

Source: Booz·Allen & Hamilton surveys. Published in *Viewpoints* by Booz·Allen & Hamilton. Copyright © Booz·Allen & Hamilton.

Exhibit 2-6 ❖ **ALLIANCE RETURN ON INVESTMENT BY INDUSTRY**

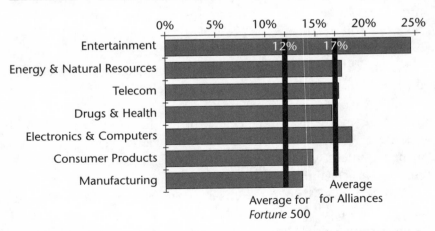

Source: Booz·Allen & Hamilton surveys. Published in *Viewpoints* by Booz·Allen & Hamilton. Copyright © Booz·Allen & Hamilton.

Exhibit 2-7 ❖ ROI vs. ALLIANCE EXPERIENCE

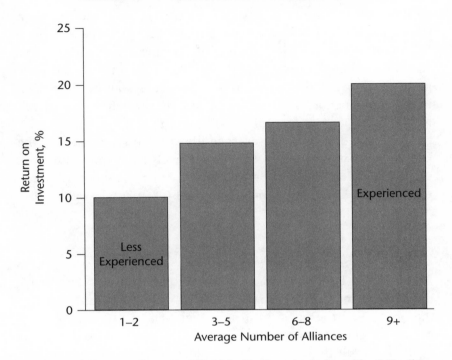

Source: Booz·Allen & Hamilton surveys. Published in *Viewpoints* by Booz·Allen & Hamilton. Surveys 2 and 3: "A Practical Guide to Alliances: Leapfrogging the Learning Curve," 1993. Copyright © Booz·Allen & Hamilton.

not a statistical fluke. Research shows that ROI steadily improves in most industries as experience increases. In some industries, the ROI for alliances of experienced firms has been four to five times the ROI for alliances of firms that have had experience with only one or two alliances.

Fact 3: Alliances have a higher percentage of winners than do either acquisitions or venture capital. In a survey of seven hundred companies, one hundred venture capital firms, fifty corporate development executives, and twenty investment bankers, we found that 60 percent of alliances were considered successful, compared with 50 percent of acquisitions and 30 percent of venture capital investments. The success rate for the top group of alliance active companies was reported at 80 percent.

THE AGE OF COLLABORATION

Real success in the twenty-first century will be less associated with the go-it-alone and self-reliance mentality that won the American Wild West in the late 1800s than with a cooperative mentality. The world has entered a new era—the age of collaboration—and companies will obtain the capabilities and resources necessary to win in the changing global marketplace heavily through alliances. Alliances are a new engine for growth, and they are not a flash-in-the-pan phenomenon. The average life span of an alliance in the United States is eight years. That's a relatively short time compared with fifteen years in Europe and Japan, but it's almost triple the three-year average life of alliances of 1983. A mental recalibration is required.

WHY ALLIANCES ARE SUCCESSFUL

Alliances can be a profitable way to expand a business. In an acquisition or merger, the partners take all—the good and the bad, the pretty and the ugly, businesses that fit and the baggage, the profitable and the unprofitable, the core capability and the unwanted branch in Somalia. Any problems, liabilities, warts, and unfinished business of the acquired company are yours, for better or for worse, from this day forward. For example, Aon acquired Alexander & Alexander in 1997; six months later, a mysterious and hidden loss of $27 million surfaced.

In an alliance, you can carve out the piece you like. You can take the prime cuts of meat and leave the liver and the hooves behind. Alliances are about combining capabilities of two or more partners. We take advantage of your strength in the market and my technology, or your cost position and my distribution. We do as Pepsi and Lipton did with iced tea—Pepsi's distribution and Lipton's product.

REASONS TO CHOOSE ALLIANCES

Our research and experience at Booz·Allen indicate seven main reasons that companies choose alliance over acquisition or internal action.

1. **Risk sharing.** Companies cannot afford the potential downside of the investment opportunity alone. Airbus Industrie, an alliance of German, French, British, and Spanish aerospace companies, was created exactly for this reason. The oil industry has long used alliances to share exploration risks in such locations as the North Sea, the South China Sea, and Azerbaijan.

2. **Acquisition barriers.** Companies cannot acquire the right partner because of price, size, unwanted businesses, government resistance, reluctance of owners, or regulatory restrictions. The GM-Toyota alliance fits almost every one of those reasons.

3. **Market-segment access.** Companies don't understand the customers or don't have the relationships or infrastructure to distribute their products to a particular market. Lipton chose PepsiCo for this reason.

4. **Technology gaps.** Companies don't have all the technology they need and can't afford the time or resources to develop it themselves. The seed company DeKalb gained access to Monsanto's biological research and gave Monsanto the ability to capture more value for its research by participating downstream.

5. **Geographic access.** Companies aren't where they want to be and don't have the resources to get there. Corning joined forces with Samsung to enter and compete in the Asian market.

   In many cases, government regulations inhibit direct access. China is a good example. Few companies have the resources, commitment, or permission to go it alone in China. Most companies welcome the government's encouragement (or mandate!) to get a local partner. CITIC is a top government agency in China, established specifically for investments in partnerships with foreign corporations, both inside and outside China, and has hundreds (maybe thousands) of cross-border alliances.

6. **Funding constraints.** Individual companies can't afford developing or launching the venture alone. Consider the Caspian and Alaskan pipelines built to bring oil from production fields to markets.

Exhibit 2-8 ❖ CROSS-BORDER INTENSITY BY REGION

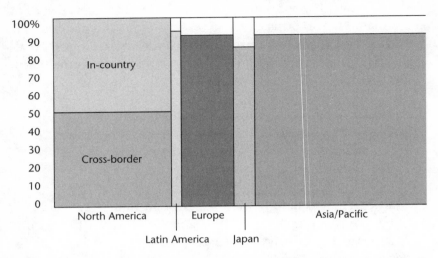

Source: Booz·Allen interviews and analysis, 1994–1997. Published in Booz·Allen & Hamilton Viewpoints.

7. Management skills. Companies need more talent to be successful. Oracle and Microsoft have several alliances with start-up technology companies to which they contribute management talent and access to their resources in exchange for proprietary access to the start-up technology.

Sometimes, these drivers are the same for both partners (e.g., risk sharing), but often they are different (e.g., one has technology, the other distribution). In all cases, each partner is looking for something that the other partner can provide. It's a targeted exercise with a specific capability or objective in mind. The search for an alliance partner is often triggered by the recognition that neither acquisition nor going it alone will work in that particular case. Hence we should think of alliances as a natural progression in the search for capabilities that can help companies win the competitive game.

THE CROSS-BORDER ALLIANCE BOOM

Nowhere are the advantages of alliances more apparent than in cross-border consolidations (see Exhibits 2-8 and 2-9).

Exhibit 2-9 ❖ ALLIANCES BY REGION AND COUNTRY

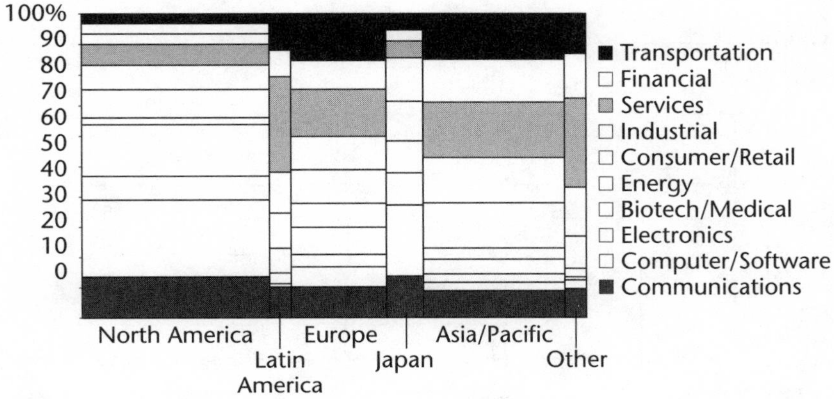

Note: Width and area are proportional to number of alliances.
Source: Alliance analyst, SDC, Booz·Allen & Hamilton analysis. Published in Booz·Allen & Hamilton *Viewpoints.*

Of the twenty thousand alliances formed worldwide in 1994 to 1996, approximately 75 percent have been across borders. The United States trails the rest of the world with about 54 percent cross-border alliances, compared with over 90 percent for Europe and the Pacific Rim.

Flourishing cross-border alliances are changing the global business environment in most industries in ways that we are just beginning to understand.

In many industries, the global demands on technology and financial resources are forcing companies to ally as industries rapidly change and acquisitions become impractical or impossible. The choice? Get with it, or get run over!

Alliance Investment Stakes and Skills

Alliance investment stakes are highest in Asia (excluding Japan) and significantly lower in the United States and Japan. The average global strategic-alliance investment by the top one thousand U.S. companies amounts to only $20 million, compared with $90 million for China and the rest of Asia (excluding Japan) (see Exhibit 2-10). The United States also lags in sales per alliance, with only $80 million, in contrast with more than $250 million for European alliances.

Exhibit 2-10 ❖ ALLIANCE SIZE BY COUNTRY
Millions of Dollars Investment per Alliance

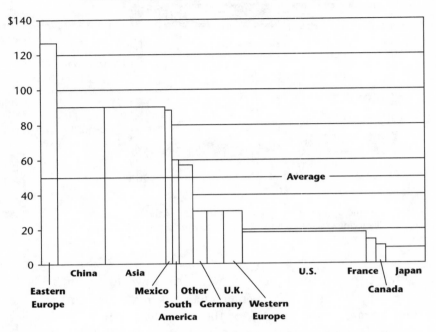

Source: Alliance Analyst, SDC, Booz·Allen & Hamilton analysis, study 2 from Exhibit 2-3.

In 1998 the U.S. average has more than doubled to over $50 million. The important point is that we should expect very high growth in alliance activity in the United States, a relative newcomer, as it catches up to Europe and Asia.

We should also not be surprised by the results of Booz·Allen's 1997 survey on alliance competencies covering the United States, Europe, Asia, and Latin America. The United States trails Europe and Asia in alliance skills. When comparing their own practices with those of companies that achieved superior alliance results, the self-assessment ratings of European and Asian companies were higher than those of U.S. companies. These findings were supported by field interviews and client work.

European and Asian companies indicated that their U.S. counterparts were behind in the critical skills of integration planning and implementation. U.S. companies are too quick to think the job

Exhibit 2-11 ❖ RACING TOWARD GLOBAL CAPABILITIES: EVOLUTION OF ALLIANCE DRIVERS

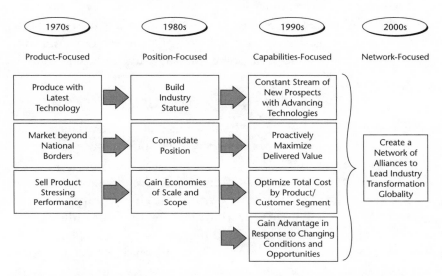

Source: Booz·Allen & Hamilton analysis, 1996–1998. Projection for 2000s by author.

is completed when the negotiations are finalized. As the Europeans and Asians know, that is just the beginning.

Looking Ahead in Cross-Border Alliances

Exhibit 2-11 depicts the evolution of cross-border alliance drivers over three decades. The 1970s was the era of product performance, in which alliances generally focused on getting access to the latest technology and selling products internationally (several alliances between U.S. and Japanese companies in manufactured products occurred in the 1960s and 1970s). But the key selling point was product performance. In most cases, the boundaries between industries were very clear-cut, so a broader set of capabilities did not need to be accessed.

In the 1980s, the emphasis shifted to positional focus. Companies sought to build industry stature, consolidate position, and often gain economies of scale and scope. Now the emphasis is on capabilities. Industry lines are blurring, and markets are becoming global. In these newly defined competitive arenas, positional assets are not enough, and new capabilities are required to succeed. The name of the game is to maximize delivered value, to minimize total costs, and to gain competitive advantage.

Looking to the future, we may expect the emphasis to shift from one-on-one alliances to networks whose objective is to lead the transformation of industries. These networks will evolve into relationship enterprises as they concentrate on establishing leadership positions.

WHAT CAN WE CONCLUDE?

The advantages and purposes of alliances just described have been around forever, yet alliances have become popular in the corporate world only recently. Why?

Three things have happened over the past decade that have given alliances a major boost in the boardroom. First, companies have come to recognize that globalization and growth mean adding more capabilities in more places around the world than can possibly be obtained by acquisition or internal development. This scramble for capabilities has been the most important driver behind the surge in strategic alliances.

Second, there is a growing awareness that ownership of foreign companies has serious drawbacks. Nationalism is the second most important driver of strategic alliances. If home-country advantage is important, alliances are the best way to obtain it. Antitrust, nationalist sentiment, and national crown jewels all favor alliances over acquisition.

Third, companies have made the stunning realization that alliances can be profitable. Booz·Allen's research showed that alliances were more profitable than total industry average ROE (return on equity). That would be enough to get any board member's attention. Not only are alliances more profitable on the whole, but companies that were alliance active were significantly more profitable than alliance neophytes.

In a brief ten years, strategic alliances have leaped onto the global business stage as one of the most important vehicles for growth and competitiveness. Alliances have become larger and closer to the strategic core of companies and have become a larger and larger part of the corporate portfolio. Alliances have several significant advantages over acquisitions. The major drawbacks—difficulty in negotiating and managing—are receiving considerable top-level attention as alliances become an ever-greater part of the corporate portfolio.

Some scholars, notably Michael Porter of Harvard, believe that alliances are unstable and will either be taken over by one of the partners or fail. Alliances have high transaction costs (academic code for difficulties in getting partners to act effectively without the power of ownership), and those costs, accompanied by partner frustration, will lead to a takeover or breakup. An owned foreign subsidiary, they argue, can be integrated into the parent's business and decision systems. Only through ownership can a company be world-class and have a sustainable international position; thus alliances are doomed to mediocrity.

Porter's observations are correct, but not his conclusions. My experience puts me in the camp with Michael Yoshino (Harvard) and Srinivasa Rangan (Babson), who in their fine scholarly work, *Strategic Alliances—An Entrepreneurial Approach to Globalization,* respond to the argument against alliances:

> Do such criticisms doom strategic alliances as a managerial instrument? Certainly not. We counter that alliances are neither mere transitional devices, destined to "fail," nor do they "deter" an alliance-seeking firm's "own efforts at upgrading" its core competencies, but that, to the contrary, alliances enable firms to focus on and invest in a few selected core competencies, leverage the competencies of other firms, and thereby grow into formidable global competitors.

The first half of their book effectively justifies this position.

Booz·Allen's research and client experience show that today alliances are more profitable than are ongoing operations, and there are ample examples of very successful alliances, both in-country and cross-border—witness Corning's family of alliances, the auto industry, telecommunications, aerospace. Clearly, there have been unsuccessful alliances. Further research has focused on why some alliances have not succeeded (see Chapter 6), but contrary to the results of acquisitions, the winners are outpacing the losers.

Throughout this book, I make the point that acquisitions and mergers will continue to be important to corporations as they expand their reach and consolidate their industries. I do believe strongly, however, that acquisitions will not be sufficient to establish world leadership in the next century. Alliances must play a major role; no company has the money, the clout, the political position, nor the willingness to take risks or to own everything necessary to achieve world leadership. To those scholars who believe that alliances inevitably fail, I suggest they redirect their research to determine: How can alliances be successful?

As the title of this chapter implies, strategic alliances as we know them today are not the endgame. The evolution will continue. Indeed, in the evolution of commercial enterprise, strategic alliances are the precursors to the trillion-dollar enterprise.

Next, the Relationship Enterprise

CHAPTER 3

The first two chapters surveyed the landscape and examined the forces that are shaping our economic and business environment and the way in which companies are adapting. This chapter reviews what business enterprises need to compete, grow, and be profitable in the environment in the beginning of the twenty-first century, and draws on lessons learned about how current business structures fare in that emerging environment—what's good and what's not. Based on these conclusions and some assumptions, specs can be drawn up for the form of enterprise that will win in the new environment.

The second half of the chapter is devoted to describing the relationship enterprise (and its logical conclusion, the trillion-dollar enterprise)—its characteristics and how it differs from the global corporation. The chapter concludes with two current examples of the relationship enterprise: public accounting and the Japanese *keiretsu*.

REQUIREMENTS FOR THE NEW ENVIRONMENT

The two dominant forces that will shape the world economy in the beginning of the twenty-first century are globalization and nationalism. A third force, consolidation, is both a cause and a product of globalization. The structure of a business enterprise should be shaped by these two forces as well. Stated another way, the business organization of the twenty-first century should be advantaged in a world driven by globalization and nationalism. These powerful winds will cause many shipwrecks, but wise captains will use them to propel their ships to safety and prosperity.

The key question is how to be successful and achieve that goal. Our list is short and simple: be global, set world standards, and be local. Let's look at each in turn.

Be Global

It's hard to imagine being a leader in almost any industry in the next century without being global. Even traditionally local industries, such as restaurants and real estate, have turned global. Just look at McDonald's and its objective of being the first choice of every kid on the planet. Security Capital Group, a U.S.-based firm that develops REITs (real estate investment trusts) and creates public ownership of vast real estate holdings, has the ambition of enabling anyone in the world to invest in apartments or hotels or office buildings or shopping centers or warehouses anywhere in the world. We don't have to stretch to understand that most of us will be competing in industries that are global. Thus, the first requirement: be global.

The tough question is: What does it mean to be global? The mandate that I envision goes something like the following:

- Serve and have access to all the major markets for my product or service, including those markets that should be using my product or service in the future. (Note that I didn't write "have an office or factory or a sales force," but "serve and have access to.")
- Understand my customers and my markets everywhere, including the opportunities, risks, and obstacles that they face now and in the future.
- Be able to meet and anticipate my customers' requirements and expectations whatever they are—including cost, reliability, service, distribution, technology—far better than anyone else in the world. Make our partnership indispensable to my customers' success and the interface between us seamless, effortless, and profitable.

- Obtain my materials and services from the best sources in the world.
- Understand all important factors and trends that will impact my business in the years ahead, including technology (product, manufacturing/processing, information), new organizational approaches, the Internet, and political and economic conditions everywhere. Recognize Didier Pineau-Valencienne's (chairman of Schneider Group of France, a global manufacturer of electrical and electronic equipment) challenge that a business can and will be impacted by developments from anywhere in the world.

Set World Standards

A principal responsibility of a leader is to set standards that others will follow. Hence, one definition of an industry leader is the individual or firm that others look to set (and follow) standards. A company will not be a leader if it aspires only to match world standards. Think about companies that have been leaders in their industries—Ford and IBM in their early years, General Electric, Toyota, Jardine Matheson, Microsoft, Corning, Bosch, Motorola, Coca-Cola, Boeing. All were standard setters. In the business context, these standards should include the following six areas:

- **Innovation.** The greatest corporate innovations are not necessarily new ideas, but the mechanisms for putting those new ideas into action. Motorola's Bob Galvin thinks of the innovation leader as the firm that can move from idea to commercial success most rapidly. The ideal enterprise must have the capability to tap sources of good ideas (intellectual capital, in the latest vernacular) from any industry and any country and move them rapidly through research, product development and engineering, manufacturing, and distribution to customers.

- **Value.** Factors contributing to value differ by product and service. Typically, they are some mixture of design, delivery, total cost, reliability, technology, and quality. Value can only be defined from the customer's perspective; hence piece cost—the easiest way for a supplier to point to value—is an inadequate measure.

In a study involving a major automotive manufacturer and five of its largest suppliers in the mid-1990s, Booz·Allen found that changing the way in which the companies interacted could reduce the total cost of materials purchased by 25 to 30 percent without affecting the functionality or style of the vehicle. For example, expensive complexity was found in areas that weren't important to customers, such as offering twenty-four kinds of carpet for trunks. Extensive duplication of costly engineering was found in both the auto company and its suppliers. OEMs (original equipment manufacturers) mandated costly and unnecessary rules on everything from billing procedures to how much inventory the supplier should carry to details of manufacturing processes. In addition to reducing costs, eliminating duplication cut the cycle time with the suppliers dramatically. None of the savings came by reducing the manufacturing cost of individual parts (e.g., gears, pistons, forgings, wires).

Given that purchased materials account for over 60 percent of cost of goods sold for most auto companies, enough savings were realized to reduce the price of the vehicle and still make suppliers and the auto company more profitable.

Motorola believes that customers value the convenience of mobile communications. Hence, a core strategy for Motorola has been to lead in designing and manufacturing products and systems that enable better, broader, more convenient, and lower-cost mobile communications. The age of Dick Tracy's two-way wrist radio is here. Motorola believes the future of mobile communications is in satellites, and it is investing $25 billion to set up satellite networks that will enable all types of communications (data, voice, image) to be at people's fingertips wherever they are in the world, at low cost, high quality, and with superior reliability. This is clearly leadership in setting world standards in value.

- **Performance.** Remember that performance is defined by the customer as well as by Wall Street. Everything a company does should be measured by its impact on the benefit-cost criteria of its intended customers. Over the past decade, businesses have been breaking down their operations by process and activity and measuring these against competitors—the benchmarking wave.

Virtually anything that can be compared quantitatively is bench-marked—cost, cycle time, market share, research spending and results, head counts, productivity (not only in manufacturing, but in everything from accounting and systems to engineering and human resources), quality, and financial results. Consulting firms have built large storehouses of benchmarks, which can short-circuit the tedious and complex task of doing it yourself. World-class means world-class in performance both in prof-itability and in the eyes of your customers. Companies should focus on those activities and operations that impact the cus-tomer's value criteria. Let your competitors spend their money on activities and operations that don't matter to the customer.

- **Processes.** More attention is, appropriately, being focused on processes. Benchmarking has broadened from quantitative measures to more qualitative processes. Some gurus preach the process gospel as the magic key to financial and market suc-cess. One of the common characteristics of processes is that they cross several functions and knit together otherwise inde-pendent or isolated activities. Good examples of important processes include product development, establishment of new businesses, international market development, information collection and dissemination, quality management, systems de-velopment, customer acquisition and retention, and manage-ment development.

  World-class means world-class processes—but with the same requirement that the customers' criteria of performance dictates. Our mythical enterprise must be able to identify new processes, adapt them for effective internal use, and spread them across the enterprise continually.

- **People.** We have known since the dawn of history in every human endeavor from war to sports to politics to business that the win-ners have the best people, properly motivated and effectively or-ganized toward a goal. So it will be in the future. The challenge will be to create conditions and an environment that will attract the best people, train and develop them to the peak of their abilities, and motivate them to achieve at their maximum level. Easy to say, tough to do. And this must be accomplished in every country in which the enterprise is participating.

- **Capabilities.** Most lists of world-class standards would put capabilities first. I think of capabilities as the accumulation of people, processes, assets, and performance. Capabilities enable one firm to serve its markets and customers better than another. Capabilities enable a firm to anticipate trends and lead its competitors. Capabilities enable a firm to create and drive new markets, to change the competitive playing field, to shape the environment in its favor. World-class certainly means world-class capabilities. The enterprise we are constructing will need to determine what capabilities are required for leadership in its industry, at what level those capabilities need to be, and how they can be built, acquired, or accessed.

Be Local

The final and possibly most difficult mandate to the global enterprise is to be local wherever it operates. The advantages of serving a market from a local base are large. True, foreign cachet is important in some products, for example, perfume, wine, sports cars, and watches. Nevertheless, in most countries the mass market shows a strong preference for locally produced goods. In virtually every country on earth, the vast majority of expenditures by consumers goes for locally produced goods and services. Globalization has not eclipsed national pride. Despite all the press and concern that globalization is hollowing out whole economies, consumption in almost every country is at least 90 percent locally sourced. There is a distinct bias in most countries in favor of home-country companies and their products because of the obvious realization that they provide the jobs that enable the citizens to have the ability to buy.

As we have seen in the previous chapters, there are other subtle and not so subtle advantages of being local in most countries. We need to distinguish between locally produced and locally owned. Employment is derived from locally produced. Special advantages accrue to *locally owned* companies. Availability of capital is one such advantage. Subsidized research is a common perk of national companies. Access to information from government and state-owned schools, tax breaks on a wide range of activities, state supported training, and the often-criticized bias on government contracts are others. Whereas most countries are not blatantly biased toward locally owned companies, all have some biases, and they are important.

What does it take to be local? There are at least six important standards that a company wishing to be local should strive to achieve:

- Understanding of specific requirements of the local customers and how they differ from those of other regions and countries, and products and services tooled to meet those requirements
- Local marketing, sales, and distribution—advertising and the distribution system are particularly distinctive
- A distinct national image in areas for which it is important to be national
- A predominantly local workforce and an image as a national employer that is attractive to the nation's most capable people and that is an employer of choice in the industry
- Access to benefits differentially available to locally owned enterprises
- Ability to operate locally in each important market

That's my list: be global, set world standards, and be local. Surely other factors are important for winning global institutions to possess, but this is a good starter set.

STRUCTURE FOR THE NEW ENVIRONMENT

Let us now explore how to put together an organization that can meet these criteria. A company can use one of four approaches:

- Build internally; develop the capability by investing, hiring, and growing current business platform.
- Merge with or acquire companies having the needed capabilities.
- Enter alliances with companies that have the needed capabilities.
- Create a network of alliances that collectively have the needed capabilities.

Exhibit 3-1 ❖ THE BEST WAYS TO BE GLOBAL

Critical Capabilities	Build Internally	Acquisitions	Alliances	Network of Alliances
Serve and have access wherever relevant	◐	◐	◕	●
Understand all my customers and markets	◔	◔	◐	●
Meet and anticipate customer needs	◐	◐	◕	◕
Provide best sourcing globally	◐	◔	◐	◕
Understand issues with important impact on my business	◐	◔	◐	●
Take and keep the lead in all important markets	◔	◔	◐	●
Total	◐	◔	◐	●

Key: The degree to which a circle is filled reflects a given approach's ability to meet the selected criterion. For example, acquisitions fail to meet the ability to take and keep a lead in all important markets, whereas a network of alliances fulfills that need.

We will examine each of the mandates—be global, set world standards, be local—individually, and rate the abilities of the four approaches to meet them (see Exhibits 3-1, 3-2, and 3-3).

Be Global

Under the rubric of Be Global, I have identified six specific capabilities, for which I've rated each approach (see Exhibit 3-1). For example, the best way to serve and have access everywhere is to establish a network of alliances (solid circle); whereas building internally or acquiring will rarely get you to a leadership position in all important markets (half circles).

The conclusion should not be surprising: choose acquisition last and network of alliances first if you want to be global. It is almost impossible to imagine a set of acquisitions in virtually any industry that could establish a global corporation that would be powerful everywhere. There are a few examples of companies that built such a position internally, such as Boeing and Coca-Cola. Other companies have had moments of global leadership—for example, Ford and IBM—and a few have a shot in the next decade—such as Intel and Microsoft.

Suffice to say that unless you have a dominant, defensible, long-term technological advantage or market franchise, you should not bet your company's future or world leadership on internal development.

Logic appears to indicate overwhelmingly that a network of alliances gives you a better chance to be global than does any other approach. You can select the best partners in each country or region. Collectively, you can understand customers and markets; you can understand developments that can impact your business; and you can lead in all important markets. One or a few alliances will not be enough. Strong global presence and market leadership will require multiple, linked alliances so that all partners benefit from the understanding, consumer insight, technology, and presence of the other partners.

Don't worry yet about how you will put together or manage such a network. My intent in the first four chapters is to demonstrate the importance and value of an enterprise built on a network of alliances. Effective management of that structure is addressed in Section II.

Set World Standards

Setting world standards is an ambitious goal. Setting world standards in more than a few areas is probably beyond any single corporation. Exhibit 3-2 shows how we can rank the various approaches for developing an organization that can set world standards in the six key areas set out in our criteria.

Internal development and network of alliances rate highest across the board. It's easy to understand why world-class financial and operating performance and processes are achieved internally.

Exhibit 3-2 ❖ THE BEST WAYS TO SET WORLD STANDARDS

Critical Elements	Build Internally	Acquisitions	Alliances	Network of Alliances
Innovation	◑	◑	○	●
Value Proposition	◑	◑	◐	●
Financial and Operating Performance	●	◐	◐	◔
Processes	●	◕	◔	◔
People	◑	◕	◑	●
Capabilities	◔	◕	◑	●
Total	◔	◑	◐	●

Key: The degree to which a circle is filled reflects a given approach's ability to meet the selected criterion.

It's tough to buy processes, and performance requires strong management discipline.

Several companies have achieved world standards in the various categories. Motorola, Microsoft, Intel, Pfizer, and Monsanto provide good examples of world-class innovation, year after year at the top of their industries. Innovation is not limited to technology; Wal-Mart, Home Depot, and Crate & Barrel changed the paradigm in retailing, UPS did it in distribution, and Toyota redefined engineering and manufacturing.

The value proposition of Dell Computers has set a new world standard for custom-designed hardware for corporations, and Federal Express set new value standards in delivery of mail and small parcels by understanding the value of time and reliability. General Electric sets standards in many categories, and its financial and operating performance is always on top.

Several companies have concentrated on building world-class processes across their businesses. It is hard to single out a few true leaders because processes are hard to compare. Nevertheless, the value of strong processes is well understood by the leading companies in every industry. Arguably, Wal-Mart, Federal Express, and Toyota owe their success to well-crafted, innovative business processes that have enabled them to outperform their competitors significantly.

Setting world standards in people and capabilities is extremely difficult by building internally, making acquisitions, or forging a few alliances. An organization must be able to tap the best and brightest from many nations to claim world class. Acquisitions are far too limiting. The same can be said for capabilities; to be world-class, an organization must have all the capabilities necessary to lead its industries at world-class levels. No individual company can aspire or acquire to that level.

The conclusion: a strong discipline internally coupled with a network of alliances is the best organizational approach for setting world-class standards in the six key areas. Careful and proper selection of the partners will enable the enterprise to fill the gaps. Each partner must understand the value of being world-class and have the discipline, commitment, and willingness to invest that are necessary to achieve those standards. Once such a network has been established, it will continue to generate new world-class standards.

Be Local

Finally, being local in many nations cannot be achieved by a single corporation. As we have defined it, being local means *being local* . . . not making an attempt to be local through foreign ownership. You can be local with a global product. Coca-Cola and McDonald's do it by local ownership of franchised bottlers and distributors. Boeing does it by partnering with local manufacturers.

As Exhibit 3-3 shows, acquisition can certainly enable a company to understand local consumers, tailor products to local needs, provide local manufacturing, marketing, sales, and distribution, and possibly provide a distinct national image (if the foreign owner allows the acquired company the necessary autonomy and freedom). However, acquisition falls far short in being the employer of choice in the local market (even if it was top dog prior to the acquisition). Operating locally in each important market would require a large number of acquisitions, each with the baggage we discussed previously. Acquisition is not the best way for a corporation to build a global enterprise that is able to be local.

Exhibit 3-3 ❖ THE BEST WAYS TO BE LOCAL

Critical Capabilities	Build Internally	Acquisitions	Alliances	Network of Alliances
Tailor to local requirements	half	full	full	full
Market, sell, distribute locally	quarter	full	full	full
Establish a distinct national image	quarter	three-quarter	full	full
Be the local employer of choice	quarter	quarter	full	full
Maintain local ownership, access to local funding, treatment as national	empty	empty	full	full
Operate locally in each important market	empty	empty	half	full
Total	quarter	half	full	full

Key: The degree to which a circle is filled reflects a given approach's ability to meet the selected criterion.

Nor does building internally offer much promise. In almost every category, building internally is the least attractive approach to being local in multiple locations. Hence, unless other countries cannot live without your product or technology or service, you should seriously consider alliances.

On a country-by-country basis, individual alliances can provide all the capabilities needed to be local. The network of alliances has advantages when multiple countries are involved. Think of the options as hub and spoke (individual alliances with each country) or as a web (network of alliances covering the countries). To the extent that there are advantages across countries, and not only with the hub or parent, then the network is the preferred approach. Since the objective is to establish an organization capable of leading (or dominating) an industry across the world, I prefer the web to the hub-and-spoke system.

Bottom line: the network is the best approach in all three arenas—being global, setting world standards, and being local.

ENTER THE RELATIONSHIP ENTERPRISE

The term *relationship enterprise* simply captures what is happening today. The relationship enterprise is a network of alliances that operate as a single entity in key areas. Four characteristics distinguish the relationship enterprise and its grown-up version, the trillion-dollar enterprise:

- **Size and global reach.** Relationship enterprises will be very big—some eventually growing into trillion-dollar enterprises. They will be well suited to operate globally with partners in major markets and regions across the world.

- **Network of independent companies.** They will comprise independent companies, large and small, based in several countries, each with capabilities that are desired by the network.

- **Common mission.** They will be bonded together by a common mission with a broad strategic agenda and a recognition that they will be more successful jointly than independently.

- **Act as a single company.** On issues related to their common mission, the member companies will develop and execute a common strategy and will act as a single company.

We have already seen an overwhelming endorsement of alliances. Growth and acceptance of alliances has been extraordinary in the 1990s. Companies are forming multiple alliances and alliances closer to the strategic core of their businesses. Networks are also forming in a few industries, such as commercial aviation and telecommunications.

THE THREE-STAGE EVOLUTION

I see the relationship enterprise developing in three stages.

Stage 1: Single-purpose alliances
Stage 2: Network of partners
Stage 3: Multiple partners acting in concert

These stages will at first evolve gradually, as partners recognize the value of their alliances and the potential for deeper involvement. Later, they will accelerate, even in convulsive upheavals, as when industry restructuring forces bold action. We are already well into Stage 1: single-purpose alliances across a range of activities.

Stage 1: Single-Purpose Alliances

Finding they can't continue to go it alone, companies are building more and more linkages with other firms to bridge traditional geographic and value-added boundaries. There has been a shift in corporate thinking on alliances. The old model was linear. If you wanted to expand internationally, the first choice was to do it yourself. If that wasn't possible, you would consider making an acquisition. Only as a last resort would an alliance be considered.

The new model is different. It recognizes alliances on the same footing as either going it alone or acquiring. The decision tree has changed. You determine what capabilities are required and pick the best way to get them. Take, for example, Corning, as it considered expansion into the Asian market for television sets. Corning invented the all-glass television tube many years ago and was a major supplier in the worldwide industry, but had little presence in Asia. Samsung was a large Korean manufacturer of consumer electronics, including television sets and tubes. Samsung wanted to expand its television manufacturing, which fit well with Corning's interest in access to the high-growth market in Asia. The alliance combined Corning's technology and Samsung's low-cost manufacturing and marketing reach in Asia. The alliance has been very successful, with sales now in excess of $500 million and a major share of a dynamic market.

Organizations across the world and in almost every industry are in Stage 1 because it is in their self-interest. They are responding to economic and political forces and are creating a new competitive dynamic. Chapter 2 was about the development of Stage 1, single-purpose alliances.

Stage 2: Network of Partners

The second stage of evolution is just beginning: networks are forming, bonds are strengthening. Communicating and doing business together becomes easier, trust builds, and the common agenda evolves.

Stage 2 is also a natural evolution. As companies add new capabilities or enter new markets through alliances, they begin to recognize the opportunities that broader and deeper involvement with their partners might offer. A good example is the evolution of the telecommunications industry globally.

Telecommunications companies began forming alliances in the 1970s to extend their services across regions. These early alliances were bilateral and specific in their objectives and aspirations. As major companies became more comfortable working together, they expanded their relationships to include technology sharing, cross marketing, and even common investments. Alliances shifted from bilateral to multiple companies. Today, several global networks are forming, each with the objective of serving all their customers' needs across the globe. Two networks centered on British Telecom and France Telecom/Deutsche Telekom are clearly in Stage 2, network of partners.

Although relatively few industries have evolved into Stage 2, we can predict the characteristics that such enterprises (and the companies they comprise) will have.

Common Systems and Standards

If several companies are to operate as a single enterprise, they must be able to communicate easily. The optimum would be a common set of systems, common technology standards, and a common language (or at least a common understanding of terms). The easier it is to do business together, the more likely firms will expand their relationships.

The development of the Boeing 777 provides a good example of how common systems work for an alliance. Boeing formed an alliance with a number of firms to design and build the new jet. Boeing and its five Japanese partners created a transpacific telecommunications system, based on a common workstation, to link their design operations. The partnership's five hundred workstations ran the same computer-aided-design, engineering, and manufacturing software. At any point in the process, Boeing knew exactly where everyone was without having to use complex reporting systems. According to United Airlines, one of the alliance partners, the development of the 777 was the fastest and most efficient construction of a new commercial aircraft ever. Also according to United, the design itself was outstanding. Virtually all United's requirements were built in at every stage of the development.

Shared Goals and Strategies

It is essential to the success of any alliance for the goals of the parents to be consistent and shared by the managers of the alliance. In Stage 2, the partners go beyond the goals of the alliance and share goals for their firms. In the telecommunications industry, each of the partners wants to provide global service to its customers. The alliances enable them to deliver on that promise. Each wants to serve customers across the globe; each wants to offer telecommunications capabilities to its customers that match or beat any competitor's offering; each wants its cost to be at the lowest level in its industry. Without the alliances, such goals would be merely dreams. No single company in the telecommunications industry could possibly afford to own or develop the phone companies, satellites, transoceanic cables, the switching equipment, and the new technologies that total, global service to BP Amoco, General Motors, or Mitsubishi implies, not to mention the legal and regulatory roadblocks to ownership that exist.

Shared Values and Trust

The United Kingdom and the United States are very close allies. The bonds extend to a common heritage, but have been forged with mutual support for the past 150 years (after the United States got over the burning of the White House and Congress in 1812!). These two countries share the same values and have a deep and enduring trust. British officers are the only military officers outside the United States who would be given command over U.S. troops, as in World War II, when command was given to Field Marshal Montgomery for Operation Overlord at Normandy Beach. The two countries share intelligence. With few exceptions, the closest relationship between the U.S. president and another head of state has been that with the British prime minister. This alignment of values and this kind of trust are necessary in the alliances that make up a relationship enterprise.

The relationship between Intel and Microsoft is a good corporate example of this kind of trust. They share their closest secrets, and the alliance is documented by a handshake.

Stage 3: Multiple Partners Acting in Concert

Once the values, goals, and systems are aligned and the members of the alliance are embarked on a direction for which their combined energies, resources, and capabilities are required, they are ready for the third and final stage: the partners recognize their potential power and begin to act together as a single company.

A relationship enterprise will actually operate more like a political federation than a business alliance. Each participating company will have its own agenda and objectives, which it will pursue independently. Each will have shareholders and other stakeholders whom it must satisfy. However, each will lend its full power to the enterprise. For an analogy, think of how the United States engaged in World War II. It honored its alliance with the United Kingdom and other European countries by devoting its considerable wealth, production capability, and military might to the common mission of freeing Europe. Nevertheless, the United States remained an independent nation, as did the United Kingdom, France, the Netherlands, and Belgium. Clearly, the power of the alliance far exceeded the power of any one member operating independently.

RELATIONSHIP ENTERPRISES IN ACTION

There are two current examples of relationship enterprises: the public accounting or auditing profession, and the Japanese *keiretsu*. Both have been around for a long time. In both cases, networks of alliances of independent firms operate as single entities. Both were created by a set of forces that drove the independent firms together in a common mission.

Public Accounting

All industrialized countries have laws regulating public accounting firms, and rightly so. Public accountants are the primary assurance that the information that a publicly traded company reports is accurate. A country's ability to attract investment funds for its local industry depends on the credibility of its financial information.

One of the common regulations of the accounting profession is that partnerships must be national, that is, for example, a Brazilian accounting firm must be Brazilian owned. When multinational companies, with operations in five, ten, twenty, even one hundred countries came along, the prospect of hiring an accounting firm in each country and having a prayer of consistency in approach, quality, or accounting standards was daunting. In response, the major accounting firms went about globalizing themselves to meet a quite legitimate need of their clients. But they couldn't acquire foreign firms or send over partners from the parent company to set up shop because of the requirement for national ownership, so they formed alliances.

Arthur Andersen is an excellent example. Arthur Andersen began as a partnership of American certified public accountants organized and existing under the laws of the State of Illinois, USA. In the late 1950s, Arthur Andersen began linking up with internationally based audit firms to enable it to serve its clients as they formed foreign units and subsidiaries. These non-U.S. partnerships would audit the U.S. clients' subsidiaries in their countries according to Arthur Andersen's standards and instructions. Those relationships, which were coordinated by the U.S. partnership, grew in number. Finally, in 1977, to address more fully the professional independence requirements while performing multinational services demanded by clients, Arthur Andersen formed a *société coopérative* (the "SC") organized under the laws of the canton of Geneva, Switzerland. The SC is the coordinating entity for the legally separate Arthur Andersen national practice entities ("Member Firms"). The SC together with its Member Firms and those entities with whom the Member Firms have exclusive representation agreements form the Andersen Worldwide organization. There are now over 150 Member Firms in the Andersen Worldwide organization, managed through either the Arthur Andersen or Andersen Consulting business units.

Today, the Arthur Andersen Member Firm in Germany, Werlsch aftsprufunggesellschaft, serves the German subsidiary of Abbott Laboratories, the giant pharmaceutical company based in North

Chicago. Arthur Andersen Member Firms in the U.S., U.K. and Japan serve the subsidiaries of Hoechst, the largest chemical and drug company in Germany.

These Member Firms have come together with a common mission, set of values, and method of operation. Nevertheless, they are independent legally and in the eyes of the nations in which they operate. They have developed common systems, a means of communicating and working together across national boundaries. Quality control is assured by standard computerized scoring systems. Disciplined procedures are in place to accept new clients anywhere in the world. All new associates receive their initial training in Andersen's Center for Professional Development in St. Charles, Illinois, together with other new associates from the countries across the globe. All staff auditors receive three weeks of training annually—training that is designed and delivered with carefully crafted specs. Even the trainers are certified by central training executives. Partners of Barbier Frinault and Associes (Arthur Andersen's affiliate in France) clearly thinks of themselves as partners of Arthur Andersen.

Arthur Andersen works hard at being an effective relationship enterprise, and the results show it. Scored against our criteria of be global, set world standards, and be local, Arthur Andersen gets straight A's. And it has done so as a relationship enterprise.

Japanese Keiretsu

The other commercial structure that is close to a relationship enterprise is the Japanese *keiretsu* and its forerunner, the *zaibatsu*. The *keiretsu* is a network of companies in which there is substantial cross-ownership and that operate in certain areas as a single enterprise. *Keiretsus* were formed after World War II when their predecessors, *zaibatsus,* or family-run enterprises, were outlawed by the Allied military occupation forces in Japan.

History traces the origins of the *zaibatsu* back almost four hundred years, to 1616, the year Tokugawa Ieyasu, the great warrior shogun, consolidated his role over all of Japan after a devastating civil war. Sokubei Takatoshi Mitsui was a descendant of the Mitsui family, which since the twelfth century had been merchants under the protection of the Sasaki lords. The Sasakis were defeated and disappeared, but the agile Mitsuis survived.

The year Japan was consolidated, Sokubei renounced his rank as samurai, or warrior aristocrat, to become a lowly tradesman. The Mitsui family chronicles recorded his speech to his family on his return from Edo (Tokyo), which marked the beginning of the Mitsui empire. "A great peace is at hand. The shogun rules firmly and with justice at Edo. No more shall we live by the sword. I have seen that great profit can be made honorably. I shall brew sake and soy sauce and we shall prosper."

By the start of the twentieth century, the house of Mitsui was established as a great and powerful force in Japan, along with three other *zaibatsus,* or family-controlled financial cliques. Mitsui played an important role in every military venture and political uprising in Japan during the first half of the twentieth century: the Russo-Japanese War of 1905; Sun Yat-sen's revolution in 1920 to overthrow the Manchu dynasty; and the restoration of the Manchu dynasty in Manchuria in 1932. Mitsui was a major factor in the Japanese war machine from 1939 to 1945. In all those wars, the might of the house of Mitsui was focused like a laser on the goal—winning the war.

Like other *zaibatsus,* Mitsui consisted of many branches of the family and was governed by a strict constitution. The Mitsui constitution, written in 1722 and revised in 1900, was the philosophical bond that kept the enterprise together. The Household Counsel acted as the board, but with power to control the personal and family lives of the members of the family as well as the operations of hundreds of alliances.

The interesting point for our purpose is that the *zaibatsu* was a large network of alliances controlled centrally by a holding company through minority investments. The glue was the family and its common purpose, goals, strategies, and values. All the elements of the full-fledged relationship enterprise were present. The member firms pursued their own strategies except when the interests of the group dictated they act as one. Their governance, their main business processes, the communication among units were all in place to operate as a single enterprise from the beginning in 1620 through World War II. Clearly, in the various war efforts Mitsui did act as a single enterprise. During World War II, Mitsui controlled about three hundred companies. Mitsui companies employed 1.8 million people in Japan and another million overseas.

After the war, the *zaibatsu*, the foundation of industrialized Japan, were dismantled and declared illegal. The families' power was broken.

Japan was faced with the following situation. The country and virtually all its industrial capacity were demolished. Over a million of its young men, who would have been the backbone of reindustrialization, were dead or maimed. Japan had few natural resources; it was occupied by a foreign country, which was setting new rules for politics, the economy, and business; and, by the way, most of its leaders had been removed as war criminals.

We know the result. From devastation to challenging the United States as the world's second largest economy in just four decades. But that's not the point. This is: the Japanese understood the forces shaping their future and turned them to their own advantage. The Japanese used their situation to bargain for temporary relief from foreign competition during reconstruction so that their industries would have the chance to get back on their feet.

The great families of the big four *zaibatsu*—Mitsui, Sumitomo, Mitsubishi, and Yasuda—faded from the industrial scene by the end of the U.S. occupation in 1952. But the directors and managers of their companies rose to reconstruct networks of companies that had remarkable similarity to their predecessors. The Mitsui Bank played the role of the old Mitsui Honsha as the hub, with cross stockholdings in enterprises in the group "to such an extent that by the mid 1950s, they owned enough of each other's stock to exert mutual control in almost every case." The old system that had worked so well in the past was revived, with a new set of legal requirements, but with the same soul and spirit. And the companies had a huge common objective—reconstruction of their country.

The *keiretsu* (the name given to the reborn *zaibatsu*) became the great enabler of the reconstruction. Each member of the group used its capital to improve its products and processes and to add capacity. In acquiring small stakes in members of the group, the banks could count those investments in their capital base for determining lending potential. Since banks typically carry loans at fifteen times capital, these investments allowed a major expansion in loans. The bank provided member firms with low-cost financing, and the trading companies provided services for marketing their products. The individual companies had no need to acquire other companies to gain control, as these working relationships gave them preferred access to the capabilities and markets they needed to grow and become stronger. Hence, while capital was being spent by companies in the United States and Europe to acquire other businesses, Japanese capital was devoted to the plants and equipment of Japanese companies. These companies in turn bought their supplies from other members of the family. These *keiretsus*, like their predecessors, expanded to include a wide cross section of commerce and industry.

Rated against our criteria for the successful enterprise structure for the twenty-first century, the *keiretsu* does well on some counts, but not so well on others.

> *Be global: good to excellent. Keiretsus* moved into foreign markets through alliances in the 1960s and 1970s. Trading companies supplied the marketing power. They gained an excellent understanding of customer requirements and delivered on those needs with innovative products. *Keiretsus* gained leadership positions in many U.S., European, and Asian markets.

> *Set world standards: good to excellent.* In the manufacturing arena, the Japanese rewrote the book from 1965 to 1990. Japanese standards *were* world-class standards. All benchmarks were based on Japanese results: quality, cost, cycle time, productivity, efficiency. In manufacturing, the Japanese led in innovation, value, processes, and capabilities. The Japanese used the weak yen from 1965 to 1985 to mount an extraordinary export economy. Then, when the yen strengthened from 1985 to 1994, they invested heavily in the United States and Asia, establishing a strong offshore production base.

The *keiretsu* has not, however, developed world-class managers and professionals outside Japan. Nor has it delivered strong financial performance.

> *Be local: very weak.* The Achilles' heel of the *keiretsu* as a global competitor is its weakness in being local. Although the trading companies and some manufacturing companies, such as Toyota, have had extraordinary consumer insight in overseas markets and their plants have operated with extraordinary ef-

ficiency, the Japanese subsidiaries are not local companies. They have few alliances with local companies. Most Japanese alliances with non-Japanese companies are licensing and marketing arrangements. NUMMI, the joint venture between Toyota and General Motors in California to manufacture Japanese-designed cars in the United States, is a move in a new direction toward broader cross-border alliances. In this case, the Japanese are fully committed to a deep and enduring alliance with General Motors.

While the *keiretsu* has many characteristics of the relationship enterprise, it is most effective within Japan and as an exporting engine, rather than as an enterprise that can dominate industries globally. The best course for *keiretsus* will be to create alliances with non-Japanese partners and become part of global relationship enterprises.

The two megatrends, globalization and nationalism, create the fertile soil for the relationship enterprise. The explosion of alliances and their changing character provide the seed to grow relationship enterprises. The harvest will come as the networks of alliances being created today work closer together and establish the bonds of common goals, common systems, and trust. The result will be a network of independent companies acting as a single company with a common mission. The result will be giant enterprises, operating globally, with enormous size and power, as relationship enterprises grow into trillion-dollar enterprises.

Industries Ripe for the
Trillion-Dollar Enterprise

Where and when will relationship enterprises appear? Conditions are fertile in a number of industries. Every company should analyze its own situation, the competitive dynamics, and the advantages and risks of moving in this direction. The purpose of this chapter is not to predict the evolution of certain industries, but to demonstrate that the forces are present to move industries in the direction of relationship enterprises, that relationship enterprises are real and could impact you, your company, and your industry.

Four important criteria signal the desirability (and inevitability) of relationship enterprises:

- **Rate of globalization.** A major driver of the relationship enterprise is the need to compete globally. Industries that are now, or are moving rapidly toward being, truly global are prime candidates.

- **Benefits from consolidating.** If there are significant economic benefits to cross-border consolidation, the odds of spawning relationship enterprises are high. Benefits from integration can be derived from cost, technology, distribution, market reach, and countless other areas that spark companies to look beyond their borders for acquisitions.

- **Big bets and risks.** Industries that face large investments and large risks are good candidates for relationship enterprises. Examples of such investments are costly first entries in countries (e.g., China or India), economically and politically risky ventures (e.g., laying a pipeline across Russia), and risky technologies (e.g., electric car, supersonic commercial jet, biotech research, satellite communications system).

- **Regulation and trade barriers.** A principal advantage of the relationship enterprise is that it is on home turf almost everywhere, which dramatically reduces the impact of regulation and trade barriers. To the extent that an industry has restrictive and varying regulations and significant trade barriers, the relationship enterprise is likely to be built around those restrictions.

Exhibit 4-1 divides numerous industries into three categories. The first category, Hot Now, includes industries that are either transforming to relationship enterprises or are highly likely to transform in the next five to ten years. Industries in the second category, The Next Wave, could move toward relationship enterprises within twenty years. All industries in this category are globalizing, and the pressure to form alliances will be high. In each case, however, one or more other factors make it less likely that relationship enterprises will form in the near term.

Industries in the third category, The Last to Go, will probably remain predominantly national. Individual companies will become international, but the bulk of the competition will be at home. Several additional industries, including publishing, metalworking, construction machinery, and financial services, could be in the second wave, but are more likely to move to relationship enterprises later (although prior to those in The Last to Go category).

There will also be alliances across industry groups; telecommunications, electronics, and computers are clear examples of industries whose borders are merging. Computer hardware and software companies may well become important partners in relationship

Exhibit 4-1 ❖ FACTORS DRIVING INDUSTRIES TO RELATIONSHIP ENTERPRISES

Hot Now	Need to Complete Globally	Benefits from Consolidation	Big Bets, Big Risks	Regulation and Trade Barriers
Telecommunications	Very Important	Very Important	Very Important	Very Important
Automotive	Very Important	Very Important	Very Important	Important
Aerospace	Very Important	Very Important	Very Important	Very Important
Banking	Very Important	Modestly Important	Very Important	Very Important
Energy	Important	Very Important	Very Important	Very Important
Commercial Aviation	Important	Very Important	Modestly Important	Very Important
Public Accounting	Very Important	Very Important	Very Important	Very Important
Pharmaceuticals	Very Important	Modestly Important	Very Important	Important
Primary Metals	Important	Very Important	Modestly Important	Modestly Important
Computer Hardware and Software	Important	Modestly Important	Important	Modestly Important

The Next Wave				
Biotech	Modestly Important	Some Importance	Important	Important
Electronics	Important	Modestly Important	Important	Important
Machinery	Important	Modestly Important	Important	Important
Apparel and Textiles	Important	Modestly Important	Unimportant	Important
Chemicals	Modestly Important	Modestly Important	Important	Important
Paper and Wood Products	Important	Modestly Important	Important	Important
Food	Important	Important	Unimportant	Some Importance

The Last to Go				
Glass	Important	Important	Important	Important
Construction	Important	Unimportant	Important	Important
Hotels	Important	Modestly Important	Important	Important
Education	Important	Important	Unimportant	Important
Publishing and Printing	Important	Important	Unimportant	Important
Electric Utilities	Unimportant	Modestly Important	Modestly Important	Very Important
Health Care	Unimportant	Some Importance	Modestly Important	Very Important
Real Estate	Unimportant	Important	Modestly Important	Some Importance
Retailing	Unimportant	Important	Unimportant	Modestly Important
Advertising	Unimportant	Unimportant	Unimportant	Important

Legend:
● Very Important ◕ Important ● Some Importance ◐ Modestly Important ○ Unimportant

enterprises in other industries, such as the aerospace, automotive, and commercial aviation industries.

We will look at four of the industries in the Hot Now category to see why and how they will evolve into relationship enterprises: aerospace, commercial aviation, automotive, and energy. It would be equally viable to look at the other six, or all ten, for in every case, the conditions are ripe. To make the discussion more relevant (and provocative), I will suggest which companies are likely to form competing enterprises in a few of the industries.

AEROSPACE

For our purposes here, the aerospace industry includes the design, manufacture, and sale of aircraft for both commercial and military markets. Relationship enterprises have already formed in the commercial aerospace industry. The two primary relationship enterprises are Boeing and its partners and Airbus Industries. Only government regulation and security concerns are inhibiting the defense aerospace industry from closer cross-border alliances. Let's explore how aerospace arrived at today's relationship enterprise position to see the path that other industries are likely to follow.

At the conclusion of World War II, the airplane was well established technologically but the age of the frequent flyer was still a few decades away. Almost all of the world's productive capacity for aircraft was dedicated to the war effort. By 1950, a commercial aerospace industry had been reestablished. The primary commercial manufacturers in the United States and the United Kingdom were Boeing, Lockheed, Douglas, Consolidated Republic, Short Brothers, de Havilland, and Hawker Siddeley. Most of these companies also produced military aircraft. In addition, several manufacturers produced only military aircraft and missiles. The largest of these were McDonnell, Hughes, Northrop, Grumman, Fairchild, Fairey, Handley Page, Folland, Avro, and Vickers.

In the United Kingdom, the industry consolidated from eighteen to five manufacturers between 1950 and 1965, and then to two by 1990, as shown in Exhibit 4-2. Other European countries saw similar consolidation.

The U.S. defense aerospace industry remained relatively stable (compared to many other industries) for almost forty years. Defense

Exhibit 4-2 ❖ CONSOLIDATION OF U.K. MILITARY AIRCRAFT MANUFACTURERS

Prime Contractors for Military Production Programs

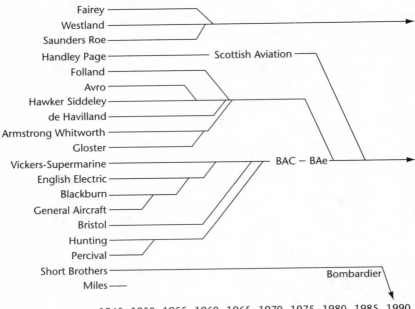

Source: Booz·Allen analysis.

budgets reflected the Korean and Vietnam Wars and the tensions of the cold war. The Reagan commitment to winning the cold war by escalating the arms race to a level that the Soviet Union couldn't sustain resulted in a robust defense market in the 1980s. Exhibit 4-3 shows little consolidation in the U.S. industry from 1945 to 1990.

The industry entered Stage 3 during the 1980s. As indicated, a crisis or discontinuity will cause alliance networks to begin operating as single entities. Two events dramatically reshaped the commercial and defense aerospace industries. First, in the early 1980s, the European manufacturers realized they could not match the United States in commercial aerospace unless they banded together. Airbus Industries was formed as an alliance of the aerospace companies of the United Kingdom, France, Germany, and Spain.

Exhibit 4-3 ❖ CONSOLIDATION OF U.S. MILITARY AIRCRAFT INDUSTRY

Prime Contractors for Military Production Programs

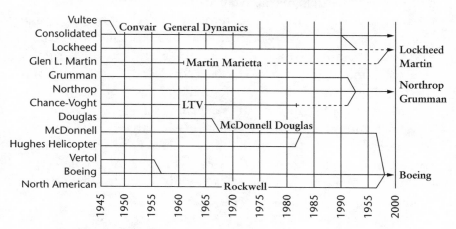

Source: Booz·Allen analysis.

Second, the cold war ended and the Soviet Union collapsed in 1989. Suddenly, the entire purpose of the military in the NATO countries had to be reassessed. A rapid reduction in arms purchases occurred throughout NATO. Military aircraft production fell sharply.

The U.S. military-aircraft manufacturing industry responded with a major consolidation, from seven fixed-wing aircraft companies in 1990 to three companies by the end of 1997: Boeing, Lockheed Martin, and Northrop Grumman. U.S. commercial-aircraft manufacturing consolidated to one firm by the end of 1997 with the merger of Boeing and McDonnell Douglas.

The commercial aerospace industry has formed two competing alliances networks, with Boeing and Airbus at their centers. These two networks are competing as single enterprises in the design, manufacture, and sale of commercial aircraft. We can rightly call them relationship enterprises.

Boeing had secured several airlines (American, Delta, and Continental) as partners in its relationship enterprise through exclusive buy-Boeing agreements. But these were broken up during the negotiations with the EC (European Community) on the European approval of the Boeing–McDonnell Douglas merger. Nevertheless, airlines will continue to participate as enterprise partners on specific new programs. For example, United Airlines was a partner in the design and development of the Boeing 777. United managers and engineers participated actively in major decisions on functions, capacity, the passenger cabin, and the flight deck of the 777. John Zeeman, then executive vice president of marketing for United, told me, "For the first time, we are a full partner in the design of an aircraft that will be key to our fleet for decades. . . . I think this [partnership between the manufacturer and customer] is the right way to go in the future." Boeing's executives agree.

We need not predict how relationship enterprises will develop in commercial aerospace—they are here today. They will, however, develop and change, particularly Airbus. In 1998, Airbus consisted of four independent companies, each with multiple alliances and vendors.

Although Airbus is a relationship enterprise, it is an inefficient one. Consolidation, probably through merger of the four partners, and rationalization of the operations and supply base would likely save $1 to $2 billion in costs annually. Possibly more important, consolidation and rationalization would improve technology development and shrink the timeline for developing new aircraft through focusing resources, better prioritizing, reducing the need for coordination, and eliminating political squabbles.

Aerospace over the next decade will be an interesting laboratory for the relationship enterprise as Boeing and Airbus race toward trillion-dollar status. Interestingly, engine manufacturers are grouping in a separate relationship enterprise that will supply both aircraft manufacturers. For example, the partnership formed for the Mach 3.5 engine includes GE, Pratt & Whitney, Rolls Royce, IHI (Japan), Fiat, and SNECMA (France).

Global consolidation of military aerospace is moving much more slowly because of the national barriers established by the major manufacturing countries. Mergers are difficult when security is involved, and secret technology pervades military aircraft and weaponry. Consequently, there have been very few (less than five) cross-border mergers of defense aerospace manufacturers in the 1990s. Alliances are beginning to become more important, but slowly.

The case for cross-border consolidation in defense aerospace is powerful. Just as consolidations within the United States and the United Kingdom resulted in substantial savings for the surviving combinations, so will broader consolidation across borders. The political obstacles are enormous, however. A merger or major alliance of DASA, Aerospatiale, and British Aerospace would result in huge savings but, at least at this time, is politically difficult, principally because of France's opposition. A merger between British Aerospace and either Boeing (McDonnell Douglas) or Lockheed would result in a defense powerhouse, but the United States would have trouble sharing top-secret designs and weaponry even with its closest ally, the United Kingdom. There is recent evidence that cross-border mergers are being tested; for example, GEC (U.K.) bought Tracor (U.S.), and Rolls Royce (the aircraft engine maker in the U.K.) may merge with Allison (of the U.S.).

Some form of alliance may be possible in defense, though, because it is easier to retain national control over highly sensitive designs and data with alliances than with mergers. For example, an international alliance has been formed by Boeing and Kvaerner Maritime of Norway to build a floating runway and troop carriers for the U.S. Navy, which would become the world's largest offshore air base. Boeing and Kvaermer are also partners in Sea Launch, an offshore satellite-launching platform. In the EC, alliances among defense manufacturers are beginning to pick up steam. For example, SAAB and British Aerospace have an alliance as do Alenia (Italy) and DASA (Germany). British Aerospace and DASA are operating as partners in many respects.

I anticipate that alliances will increase rapidly in the defense industry within countries. Given the overlap between defense and commercial aircraft design and manufacturing, we should see the emergence of giant relationship enterprises serving both defense and commercial markets.

COMMERCIAL AVIATION

Since we are discussing airplanes, let's look at the industry that uses the airplanes. Commercial aviation is well into Stage 2 of developing relationship enterprises. It entered its age of collaboration in the mid-1980s. Today, the commercial airline industry is solidly in Stage 2 of development of its relationship enterprises. Let's examine how it got there and what it will take to move it to Stage 3.

Like several other industries, its history of consolidation was principally through merger and acquisition. Many of the great names of U.S. aviation—names such as Capital, Pan Am, Eastern, National, Southern, Republic, Piedmont—are gone, merged into more successful companies. In the airline industry, many carriers have gone bankrupt but somehow keep flying. Deregulation in Europe is just beginning to take hold. We should expect fewer mergers there than in the United States because most countries wish to retain their national airlines. Belgium appears to be the exception. Rather, we should expect a scramble (already under way) of cross-equity and other alliance arrangements designed partially to achieve better economics but principally to survive. Who can imagine France, the United Kingdom, Germany, Italy, and the Netherlands without Air France, British Airways, Lufthansa, Alitalia, and KLM? Certainly not the French, British, Germans, Italians, or Dutch!

The primary force for consolidation now and into the twenty-first century is globalization. Although mergers will continue within countries, the only solution available for global consolidation is the alliance. Every country on earth reserves the right to approve or disapprove the sale of its airlines, and most say no. The United States has a law prohibiting foreign ownership over 25 percent. Can you imagine buying Japan Air Lines?

In our research at Booz·Allen, we were able to find few airlines that flew beyond their own borders that did not have alliances with carriers of other countries. The average number of alliances is about five, and many have over ten.

The requirement for alliances is clear. The big question is the endgame. Will the industry continue to evolve into a spaghetti bowl, with each carrier setting up many bilateral alliances resulting in an incoherent scramble of relationships, or will alliances be rationalized around a few relationship enterprises? I believe that the power of global coordination will move airlines toward relationship enterprises, and that we are in the second of a three-stage evolution that will result in the world's airways being dominated by relatively few relationship enterprises.

In the late 1980s and early 1990s, code-sharing alliances swept the industry as airlines sought to offer seamless travel anywhere in the world. A passenger could board United Airlines in San Francisco, fly to Frankfurt, and change to a Lufthansa flight to Athens all on a United flight number. Baggage was automatically checked through. The passenger might not even be aware of the need to switch carriers—at least not until she looked for her United flight to Athens in the Frankfurt airport. These alliances also involved frequent-flyer miles (our Chicago-Frankfurt-Athens passenger received United Mileage Plus credit for the whole trip, even the Lufthansa leg). Marketing programs by both companies added flights across their combined network; for example, Lufthansa advertised flights from Munich to virtually any city in the United States (unsaid: by connecting with a United flight in the United States).

The second stage of the evolution increased the support between partners. Examples include KLM and Northwest, U.S. Airways and British Airways (since broken up by British Airways in favor of an alliance with American Airlines), Delta, Singapore International, and Swissair. Further nonequity, cross-border alliances were forged by virtually every major airline in the world. United and Lufthansa won antitrust immunity in the United States and Germany, allowing the two airlines to schedule flights and collaborate on pricing. Joint marketing agreements were established, whereby one airline markets for both in its home country (or continent), allowing partners to close ticket offices and reservation centers, and to rely on partner services in the airport, such as baggage handling, check-in counters, and passenger services. One result of these alliances: few, if any, Lufthansa employees work in the United States and few United employees are in Europe.

Stage 2 witnessed a giant leap in the number of alliances, but the airlines' spaghetti-bowl approach to alliances has resulted in limited attention and investment in making the network of alliances successful, and it will take a lot of untangling to reap the benefits of Stage 3. A few networks are already evolving and are poised to move to Stage 3, potentially leaving those in the spaghetti bowl behind.

Stage 3 will see the spaghetti bowl sort out into a few networks of carriers that will operate as single firms—as relationship enterprises.

The enterprises will have central scheduling, coordinating national and international flights to ensure effective, customer-friendly connections, and a common marketing strategy. They will organize selling, reservations, customer service, and airport functions to eliminate duplication and operate at the lowest possible cost. Fleet plans and interior designs will be coordinated. Maintenance will be planned centrally and delivered in the most economic fashion globally. Finally, international flight crews will be planned and scheduled centrally. We should see U.S. crews on Japan Airlines planes.

Every airline would like to become the hub for its alliance network. For example, Malaysian Airlines would like to pick the best carriers in Europe, the United States, Latin America, and other Asian countries as alliance partners so that its passengers can fly anywhere in the world under the Malaysian flag.

Now let's take the perspective of a major carrier toward an alliance with Malaysian Air. For such a carrier, Malaysian Air would provide passengers connecting through its networks, but there would be little advantage in Malaysia, since in-country connections are more frequently by car or horse than by airplane. If you are British Airways, the value of an alliance with Malaysian Air drops precipitously if Malaysian also has alliances with Lufthansa, Iberia, SAS, KLM, Air France, Thai, Air India, Cathay Pacific, Delta, and Northwest. Why? Because British Airways (or its partner, American Airlines) would have to share the interconnecting passengers with all Malaysian Airways' other alliance partners. The dilution in volume would lead quickly to evaporation of interest, and would certainly reduce investment (e.g., marketing for Malaysia in Europe) quickly to zero.

Alternatively, Malaysian Air could become a member of the British Airways–American Airlines relationship enterprise and provide the enterprise with links in Southeast Asia. Under the first scenario (Malaysian Air has its own alliance network, including Air India), the London-Delhi-Malaysia passenger flies Air India and Malaysian Air. Under the second scenario (Malaysian Air as a member of the British Airways relationship alliance), the passenger uses British Airways and Malaysian Air. Malaysian Air loses nothing, but enters a partnership that would be willing to invest in its success because it would be an important link in the global network.

Recognize that Malaysian Air has competitors for the partner slot in Southeast Asia; Singapore, Thai, and Indonesian airlines could also fill that role. Consequently, there is real value and some urgency for airlines to align with a strong network—a far better course than deciding on alliances independently on their own apparent merits.

The two largest relationship enterprises are already taking shape. One, called Star, will include United, Lufthansa, SAS (Scandinavia), Varig (Brazil), Lan-Chile, Air Canada, Thai Airways, and eventually several others. The second enterprise will include American, British Airways, Japan Air Lines, Qantas, Aerolineas Argentinas, and four or five others to be selected. Other groups will form to compete globally, but will lack the power and customer base to play in the top echelon.

These two behemoths will compete head to head for dominance of international air travel. They will use their leverage to attract the best new partners in important markets, to raise capital at low cost, to have the best distribution economics (even power over travel agents!), and to gain the preferential treatment of a local airline in countries of their partners.

Just imagine if you were Korean Air or Aer Lingus, how important it would be to be a part of one of the winning groups. I even envision a consolidation of U.S. airlines through a combination of mergers and alliances, melding several of the biggest U.S. carriers into the two relationship enterprises. We have seen the first shots over that bow with the pending alliances in 1998 between American and U.S. Airways, United and Delta, and Continental and Northwest.

Not so incidentally, the winning enterprise will be the group that is best able to operate as a single airline (unscramble the spaghetti bowl) and that best leverages the inherent advantages of the relationship enterprise.

AUTOMOTIVE

The automotive industry is in Stage 1 of relationship enterprise development but is moving quickly to Stage 2. The forces for consolidation are powerful but the desire to retain independence and control is also strong. Entry into Stage 3 is probably ten years away. Contrary to current thinking in the industry, I believe Stage 3 is inevitable because of the overwhelming economics and the forces of nationalism.

Alliances are old hat in the auto industry. Henry Ford and Harvey Firestone formed an early alliance to produce a car that workers could afford so that production could grow. Ford agreed to use Firestone tires, which enabled Firestone to launch the tire industry in Akron, Ohio. Nevertheless, alliances were rare then, and Ford was predominantly an integrated manufacturer. In Ford's view, he wanted to own and control as much as he could. Ford's River Rouge plant produced the steel, glass, castings, and plastic that went into sheet metal, windows, engines, trim, brakes, drive train, suspension, and a wide range of parts for all of Ford's cars.

While Ford built from the ground up, the primary evolution of the rest of the industry came through acquisition and mergers, starting with the formation of General Motors in 1908. Over a two-year period, Billy Durant, the founder of Durant-Dort Carriage Company, incorporated General Motors Corporation and merged into it twenty-five companies; eleven were automobile companies and the remainder were parts and accessories manufacturers. Many of the early pioneers joined Durant's dream and traded their independence for shares of General Motors. Some names remain today—Buick, Olds (now Oldsmobile), Cadillac. Oakland became Pontiac. Many names are only marked in history books—Marquette, Ewing, Randolph, Welch, Rapid Motor, Reliance Motor Truck, McLaughlin of Canada. In 1911, Durant financed Louis Chevrolet to experiment with a light car. The Chevrolet Motor Company became very successful and exchanged stock with General Motors in 1916, which led to a merger in 1918.

Throughout the next sixty years, the industry continued to consolidate through mergers. Names such as Chrysler, Dodge, Plymouth, Nash, Jeep, Studebaker, and Packard melded into the Chrysler Corporation. Eventually, the U.S. auto industry's Big Three became the only three.

Through 1970, a Ford car was produced by Ford Motor Company, a Chevy by GM, and a Plymouth by Chrysler, bumper to bumper. As recently as the late 1970s, a lawsuit accused GM of installing a Chevy engine in an Olds 88. The mentality in the market and among the auto companies was that products were proprietary. Even tire-tread designs were proprietary to individual car lines. Cross utilizing an important component such as an engine was a big problem.

Along came the oil shock of 1973, and the invasion of the U.S. market by reliable and low-cost Japanese cars. The U.S. car makers watched their market share drop from 85 percent in 1970 to 75 percent by 1980. The second oil shock in 1979 and the recession of 1980–1982 bankrupted one of the U.S. Big Three (Chrysler) and made a major dent in the pride and financial strength of the other two. Ford and GM were perilously close to the financial brink in 1981. The fourth U.S. car maker, American Motors, was bought by the French company Renault and subsequently sold to Chrysler. Interestingly, the government loan guaranty that saved Chrysler in 1979 turned out to be a terrific investment for the U.S. Treasury. Chrysler calculates that the government netted $330 million in fees and profit on Chrysler warranties without actually investing even one dollar.

The U.S. Big Three struggled throughout the 1980s to regain their position in the U.S. market. During that decade, they spent over $100 billion improving their operations, reducing the cost of their manufacturing facilities, and upgrading their products to be competitive with the surging sales of lower priced and more reliable imports. Their share dropped another ten points to 65 percent. The auto companies began to recognize that going it alone might not be the best strategic course.

Strategic alliances in the U.S. auto industry began cautiously in the 1960s. GM took an equity position in Isuzu and Chrysler invested in Mitsubishi. Ford formed an alliance with Nissan Toyo-Kogyo (now Mazda) to manufacture automotive transmissions under a Ford patent. Ford forged much stronger links with Mazda by buying 25 percent of its stock in 1979. Recently, Ford upped its ownership in Mazda to 33 percent, which allows Ford management control.

In the 1980s alliance fever struck the entire industry, and it reached epidemic proportions by 1990. In the late 1980s, the alliance network crisscrossed Europe, Japan, and the United States, with a number of other countries also participating.

For example, Ford had equity in Mazda and Kia, and bought Jaguar and Aston Martin; had joint ventures with Mazda, Nissan, and Volkswagen, and marketing and distribution agreements with Kia and Mazda.

European auto companies were no different. By 1990, Volkswagen had equity in BAZ and Skoda (Czechoslovakia at that time); joint ventures with CNAIC, First Auto Works (China), Ford, and Mercedes-Benz; marketing and distribution agreements with Skoda and Toyota; technology alliances with First Auto Works, Porsche, Skoda, and Toyota; and manufacturing and assembly alliances with BAZ, First Auto Works, Porsche, Skoda, and Toyota. All this in addition to the major supply agreements with Ford, Nissan, Rover, and Volvo.

Probably more important than the absolute number of alliances is the change in the nature of alliances. Today's alliances go deeply into the core of R&D, product development, engineering, parts manufacturing, and assembly. Whole cars are designed and manufactured for alliance partners. Alliances are far more strategic and longer term. The Chrysler Sebring Coupe and Avenger are produced by Mitsubishi; the GM Prism is produced by NUMMI, the GM/Toyota joint venture in California. The GM/Suzuki joint venture (CAMI) produces the Metro and Tracker. No longer are alliances limited to suppliers, now they may even extend to archenemies. Sales among major auto companies have risen from ground zero in 1980 to billions in 1995. Toyota and GM are among each other's largest customers. Virtually every auto company in the world has alliances with competitors, suppliers, technology firms, distribution channels—in an industry that was "proprietary pure" just twenty-five years ago.

What about the future? I see nothing that will reverse the current course toward consolidation through alliances and closer relationships among auto producers and their supply chains. We can expect a major reorganization of alliances into a few multicompany networks—a major discontinuity that will be equal in magnitude to the acquisition binges earlier in the twentieth century.

Some auto executives, like Ford's CEO Alex Trotman, believe that the auto industry will continue to rationalize with mergers, takeovers, equity stakes, and alliances. But Trotman states, "The alliances are specific, such as our alliance with Volkswagen on the production of a European mini-van, and the alliances have sunsets."

The real value of a network of alliances is unlocked when the partners are able to plan together, to rationalize product lines, platforms, engine families, and distribution systems. The auto industry today has eighteen major companies and an equal number of smaller automakers. Each designs, develops, engineers, manufactures, and sells its product line. Today's alliances reduce the costs and risks of being truly independent, but the big bang comes with reducing the complexity, gaining scale, and combining efforts to design and produce cars and trucks in significantly larger volume.

The answer for the industry is to consolidate alliances into large competitive enterprises—relationship enterprises—which can reap the benefits of rationalization of platforms, engine families, and distribution systems. I anticipate four or five great auto enterprises with members from the United States, Europe, and Asia to be in place in ten years. Suppliers will align themselves with one of these enterprises for the dominant share of their sales. Sharing of technology and information will grow, cross-production will increase, and product development will be collaborative. There will be substantial rationalization in manufacturing and common platforms and parts. The actual number of platforms and engine families will be a fraction of the number produced by today's independent companies. Distribution and sales systems will at last be revolutionized.

The consolidation may occur by the creation of large joint ventures, as auto executives such as Ford's Alex Trotman suggest, or by alliances among manufacturers to work jointly on major programs.

The forces propelling these changes are both economic and political. One of the most important drivers of design and manufacturing costs is the number of platforms (the structure of the vehicle, including the frame, the housing for the engine, and the suspension system) and power trains (the engine, fuel intake, and transmission systems). Most of the expensive engineering and tooling go into the platform and power train. U.S. and European full-line auto companies might each have ten or fifteen platforms and almost that many engine families. Japanese auto companies have half that number.

The customer doesn't see platforms or power trains, only style and performance. A relationship enterprise of four or five auto companies and several suppliers could offer an unlimited range of vehicles (subcompact cars through medium trucks) and unlimited models and styles on fewer than ten platforms with a few minor tweaks and as many engine families. Just think about the cost savings that this kind of simplification can bring about. A relationship enterprise with five OEM partners could reduce the number of platforms from sixty to ten and the number of engine families to the same degree. Investment could be focused on fewer projects; hence, efficiency and performance could be expected to be substantially better. Competition will be based on style, performance, features, and price, which can be built on any platform and engine.

Auto companies are a major source of employment in their home countries. Even free traders like the United States erupt when that employment base is threatened. The relationship enterprise allows Japanese members to remain Japanese and German members, German, with all the home-country benefits and protection.

Beyond the relationship enterprise, I see the emergence of trillion-dollar enterprises in the auto industry, and believe that consolidation toward them is occurring today. At least two giants will emerge—each with one U.S. company (Ford or GM), one Japanese company (Toyota, Honda, or Nissan), and two European companies (pick from about ten). A number of smaller automakers from the emerging economies will join the club. A third giant around Chrysler/Daimler could well emerge. Each trillion-dollar enterprise will have a set of major suppliers from the United States, Europe, Japan and the emerging countries, and each will create joint-venture marketing companies for large emerging markets such as China, India, and Indonesia. Each will attempt to rationalize the distribution systems in Japan, Europe, and the United States. Each will have financial partners (banks, credit companies, insurance companies). Tentacles are already stretching throughout Southeast Asia, Eastern Europe, and Latin America, with alliances among suppliers, OEMs, and distributors.

ENERGY

Energy is an example of an industry that has been in Stage 1 of development for a long time. Only recently have there been signs of evolution into Stage 2 networks. I expect further evolution to take years, possibly decades. Even though the economics of consolidation are very strong, the industry's history of single-purpose alliances and spaghetti bowl of cross alliances are hard to reverse and untangle. Strategic alliances have long been a feature of the petroleum landscape. Most of the great petroleum basins in the world have been developed by alliances of exploration and production companies. Caltex was formed by Chevron and Texaco in 1936. The North Sea was developed by many sets of alliances; the biggest players were British Petroleum (BP), Statoil of Norway, and Royal Dutch Shell, in alliances with oil companies around the world.

Low oil prices and shareholder demands for better financial performance led to the rapid expansion in alliances in the 1990s. During the 1992–96 period, alliances among energy companies grew at an annual rate of 42 percent. Among oil companies, upstream (exploration and production) alliances increased by 50 percent and downstream (refining, pipelines, and marketing) alliances by about 40 percent and have accelerated since then. Traditionally focused on upstream operations in a single country, oil companies have broadened their alliances to be regional in scope.

As Exhibit 4-4 illustrates, the oil industry has engaged in all types of strategic alliances. Examples of shared-equity (or joint-venture) alliances in the early 1990s include the creation of Uno-Ven by PDVSA and Unocal of Star Enterprises by Texaco and Saudi Aramco, and more recently, Quaker State and Pennzoil in lubes. Examples of cross-equity alliances include Arco's relationship with Lukoil, which entails an investment in Lukoil by Arco and joint funding of future projects. There are countless shared-resources alliances in the energy industry; BP and Statoil's joint marketing and E&P (exploration and production) in frontier regions is one example.

Most of the big alliances in the energy world have been cross-border alliances, which isn't surprising since few countries have more than one major oil company. The United States is an exception. Exhibit 4-5 shows that U.S. cross-border alliances have tripled from 1992 to 1995 while alliances among U.S. companies have doubled; cross-border alliances among non-U.S. companies have doubled in that time frame.

While upstream alliances continue at a brisk pace, downstream alliances in refining and marketing are accelerating as oil companies

Exhibit 4-4 ❖ ALLIANCES IN THE OIL INDUSTRY

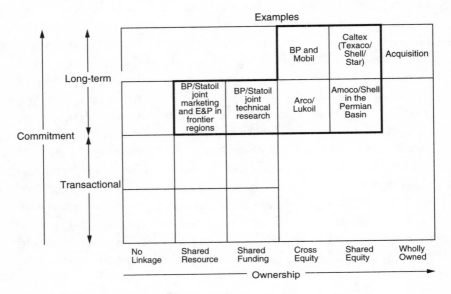

Source: Booz·Allen & Hamilton analysis.

Exhibit 4-5 ❖ ALLIANCE TRENDS IN THE OIL INDUSTRY

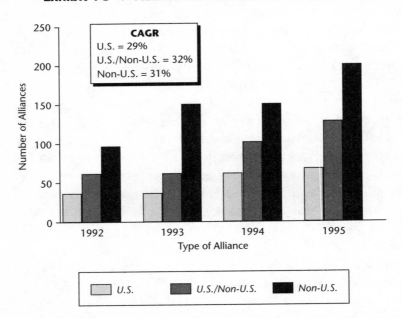

Note: Includes deal signed, waiting approval, and letter of intent alliances.
Source: Securities Data Corporation, Booz·Allen & Hamilton analysis.

strive to solve the nagging problem of low returns on downstream assets. In the last few years, there have been announcements of the innovative BP-Mobil arrangement involving European downstream and lubricants, the Shell-Texaco-Star alliance in U.S. refining and marketing, forming two joint venture companies, Equilon and Motiva, numerous alliances among oil-field service and equipment manufacturers, the Chevron–Natural Gas Clearinghouse, and the Mobil-PanEnergy alliances in natural gas marketing. In addition, Ashland and Marathon, Diamond and Ultramar with Petro Canada, which together have the second largest service station network in North America, have all announced joint ventures. More are coming.

The economics of downstream refining and marketing are driving firms to form alliances. Refining in the United States and Europe has had low profitability for a long time, and there is little hope for a major upswing. Imports drive overcapacity for most fuel grades and keep prices low. U.S. refining capacity has begun to tighten, but engineers are able to increase output on existing refineries, resulting in more capacity (called "creep" in refinery jargon). The cost of shutting down capacity (environmental cleanup for a closed refinery is a nightmare) is high enough to keep all but teakettles operating. In addition, environmental requirements for operating refineries keep increasing, resulting in added investment just to stay in business, with little or no economic return.

Refineries performing in the top quartile (in productivity, operating cost, downtime, overhead cost, safety) in the industry will probably return cost of capital, but those in the other three-quartiles will struggle to make any money. Industry executives have come to the same conclusion and are searching for escape hatches. Investing a dollar (or a billion) in exploration and production has a lot more appeal than putting the same money into a third- or fourth-quartile performing refinery, so guess what gets starved?

Marketing (i.e., service stations) is also tough in the oil industry. Wholesaling gasoline to independent station owners gives the oil companies razor-thin marketing margins. On the other hand, ownership of stations requires investment—over $1 million a pop in today's economics. You only invest if marketing margins are really good—which they can be if you have the right location. Other forces are at play, also. Modern service stations must be well-lit at night, attractive, clean, and have up-to-date equipment (e.g., the pumps should operate at faster than drip speed, cashless transactions should be offered, pumps need to be available when customers drive in). Still, that's not enough to make money. Current wisdom says there has to be a convenience store on site—not just a gum and tobacco counter, but a full-fledged (though mini) grocery store. And that takes investment and a set of capabilities that aren't native to oil companies.

To make matters worse, there are threatening armies on the horizon. The majors have always had to fight the independents, but the rules of the game were well defined and understood by both sides: good dirt (jargon for location), attractive facility, and price (the principal point of combat). The majors promoted their quality—why pay $25,000 for a car and risk its future by saving five cents per gallon? The independents promote economy—why pay more for the same quality gas? As in most industries, the customer chooses.

Well, along came the hypermarket in France and England. The hypermarket is a huge (monstrous?) store that sells everything from tomatoes to truck tires. The parking lots are equally huge. Suddenly, gasoline pumps were put over in the corner, with gas selling at prices substantially below those of regular service stations. Hypermarkets didn't need new dirt; they already plenty at low cost. They didn't need a convenience store; the hypermarket had roughly a thousand times as many items. As for cashless transactions, most people used credit cards, and they had the bonus of a twenty-four-hour operation. Hypermarkets took the approach, "If you want your engine checked, go somewhere else; we pump gas—cheap."

Hypermarkets pump three to five times as much gasoline per pump as service stations. The economics are overwhelming—and that is the army on the horizon. In France, the hypermarkets captured over 50 percent of the gasoline market in less than ten years. Hypermarkets in the United Kingdom have about a 25 percent share. Just think about those companies that used to have 100 percent of the market and now have 50 or 75 percent but still have the distribution and service-station capacity.

You now understand why oil company executives are searching for solutions to the refining and marketing problem. The recent rash of alliances in the downstream business is a response.

What is in the future for the oil industry? I don't think it is too far-fetched to believe that there will be a major disaggregation, followed by a wave of consolidation. Let me explain.

Oil companies are already disaggregating by spinning off refining and marketing into joint ventures with the refining and marketing groups of other oil companies. There aren't many buyers for refining assets, so joint ventures are an attractive exit. Disaggregation can be expected to continue both for the reasons just mentioned that are causing oil companies to disinvest (or slowly strangle) these businesses and because separation from oil parents may be the best hope for turning the downstream into a viable, profitable business.

Enter consolidation. We now have an oil industry split into two parts: exploration and production companies and refining and marketing joint ventures. We're not sure where the industry's chemical companies will land, but that is not essential for this discussion. The right next move for the refining and marketing companies will be to consolidate the industry and rationalize refining capacity. This consolidation can occur partly by merger (no one should spend cash on acquisitions), but mostly by alliances.

We can envision a North American refining and marketing industry consisting of two or three relationship enterprises that have a capacity that allows profitable returns and multiple marketing formats. The mission shifts from selling the gasoline that the oil the companies produce ("balancing" in industry jargon) to serving the customer in the best way possible and maximizing the returns from an extensive real estate portfolio. Partners in the relationship enterprise could include independent marketers, shopping malls, chemical companies, pipelines, transportation companies (e.g., railroads, barges, trucking), REIT real estate investment trusts, (e.g., for storage, ownership of service-station real estate). State companies in Europe will be happy to spin out refining and marketing assets into these relationship enterprises. The consolidation will sweep Europe more quickly than the United States because the inefficiencies there are significantly greater, even though cross border combinations take more time.

The majors will become exploration and production companies with long-term contracts to supply refineries. Unlocked from downstream assets, the oil companies will realign and consolidate their industry. There will be mergers, but mergers and acquisitions will not be the dominant path of consolidation. Alliances will—particularly networks of alliances—result in relationship enterprises. E&P operations move naturally into alliances, so the leap to relationship enterprises will not be as great as for the downstream businesses. The major adjustment—and it is indeed major—will be the shift from episodic alliances to long-term relationships. This shift could take decades.

The move toward relationship enterprises will take place at different speeds in different industries. I have nominated ten industries to move quickly—the Hot Now group. Ten more industries are in the wings and will follow close behind the first group, probably learning a lot from the missteps of those who go first.

As illustrated by the four industries reviewed here, each industry is driven to evolve relationship enterprises by specific circumstances, but the broad forces are the same: urgency to operate globally, benefits from consolidation, the requirement for big bets and big risks, and regulation and trade barriers.

You, the reader, should determine where your company and industry fit the timetable. If you are in the Hot Now or The Next Wave groups or your success depends on those industries, study the next sections very carefully, because the future is upon you. No one, however, even in The Last to Go group, can relax, as the timing I present may be off or you may find yourself working with one of the fast-track industries on your next job.

What the Rise of the Trillion-Dollar Enterprise Means to You and Your Company

— ❖ —

The world in the age of collaboration and the age of the trillion-dollar enterprise will be very different from today's world. Almost no one will argue with that. Just think about business life three decades ago compared with that of today. Why shouldn't our world three decades into the twenty-first century be at least as different?

In the 1960s, we had the organization man, a product of the stable, well-structured, disciplined organizations of the times. You could plot your career through a set of organizational boxes with confidence that those same jobs would exist five, ten, fifteen years into the future. Communications were formal—remember life before Xerox?—policies were strict; behavior was predictable. Employment was stable, often for one's entire career. When my father received his fifty-year pin from the Chicago Motor Club in 1969, he shared the honor with two other fifty-year employees, in an organization of about one thousand people. Not uncommon in those times. Unheard of today.

Today, organizations are in constant flux. Lines of authority often go to groups rather than to individuals. At

Monsanto, all business units have at least two heads and sectors are run by boards consisting of managers from within and outside the sector. At Amoco, over fifty business units report to a strategic planning committee. Cross-functional, cross-geographic teams are a common vehicle for addressing complex strategic problems or opportunities. E-mail has become the common method of communication. Anyone can initiate e-mail and only a few keystrokes are required to send a message anywhere or everywhere in the organization. Electronic links exist between companies and suppliers, customers, alliance partners, shareholders, government agencies, the president of the United States—who knows, even God may be on the Internet.

Fast-forward ten, twenty, or thirty years to a world of relationship enterprises. Although hard to imagine, the pace of change is likely to be greater than it was over the past thirty years. Business entities will be owned by two, four, even six parents who are members of the enterprise. Career paths will be totally different and very mobile. The organizational structures that will be used, along with compensation systems and communications, haven't even been conceived today. The amount of knowledge that managers will require at their fingertips will be orders of magnitude greater than what is required today.

The intent of this section is not to predict the world of the twenty-first century, but to suggest how to prepare for one element of it, the arrival of the trillion-dollar enterprise. We begin in Chapter 5 by addressing the question, How should you go about creating a relationship enterprise?

Chapter 6 looks at how life will be different in a relationship enterprise and what issues should receive priority attention. The Achilles' heel of alliances is their management over time. Effective management of alliances is significantly more important for relationship enterprises because of the heavy interaction of multiple alliances and partners.

Chapter 7 discusses the requirements for managers in the world of relationship enterprises. We consider all managers who work in or interact with relationship enterprises, whether as employees, suppliers, or entrepreneurial competitors. All must understand how these enterprises work in order to deal with them effectively. What skills are required and how can these skills be developed? Chapter 7 addresses the issue common to individual managers: "Just when I thought I knew the answer, they changed the question on me!"

Chapter 8 focuses on the changing role of the CEO. Where will authority for decisions rest in the web of ownership and interdependent interests? We explore new models. The closest analogue to today's CEO is the European king of the Middle Ages—plenty of pressure from the outside, but absolute power within his own domain. In the relationship enterprise, the CEO's job will be more like that of the leader of a factious political party, creating coalitions to get an agenda implemented.

Next, in Chapter 9, we examine changes in governance. We look to the future through the prism of the past. Governance has evolved throughout the twentieth century and will continue to evolve as relationship enterprises are created. The potential conflicts are obvious; directors must serve their shareholders and deal cooperatively with competitors at the same time. Governance of the overall enterprise itself presents an interesting problem.

How to Build a Relationship Enterprise

All companies that compete internationally should be thinking about how to prepare for relationship enterprises in their industries. Consolidation trends of the past fifteen years, coupled with a number of interviews with CEOs and other business leaders, lead me to conclude that in many manufacturing and service industries *three to five enterprises will control two-thirds of the industry's global market within twenty years.* The definition of these industries will change as lines between them blur, overlap, and consolidate; hence we cannot extrapolate from today on a straight line. The world won't be the same in twenty years.

THE PURPOSE OF THE RELATIONSHIP ENTERPRISE

As you consider how to create and build a relationship enterprise, you need to step back and determine what you want *your* relationship enterprise to do. Most candidates for membership already have alliances. Hence, the decision is not to become active, or even more active, in alliances; the decision is to plan and prepare consciously to build the foundation that will enable you to develop into a successful relationship enterprise. That is the purpose of this chapter.

There are five steps in developing a successful relationship enterprise:

- Develop a vision for your industry.
- Imagine what the undisputed leader in your industry twenty years out will look like.
- Become expert in establishing and managing alliances, particularly cross-border alliances.
- Build bonds and common processes for communicating and doing business through an alliance network.
- Bring together the key partners to chart and execute an enterprise strategy.

Next, let's discuss each of these steps, including a plan for developing the relationship enterprise.

STEP 1: DEVELOP A VISION FOR YOUR INDUSTRY

The first step in building a relationship enterprise is to understand the context in which you must compete and the challenges facing your industry. Your vision should address technology, economics, growth, changing customers and customer requirements, and potential discontinuities. Quite likely the boundaries of your industry will change; it may annex parts of other industries and cede other parts away. New competition may arrive from unexpected sources through channels such as the Internet. Ten years ago, who would have predicted that grocery stores would enter gasoline retailing and capture 50 percent of the French market from the entrenched major oil companies? The following questions provide a useful framework for developing a vision for your industry:

- What will drive demand and determine industry boundaries over the next fifteen to twenty years? How will the requirements of customers change? What will be necessary to satisfy those demands—technology? distribution? volume? What impact will globalization have?

- Where will growth and new revenue come from (geographic expansion, new products, technology, changing customer requirements)? What are the major threats to industry growth?
- What capabilities will be required to be a global winner in your industry and how can those capabilities realistically be built or obtained? What will be the investment (in product, technology, facilities, systems, training, people) required? How much capital is available to fund those investments?
- How will the competitive structure of the industry change? What will be the impact of nationalism, of privatization, of regulatory changes? How will consolidation occur? Who will be the new competitors? What role do you expect alliances to play?
- How will the economics of the industry change? What will impact price and cost levels? How will the value chain change from raw materials to products or services in the hands of consumers? How will the Internet, new venues, or technology change the way in which products and services are distributed to customers?
- What major discontinuities might occur, either through competitor actions (e.g., Walmart in the retail industry), through new technology (e.g., electronics in the twentieth century), or through political change (e.g., world wars or the fall of communism)?

One of the best ways to sharpen your vision of your industry is through war gaming, or strategic simulation. War gaming originated in the military during the Second World War. I suppose a pure historian would argue that it began with Cyrus the Great as he reviewed scenarios with his generals before attacking Babylon; nevertheless, I will stick with modern war gaming. Top military and intelligence personnel would divide into teams representing allies and enemy governments and armies. A situation would be set up for which they wanted to test potential outcomes. Members of each team would play their roles as they imagined their real-life counterparts would. The result was an excellent understanding of how an invasion, a battle, a troop movement, an air attack, or whatever would play out. Many governments still use war games, now far more sophisticated than their predecessors and reasonably robust in their ability to live the future without live ammunition.

About fifteen years ago, Booz·Allen transplanted the war-gaming process and technology to commercial enterprises. The idea is the same: the executives and managers of the company divide into teams representing competitors, suppliers, customers, regulators, and other groups that will have an important impact on how the future will unfold. A simple model of the economics of the industry or area being studied is developed to compute market shares, sales, income, and other factors that are to be measured for the participating companies.

The real value of the game, which is called a strategic simulation, is the interaction among competing companies and their responses to the actions of others. Within a few days, a company can experience the future for five to ten years under several scenarios, with industry shocks and new entrants, with consolidations or spin-offs and discontinuities. Options for action and surprises are unlimited.

The key message for creating a vision for your industry: Break the mold. Recognize that change will be great and that there will be significant discontinuities.

STEP 2: DEVELOP A VISION FOR A WINNING RELATIONSHIP ENTERPRISE

Your vision should not be an extrapolation of current trends. The relationship enterprise is certainly a product of those trends, but it represents a discontinuity—a step change in capabilities; a step change in the way industries are structured; a step change in outcome. Successfully executed, the relationship enterprise can aspire to controlling 30 to 40 percent of a global industry. It can consolidate the best players into a dominant force. It can change the rules of the game in its favor.

Consequently, your enterprise vision should be bold: bold in aspiration, bold in degree of change, bold in its membership. The vision should reach out ten, fifteen, twenty years. Bob Galvin, Motorola's former chairman, would tell you fifty years.

At the Booz·Allen advisory board meeting in Paris six years ago, Bob Galvin told us that the secret of competing successfully in the future would be to shape the environment in which you wish to play rather than to react to conditions someone else imposes. He was right, but that's certainly easier said than done. He urged us to think boldly about human resources and knowledge and to consider approaches to leading the enterprise that have never been attempted.

Imagine yourself as the leader of a relationship enterprise with 40 percent of the global market in the year 2020. Put yourself in that future and describe your situation—the markets, products, and technology, the capabilities that gave you that leadership position, and the obstacles that you had to overcome to get there. These questions may help:

- Where are your markets and how large are they? Who are your customers? How do you reach your customers (e.g., understand their requirements, sell, conduct transactions, service their needs)?
- What kind of products and technologies do you have that enable you to lead the industry? How and where are your products designed, engineered, manufactured, distributed, serviced?
- What obstacles have inhibited your effectiveness (e.g., regulations, trade barriers, capital limitations, inadequate infrastructure, weakness in key markets, cost, attracting outstanding people)? How have you overcome those obstacles?
- Who are your principal competitors? (Remember, be bold!) Describe their alliance networks. How do your economics and capabilities compare with those of your competitors?
- Whom do you want as your partners? Describe your trillion-dollar enterprise.

With these answers, you should be able to define what it takes to lead your industry in 2020. You should be able to determine whether a single company can realistically achieve global leadership of your industry, or whether a network of alliances is necessary. You would have identified the obstacles in achieving the size and scope necessary for leadership and no doubt would have given up the thought of having your company become a leader on its own through acquisitions, however large your funding sources. You will have identified your partners in your trillion-dollar enterprise.

The key message in the vision for your trillion-dollar enterprise: Be imaginative. Be bold.

STEP 3: ACTIVELY PURSUE TARGET ALLIANCE PARTNERS AND BECOME EXPERT IN ESTABLISHING ALLIANCES

If your company is going to lead or be an important part of a relationship enterprise, it had better be expert in establishing and managing alliances. Alliances are the fabric of the relationship enterprise. This chapter focuses on creating the relationship enterprise, on establishing alliances. The next chapter deals with managing alliances within relationship enterprises.

Since alliances are major factors in business across the world, we can observe what works and what doesn't in establishing them. As indicated in Chapter 2, Booz·Allen has conducted a number of surveys on alliances. In addition to obtaining data on alliances, the research team collected information on management processes and practices in establishing alliances—a classical best-practice exercise. The objective was to understand how the best performers are building institutional capabilities in alliances. The results of these surveys have been presented at the Conference Board in New York over the past three years. The comments in this section are derived from those surveys and from Booz·Allen's experience with clients in alliances.

The companies best at establishing alliances use a process consisting of four stages: identification, evaluation, negotiation, and implementation. These stages comprise eight major steps, shown in Exhibit 5-1.

The research further revealed that each step can be broken down into a series of key tasks and subtasks, each an essential element of successful alliance formation. We have developed best practices for each task of the alliance process. For example, Exhibit 5-2 shows the breakdown of tasks for opportunity definition. This step comprises three tasks: risk assessment, value creation, and value sharing. Risk assessment is divided into seven subtasks.

In all, one hundred subtasks have been defined for creating and managing alliances, and best practices have been researched and identified for each of them. As an illustration, Exhibit 5-3 shows the best practices for five subtasks of risk assessment. The range of practices observed have been and arrayed from level 1 (neophyte) to level 5 (future best practice). Since standards don't remain constant—the

Exhibit 5-1 ❖ ALLIANCE-FORMATION METHODOLOGY

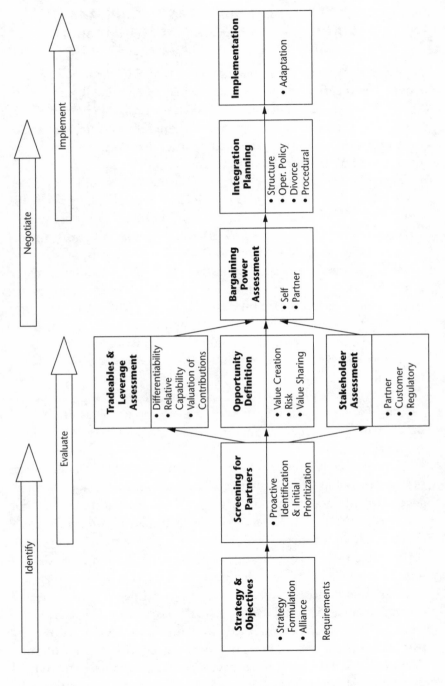

Source: Booz-Allen & Hamilton Best Practice Survey of Alliances, 1997.

Exhibit 5-2 ❖ ALLIANCE BEST PRACTICES: OPPORTUNITY DEFINITION

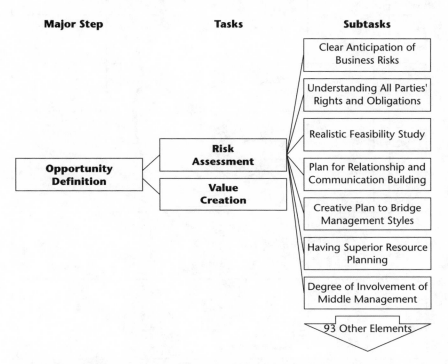

Major Step	Tasks	Subtasks

Source: Booz·Allen & Hamilton Best Practice Survey of Alliances, 1997.

bar rises almost every year in the fast-moving world of alliances—companies that achieve current best practice cannot rest on cruise control. Nevertheless, the right place to focus at the beginning is on current best practice.

Take the first element in Exhibit 5.2, Clear Anticipation of Business Risks, as an example. The research of company practices in alliance formation found that at minimum, companies develop lists of business risks (e.g., the technology pipeline is weak and may require major investment, or the plant in Reims is old and out of date, or will the alliance hold together in view of the different aspirations of the parents?). Level 2 companies do a good job of assessing the probable success of the alliance (e.g., will the alliance achieve the sales and profit goals we have agreed on? or, will the alliance solve our entry into China successfully? or, will the capabilities in the alliance be

Exhibit 5-3 ❖ SAMPLE BEST-PRACTICE TEMPLATE, RISK ASSESSMENT

Element	Other Widespread Practices			Current Best Practice	Future Best Practice	Importance to Business Performance	Average Level Achieved	Lowest Level Achieved	Highest Level Achieved	Level of Best Competitors
	Level 1	Level 2	Level 3	Level 4	Level 5		(Rating: 1 to 5)			
Clear Anticipation of Business Risks	General statement of risks to alliance success	Clear and detailed statement and analysis of the probability of alliance success	Alliance impact on successful performance of other domestic businesses	Alliance impact on successful performance of other international businesses	Impact on future attractive opportunities—corporate, domestic, and international					
Understanding All Parties' Rights and Obligations	Having vague and general rights and obligations	Better understanding of rights, but unclear understanding of obligations	Clearer description of rights and obligations, but not easily understood by other partner	Detailed description of rights and obligations, but convoluted legalese requires court arbitration	Detailed description of levels of contribution and rights, which is clearly understood by all partners					
Realistic Feasibility Study	No independent analysis—conception assessment control by corporate staff	Limited operational analysis based on prior alliance experience (ad hoc stage)	Operational analysis with focus on performance, but limited in tactical emphasis	Balance between corporate definition and operational & tactical know-how	Open discussion between partners of plans—sharing of assumptions & analysis					
Plan for Relationship and Communication Building on all Levels	No plan for relationship building, adopt informal approach at all levels	Recognize need for communications- periodic high-level/ board meetings, still utilize informal approach even in crisis periods	Plan to meet formally on a regular basis at key levels of organization to share progress	Meet on a regular base at key levels of organization but also schedule informal get-togethers to learn about each other	Establish frequent formal & informal get-togethers and other avenues of communications (e-mail, lists) on key levels					
Creative Plan to Bridge Management Styles of Partners	No plan to bridge partners' management styles in alliance	Knowledge of partners' management styles and culture, little understanding of impact on alliance and history of success	Executive profiles, organizational structure, cultural and working environment, reward and promotion programs matched with alliance needs and priorities	Interactive planning highlighting partners' organizational structure, cultural and working environment, reward and promotion programs compared to alliance needs and priorities	Adopt appropriate alliance structure to meet goals and objectives of venture					

To be filled in by each company to measure level and priority

Source: Booz-Allen & Hamilton Best Practice Survey of Alliances, 1997.

adequate to achieve competitive leadership?). Level 3 and 4 companies focus on the broader implications of the alliance on the rest of their business (e.g., what is the impact of the alliance on my other domestic or international businesses?). They examine the probable ripple effects, for example, on funding capacity, on competitive or customer response, or on other alliance partners. Level 4 is best practice among the companies surveyed. The highest level, future best practices, projects where the best companies will be in three to five years. Companies will anticipate the impact of the alliance on future opportunities, such as on markets the company may enter, on other potential alliance partners, or on the capacity to fund high-value projects in future years.

Check the practices for the other tasks shown on Exhibit 5.3. You can see the progression. It is important when assessing your own company's performance to be objective about where you stand. If you are to be a leader in the relationship enterprise game, you must be expert in alliances.

The final columns in Exhibit 5-3 allow you to rate the importance of each task to business performance (everything can't be top priority!), evaluate where your company stands on the scale (be ruthlessly honest), and rank the performance of your best competitors.

This method of analyzing your own company's performance and positioning and making comparisons with your best competitors is an excellent diagnostic tool for understanding the requirements for becoming expert in establishing and managing alliances. You can understand where you stand, which areas need improvement, and which are most important to you. These answers will allow you to set up a game plan (investments, training, capabilities) to become best in class where it matters most.

To make this framework come alive, consider Motorola's approach to partner screening. Motorola has over four hundred alliances. Its approach to partner screening uses two criteria: fit with value-creating capabilities and willingness to ally. As shown in Exhibit 5-4, Motorola develops its list of potential partners based on its strategy and objectives and then screens them against these two criteria. Based on ratings of low to high for these criteria, the short list pops out in the top right quadrant.

Exhibit 5-4 ❖ **MOTOROLA PARTNER ALLIANCE SCREENING**

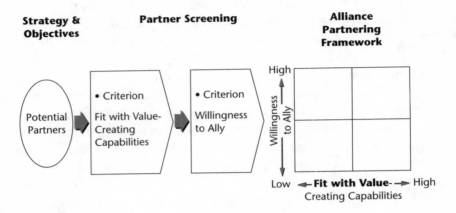

IMPACT and RATIONALE INCLUDES
- Total value proposition determines potential partner, i.e., strategic fit, alliance experience, culture, customer and market focus
- Willingness to ally accelerates pace of alliance formation

Source: Booz·Allen & Hamilton interviews and analysis.

Fit with value-creating capabilities is almost always the reason for seeking a partner in the first place. In jargon, it's the "value proposition," or why the two partners together can make more money or capture more market share or have a better cost position than the two can independently. Motorola looks at strategic fit, alliance experience, culture, and customer and market focus. The willingness to ally accelerates the pace of alliance formation.

Ten Commandments for Creating Successful Alliances

Since one hundred best practices are probably too many for anyone to focus on, I've boiled them down to the Ten Commandments for creating successful alliances. These commandments cut across the methodology I just showed you. The discipline of the methodology is very important. The spiritual guidance of the commandments can be your moral lighthouse. The truly serious among you will dig much deeper and broader into the best practices for forming alliances.

1. **Know what you want in an alliance partner and why.** Vision is crucial. A good grasp of how this alliance fits with your vision for your relationship enterprise as well as of the alliance's particular benefits is necessary. Understand what you want. Be realistic. Be clear. Understand why an alliance is important to achieving your vision.

   Think of the vision as a giant jigsaw puzzle. Each piece is a capability, an asset, a market access, a home-country position, all of which you need to create your successful relationship enterprise. Each potential alliance is a collection of these pieces. Each alliance must fill in a critical part of the giant puzzle. To make this analogy work, however, you have to modify your static view of jigsaw puzzles, because this puzzle is in constant motion and no piece maintains its shape for very long.

2. **Pick your partners for positive reasons.** Motorola has its two criteria. You may want three or even five. The criteria should be positive: fit, value, capabilities, willingness, competence, flexibility. Don't choose a partner because it's the best one available or because someone else will grab it if you don't or because you can fix its warts after the alliance. Develop your own positive criteria and stick with them.

3. **Ally for the long term and do your homework.** Go in with the belief that the alliance will last as long as the business opportunity. Consider an alliance a marriage, not a temporary arrangement. Understand and agree on mission, performance criteria, and links to the parents before you close the deal. Understand and value the contributions of both partners. Objectively assess the value creation potential. Consider how value will be shared. Due diligence for alliances requires more homework than acquisitions. Most of the homework for acquisitions is spent on defining the terms and price of the deal; most of the homework for alliances is spent on mission, vision, strategy, and relationship.

   Without question, the most common source of failure in alliances is inadequate or sloppy homework before the deal. In Booz·Allen's survey on alliance capabilities, the alliances studied were divided into successful and unsuccessful based on financial results. The single biggest difference between the groups of successful and unsuccessful alliances was the depth of understanding and agreement of both partners at the outset of the alliance. Differences in practices between the two groups were a good indicator of what separated the wheat from the chaff. Remember, the average ROI was 21 percent for the high-success alliance companies in the study and 12 percent for low-success alliance companies.

In a survey of over five hundred CEOs on the key reasons for alliance failures (over the 1990–1996 period), virtually all the factors cited were pre-agreement, as shown in Exhibit 5-5.

4. **Make the benefits and risks equitable.** Construct the alliance to serve the interests of all parties as equitably as possible. Companies, like people, tend to act in their self-interest. An alliance partner that believes it is being taken will devise means to get even or get out, two undesirable outcomes. Structure the division of value created so that you would be willing to accept either partner's position.

Exhibit 5-5 ❖ **OVER 500 CEOS' KEY REASONS FOR ALLIANCE FAILURES**

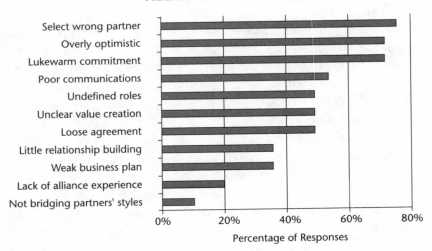

Source: Booz·Allen & Hamilton Best Practice Survey of Alliances, 1997.

This perspective is quite different from that of an acquisition, when price (the ultimate point of negotiation) is virtually a zero-sum game; the buyer wants to pay as little as possible, and the seller wants to get as much as possible. In most acquisitions, the selling shareholders have little or nothing to do with the organization after the transaction. It's much different with alliances, because you have a partner.

A small (or huge) footnote: risk sharing is just as important as sharing the spoils of victory.

5. **Offer the best and the brightest and you don't have to be the boss.** Put your top people into the alliance; it is the best way to tell your partner that the alliance is important. And if you are unwilling to put some of your real comers into the alliance, you are probably admitting that the alliance is not so crucial to your firm's future.

But that's not enough. Plato told us 2,500 years ago that brilliance alone was insufficient; brilliance augmented by excellent training produced the best leaders. The skills necessary to be a successful manager in an alliance are neither inbred nor part of the U.S. or European MBA academic culture. More will be said about training in Chapter 7.

Trust is key. If you have trust in your partner, you should be ready to have that partner run your plants in Germany, if that is what is best. Assign people to win. Being king of a losing cause is likely to be far less rewarding than being a platoon leader in the winning army. Remember that a relationship enterprise will have many alliances and will need many leaders.

6. **Make sure the parents and the alliance have common objectives.** Alignment of objectives on paper is not enough. You need to understand why your partner wants the alliance and you need to be sure that your partner's objectives are consistent with yours. The managers in the alliance must also share these objectives and aspirations. In addition to clearly telling the managers what is expected, the parents can use two important levers: oversight through a board or other supervisory link and the reward system. Make sure that rewards are paid for performance and actions you want.

7. **Communicate.** Invest in the infrastructure that makes it easy to communicate and do business together. Remember, your goal is to build alliances that will eventually grow into a relationship enterprise. The easier the alliance works, the more likely the partners will do more things together. Good communications give partners confidence, understanding, and trust. There is more on communication in Chapter 6.

8. **Hope for the best and prepare for the worst.** Prenuptial agreements are as difficult and unromantic in alliances as they are in marriages. Good prenuptial agreements in alliances identify specific conditions that could trigger a breakup and make specific provisions for breakups. Occasional or vague dissatisfaction, which will invariably occur, should not trigger dissolution.

In many cases, the alliance itself cannot be unwound. Then provisions for valuation and sale to one of the partners or a third party need to be defined. A good example is Elenco, a joint venture formed by Eli Lilly and Dow in agribusiness. At the outset, both companies placed a high priority on the agribusiness sector and each brought special capabilities to the alliance. In the mid-1990s Eli Lilly changed its corporate priorities and wanted out. The original alliance agreement included clear steps and rules for managing a breakup. Dow purchased Lilly's shares according to a prearranged formula. Elenco continues successfully today.

Despite their importance, I suspect that fewer than half the alliances being formed today have adequate or appropriate breakup provisions.

9. **Invest.** Recognize that the launching of an alliance is but its first step. Virtually all alliances require continued investment of money, people, attention, and oversight. Alliances are typically more dependent on their parents than are acquisitions. They rely on their parents for their lifelines—technology, funding, personnel, and special capabilities such as public relations, treasury, and public reporting. Often they look to parents for shared services, such as legal, accounting, employee benefits, and pur-

chasing services. Alliances, like companies, periodically require redirection, renewal, and rewards. Keep the alliance's vision in your sights and the alliance's role in your vision. Don't enter an alliance with the expectation that the alliance will manage and fund itself without your continuing support and investment.

10. **The devil is in the details.** Success is performing a thousand deeds better than anyone else. Our one hundred tasks for alliance formation constitute a good list of the things that must be done well. Alliances cannot be formed from sixty thousand feet. All parties need to examine the details, both to understand what they are getting into and to set appropriate expectations. The alliance is crucial to your company's success, or you shouldn't do it. If it is crucial, then you need to spend the time to make sure it is the right alliance done correctly, that it is well resourced, its mission and goals are appropriate, its strategy is on target and its tracking and performance measures and rewards will produce the right results.

As with the Ten Commandments that Moses brought down from the mountain, it is hard to imagine any company performing perfectly against this list, even though many of the commands appear to be common sense. I never cease to be surprised by well-managed companies that slip up on one or more of these commandments, to the regret of themselves and their shareholders. For example, two leading oil companies formed a venture based on a vision of lowering unit costs dramatically; the strategy of the offspring was to grow through acquisitions. The resulting strain brought a venture with great promise close to failure.

Companies that develop a strong, deep capability in forming alliances successfully are well ahead of the pack in developing a relationship enterprise. Companies should view this capability as seriously as they do other core competencies on which their success depends. They need to study, to plan, to invest, to hire and train experienced and capable people, to develop business processes for building alliances. Most companies understand that capabilities are hard to develop, particularly at world-class levels. Few companies have focused on developing a world-class alliance capability. Many companies (though the numbers are dwindling) act as though alliances require no new skills. The attitude of "We're good managers and we can manage anything" is more prevalent in practice than anyone would admit in public. Remember, a strong and deep capability in forming and managing alliances is the cornerstone and foundation of a strong relationship enterprise.

STEP 4: BUILD BONDS AND A COMMON PROCESS FOR COMMUNICATING AND DOING BUSINESS TOGETHER

A company is bound together culturally by a common heritage, values, tradition, and a wide range of common systems and activities. Well-led companies try hard to create bonds between the employees and the company and among employees. Stock options, bonus systems, 401(k) programs with matching contributions of company stock, common benefit programs, company newsletters, the annual report (which is directed as much to employees as to stockholders), staff meetings, and even the office picnic are some of the formal and informal ways in which companies forge those bonds. Companies have one name, a logo spread on everything from advertising to the company letterhead to T-shirts at the picnic. Think about the value of such names as Coca-Cola, Ford, Sony, Guinness, Chanel. Companies rally behind common charities and have PACs (political action committees). A company's headquarters are often as revered as St. Peter's in the Catholic Church.

Companies work hard to make communications easy because they realize that good communications make businesses stronger and employees closer. They build common computer networks, intranets, e-mail, telephone and fax systems. The first step in integrating a newly acquired subsidiary is to put the company on the parent's communications networks.

Companies spend millions every year to bond employees to the firm and to one another and to ensure that internal communications are rapid, efficient, and effortless. Companies make this investment because they know it will pay back handsomely. If units within the company work well together, the company will reap benefits in increased productivity, creativity, and swifter implementation of good ideas, which result in growth and profit.

If you want to build an effective relationship enterprise, do exactly the same things that you do to build an effective corporation: forge bonds among the members of the enterprise and build a strong communication system linking the enterprise together.

I doubt that you'll have enterprise logos or picnics, but you certainly can have an enterprise annual report, a newsletter, an intranet, an e-mail system. Boeing has common workstations with its partners. Motorola has an indoctrination program for all its alliance partners at Motorola University. Microsoft, Intel, and their countless partners are bonded at the hip with e-mail, telecommunications systems, joint projects, and a common set of goals and strategies. Alliance partners can have common training programs, for example, by joining together in an alliance with a university capable of distributed learning. (Thunderbird or Kellogg would be my choice.) Employees can be transferred among partner companies yet maintain their pension benefits through a common defined contribution plan and maintain their ties to their host company by continuing their stock options. Partners can have enterprise stock by creating a mutual fund of the member companies. Such a fund would include stocks from many countries and from a wide range of member companies—from entrepreneurial start-ups to giant corporations. The fund could be used to finance start-up members. Just imagine an enterprise that included Microsoft and took stock into its enterprise mutual fund in return for launching Microsoft in its early years.

The relationship enterprise offers plenty of opportunities for creating bonds and developing strong communications. Just as with corporations, creativity and good execution will separate the winners from the also-rans.

STEP 5: BRING TOGETHER THE KEY PARTNERS TO CHART AN ENTERPRISE STRATEGY

Two factors are required to enter the final stage of development of a relationship enterprise: trust and a precipitating event (good or bad). Trust must be established in the earlier alliance stages. Without trust, no contract can adequately bond companies in these uncharted waters. Trust must be two-way and must permeate both organizations at virtually all levels. Reliance on partners to perform to an agreed standard with common goals and values without detailed oversight is mandatory. Many alliances have achieved this level of trust—Intel and Microsoft, most of the Corning alliances, ADM and Toepfer (the Germany-based agribusiness giant). Bob Galvin said that the one thing that could transform a company into greatness was trust pervasive in the organization.

Building trust takes time, patience, and will. The organizations must have good experiences over years. You can't storm the corporate headquarters of an alliance partner to correct their erroneous ways or change the top gun. Trust is built by meeting commitments, by constant integrity and honesty, by real concern about partners, by sharing and trusting in return.

The other factor needed to bring together key partners is a precipitating event. Even though the forces of consolidation, globalization, and nationalism will lead naturally to the relationship enterprise, networks of alliances won't take the final step to operate as a single enterprise unless something compelling happens. The final step is a truly big step. It involves ceding some of the independence that corporations have enjoyed forever. It's no longer *my* strategy, but rather *our* strategy; control over *my* future is not mine alone, but shared; *my* performance depends on *our* performance.

A number of events could cause the spark that ignites a relationship enterprise. Legal and regulatory rules restricted public accounting firms from acquiring international practices. The spark that caused them to form relationship enterprises was the demand by their global clients for consistent audits across the world.

In the commercial aviation industry, alliances are quickly turning into networks as economics and customer service drive airlines to become global providers. The number of potential partners is limited, and most countries have only one good airline candidate. The spark to a true relationship enterprise will be a breakthrough in union relations that will enable sharing flight crews and maintenance work.

In the auto industry, the trigger is likely to be a move by one network of alliances to broader cooperation, which will cause the second network to become more aggressive, which will quickly escalate to the kind of enterprise activities discussed in Chapter 4.

Regulatory changes in telecommunications and electric utilities, changes in antitrust laws, and a major new technology are other probable sparks that may lead to the final stage of the relationship enterprise, in which networks of companies begin to act as a single entity in important areas.

There may be one other way of starting the ball rolling that is less traumatic than a crisis. Send a copy of this book to the core partners you'd like in the relationship enterprise with a simple note attached, "Let's talk."

Life Will Be Different in a
Trillion-Dollar Enterprise

CHAPTER

6

The trillion-dollar enterprise and its precursor, the relationship enterprise, will change your job, your company, and your life. We can only speculate how the changes will unfold. I foresee profound changes in the way companies are managed as members of relationship enterprises—in the job of the CEO, in the skills required of managers, and in the form of governance that will be necessary to oversee the enterprise.

It is important to distinguish the philosophy for managing a division or subsidiary from that of managing an alliance and leading a relationship enterprise. The purpose of this chapter is to establish the requirements for managing alliances and leading a relationship enterprise. It concludes with a discussion of the skills required to be an effective manager in these organizations.

Let's begin by examining the requirements for managing an alliance. For simplicity, we will consider two forms of strategic alliances: first, an alliance that is set up as a separate company or joint venture with two or more owner-parents, such as Dow Corning (the offspring of Dow Chemical and Corning formed to produce silicon products) and FujiXerox (the joint venture between Fuji and Xerox to manufacture and distribute Xerox products and technology in

Asia). The second is an alliance in which the people remain employees of their home companies, such as Global One (the alliance among telecommunications companies led by France Telecom, Deutsche Telekom, and Sprint), Star (the alliance of several airlines led by United and Lufthansa), and Airbus. In the latter case, the primary linkages are systems and the individual companies deal with each other in the alliance through the system. The trillion-dollar enterprise will have a full share of both kinds of alliances.

SEPARATE-COMPANY ALLIANCE

The separate-company alliance is much like a subsidiary that has two or more owners.

Common Understanding

In this kind of alliance, the crucial issue is agreement between the owners about the mission, goals, and strategy for their offspring. Common values and culture are also important, but are much more difficult to mandate. A management team needs both to understand and to embrace the desires of the parents.

Although this sounds basic, the management of an alliance does not always understand the objectives of its owners. In my experience, the time spent ensuring that the parents agree on the mission of the joint venture and that the management team is both selected and instructed to guarantee that the mission is carried out is the most valuable time spent in the entire process of establishing the venture.

Communications

A common understanding of mission and goals should be handled up front by the parents through good communications in establishing the alliance and putting a management team in place. Communications remain important throughout the life of the alliance.

Five rules of good communication are that it must be:

- Accurate
- Timely
- Relevant
- Open
- Two-way

Good communication doesn't mean you have to have lots of long talks or thick memos. To the contrary, the five rules can best be met with frequent, short, and to-the-point exchanges.

Values and Culture

Values and culture deserve special mention because they are crucial to business success and even more important to long-term satisfaction with the alliance. When you think about it, an alliance presents an extraordinary opportunity to create a culture that will be just right for the competitive world in which it will operate.

The principal values and cultural issues include:

- National and religious norms and customs
- Attitude and behavior toward customers
- Employee treatment and relationships
- Management style
- Legal and ethical standards and practices
- Language

Alliances, particularly separate joint ventures, present unusual and often very large challenges when it comes to principles and culture. The two or three parents have their own ways of doing things, which they usually feel are pretty good. Despite the common complaints of managers that "we need to change the culture around here," they don't mean that they would like to substitute a French or Japanese or Egyptian model for theirs. In your own environment, you don't even think about these issues. Policies and expectations are set, and, usually, violations are obvious and the penalties from frowns to firing are well understood. Unless these issues are addressed and expectations are clear in the alliance, simple problems can become overwhelming and competent people become stymied or leave. It is worth spending a few pages on values and culture to see where the impediments lie.

National and Religious Norms and Customs

These customs are the most obvious and often the most difficult to understand. The first rule is to recognize that national and religious norms and customs are important and deserve serious attention. We all have had run-ins with cultural norms that we did not anticipate. When you are working together with people who view the world differently from you, every day is a challenge. The need for understanding is paramount—and this is what your focus should be. You can't give too much cultural training to managers and executives who are entering into these alliances. A true understanding of the Japanese (American, French, Algerian, Indian—you fill in the blank) mind would take years of study. Since you likely don't have years to prepare, you'd better find an expert from your country on the other country's culture and religious norms.

Just any book or any expert won't do, because it is the juxtaposition of the other culture's way of thinking on your traditions and values that gets at the subtleties you will face. A Japanese scholar of India and Hinduism may be world-class, but is not going to be much help to the manager from Calgary who is slated to be the technology chief on the aircraft joint venture based in Calcutta. The requirements run far deeper than avoiding use of sports analogies to make a point. The challenge is not to "teach them how to think like we do" (i.e., the right way), but to understand how others think so you can get the best out of them and be as effective as you are back home. Motorola University offers a major program on cultural understanding for its employees and conducts seminars for joint-venture partners on what it means to work with Motorola.

There is a burgeoning cottage industry in cultural awareness and behavior. It comes in many flavors and levels of competence. Most senior executives still denigrate such soft stuff. They don't understand it and aren't comfortable with it because it can't be measured in economic or quantitative terms. In the past, cultural training meant a week or so of education in the new country for a manager and spouse so the spouse would be comfortable there and not demand to come home after three months of frustration. Make no mistake, we are no longer talking about the success of individuals living beyond familiar borders in a wholly owned subsidiary but about the success and viability of strategic alliances, which have become core to how we build a global enterprise.

One word about religion. Almost every country has a foundation of religion. The Islamic nations are the easiest to recognize because there, religion is often integrated with politics. India has multiple religions. China, while officially secular, has deep religious roots. Seventy years of Communist rule attempted to kill religion in Russia, but the Russian Orthodox church survived to be named the official church in Russia only recently. The United States was founded on religious freedom, but has a strong base in Christianity and Judaism. Slights to local religious customs, even if unintentional, are profoundly objectionable. Lack of knowledge or understanding is not an excuse for a business that intends to build a market in a country.

My counsel: take it seriously, investigate ways to bridge the cultural chasms, and invest in programs, processes, and people. The companies that build the best capabilities in this arena may well be among the most successful enterprises of the next decades.

Attitude and Behavior toward Customers

There is remarkable variation from country to country and even among industries and companies within a country in attitude and behavior toward customers. The more choices customers have and the more valuable they are perceived to be, the more likely it is they will be treated well. Airlines historically treated most passengers like cattle and have only recently begun to reward their frequent-flying business customers with more than free miles. In France, if you are a guest at La Réserve in Beaulieu-sur-Mer or are being fitted for a couture dress on Avenue Montaigne in Paris, the service will be spectacular. Drop down a few notches and your inquiries are rebuffed with "Comme?"

In most countries, including those in the industrialized world, the customer is just beginning to rise in priority. The issue in the joint-venture alliance is what the policy and strategy toward customers should be. Although the answer may seem obvious to you, in practice, it isn't. You may come from an environment that deals with a customer complaint as an opportunity to demonstrate how much you care, whereas your partner may forward all complaints to the legal department. You may wish to invest in systems that smooth the interface with the customer; your partner may view customer relations as a cost to be cut. Unless you explicitly address this issue up front, you won't know there are differences until substantial damage has occurred to your franchise.

Employee Treatment and Relationships

In a relationship enterprise, policies and practices with employees will become one of the most contentious and difficult problems. Employee treatment and relationships clearly differ from country to country and company to company. Slave labor has been outlawed in most civilized countries (give or take a few that view prisoners as free labor), but the treatment of employees in some countries is not far from that horrible past. Even the enlightened industrialized countries treated workers like farm animals a century ago. Many countries in Africa and Asia (names excluded to protect the guilty) still view employees as units of production.

In some countries, such as Japan, job security (i.e., lifetime employment) drives employee relations. The flip side of job security is that employees are expected to stay with one firm, and switching firms is still considered unusual in Japan. In other countries, such as the United States, company performance drives employee relations. The U.S. executive thinks nothing of laying off one thousand or ten thousand people, which would cause an earthquake in Japan. In Western Europe, government mandates many of the terms of employment, particularly social benefits and disengagement. The terms are so onerous to employers that large-scale layoffs are rare. In China and India, the labor pool is so huge that pay and working conditions can be miles below Western standards.

In an ideal model, firms would give their employees the security, freedom, motivation, training, compensation, information, and trust that would enable them to perform at their highest potential. Few firms would rate 10 on all these dimensions in employee surveys, but many are striving and some, such as Monsanto and Microsoft, come close.

You can't use the pay scales and work practices of the highest-cost location as the standard for the venture. But if you use the seven dimensions of employee relations as a framework—security, freedom, motivation, training, compensation, information, and trust—you can develop a workable policy for the alliance with your partner.

Debate and decide what is best for the alliance given its location, its competitive situation, its labor pool. The parents should be

---

Exhibit 6-1 ❖ **THE ERWIN CERAMICS PLANT VISION STATEMENT**

We, the people of Erwin Ceramics Plant, have a set of beliefs and rights that we value and are fundamental to our future.

It is the Right of all Employees to:

- Work in a clean, safe and healthy environment
- Work in a facility free of drugs and alcohol
- Be fully trained and equipped with the proper tools
- Work with fully trained, competent and dedicated people
- Access information that will improve employees' understanding of our business
- Challenging and meaningful work with systems that provide an opportunity for growth
- Be treated with dignity and respect, free of harassment and intimidation
- Participate in decisions that affect their worklife
- Expect long-term employment

Source: James O'Toole, *Leading Change—Overcoming the Ideology of Comfort and the Tyranny of Custom,* Jossey-Bass Publications, San Francisco, 1995.

---

involved, particularly if a core value—as trust is for Motorola—is involved; but the alliance management should make most of the calls.

An excellent example of the power of employees' making their own policies is provided by the Erwin Ceramics Plant of Corning. The plant was failing and about to be closed because of high costs and low quality. A group of eight salaried employees and eight union employees was assembled to write a vision for the plant. Group members talked to most employees and came up with the statement shown in Exhibit 6-1.

Although none of the points in the vision dealt with the problem—cost and quality—the result was striking: eighty jobs were eliminated (by attrition), defaults were decreased by 38 percent and the plant survived. This lesson has clear application to alliances.

Management Style

Within the wide spectrum of management styles lie plenty of rocks and shoals on which the alliance can run aground. Japanese consensus management drives most U.S. executives to the brink. The mandarin-style autocracy of the Chinese families in Asia is reminiscent of modern autocrats such as Chainsaw Al Dunlap. They are, unfortunately, often imitated but rarely admired. The Medicis' approach was similar some three hundred to four hundred years ago. Although Margaret Thatcher led the United Kingdom away from a labor-dominated economy in the 1980s, trade unions have shaped management in Germany, Italy, the United Kingdom, and much of Europe.

In my definition, management style includes the authority to act and the expectations that limit action. CEOs in the United States probably have the fewest limitations on bold action, and CEOs in Japan have the most. CEOs in Japan are limited by consensus within their firms, by extraordinary peer pressure from their colleagues in the Keidanren (the association of business leaders in Japan), and by the government (particularly the Ministry of Finance and the Ministry of International Trade and Industry).

We have an excellent current example in the Japan of 1998. Virtually every economist, politician, and businessperson on the planet, including those in Japan, believes that Japan's economic problems would at least be reduced (and possibly turned around) if Japan stimulated its economy, decreased restrictive regulations, opened its borders to freer trade, and reduced its massive trade surplus with the world. Yet Japanese executives feel impotent to do anything about it.

Management style is affected by cultural and religious norms as well. A CEO in a Muslim country would never interfere with religious practices of his employees, whereas a CEO on Wall Street wouldn't hesitate to have employees work on Christmas or Hanukkah. And although women probably don't have true equality of opportunity anywhere, the distance from true equality in the United States is vastly different from what it is in the Middle East or in several Asian countries.

Companies are striving to bridge the management styles of alliance partners. Recently, Booz·Allen did an analysis of best practices in this area for a major international client in the telecommunications industry. Senior management rated itself at level 2 for the best-practice element, Creative Plan to Bridge Management Styles of Partners (see Exhibit 5-3). In the study, 50 percent of all companies said they had no plan to bridge management styles in their alliances (level neophyte) and another 20 percent said they had some knowledge of their partner's management style and culture but little understanding of the impact on the alliance (level 2). In those cases, companies read a few books and possibly had training sessions on "how those guys behave." However, when Booz·Allen examined how important this best practice was in achieving alliance success, it rated among the highest in importance. The client is in the process of building this capability in a disciplined manner.

The management style of the alliance should be decided jointly by the parents and the managers of the alliance. There is no single correct answer, although culture, the competitive environment, and the mission of the alliance should be the deciding factors.

Legal and Ethical Standards and Practices

Laws of nations vary widely, and ethical standards vary even more widely. There should be no question about compliance with local laws. Legal issues rest with courts. The questions arise around just how close you can come to the line between legal and illegal. Often, that line is not clear, and there is a murky region in which honest people can disagree on what's legal or not. Similarly, there may be a law in the country of the parent that the parent wishes to enforce worldwide, whether the local country has the law on its books or not. In the case of the United States, environmental regulations, the U.S. Foreign Corrupt Practices Act, and regulations governing the handling of intellectual property rights are good examples. A French partner, however, would have no such laws and wouldn't want to impose them on its venture in Brazil with a U.S. partner. You can imagine the discussion. In my view, the murky area between law and lawless is the toughest problem. For example, many companies avoid taxes by engaging in practices that are contrary to the spirit of the law. What do you do if your policy is to abide by the spirit wherever you do business, but your partner in the alliance uses any and all means to avoid taxes?

Legal standards and practices need to be worked out in advance. Certainly, every possible problem cannot be foreseen, but principles can be agreed on and a mechanism for peaceful and reasonable adjudication can be established to handle almost everything.

Ethical standards and practices are becoming the cause célèbre of many countries and companies. The debate began over bribery and has extended to human rights, arms trading, contract compliance, sexual harassment, and other areas in the uncertain region between common practice and jail. The difficulty is the lack of a common foundation in philosophy. What is common practice in one country (baksheesh) is a bribe in another. In Brazil, there is a whole profession of people called *despachantes* who help you get through customs; you pay them for service, they oil the gears of the customs department, and out come your household effects that were "stuck" for three months. Similarly, foreign corporations are required to engage agents to contract for projects in Saudi Arabia. You pay them 5 or 10 percent for their services and, presto, life is easy. Is it unethical to engage these services? In Russia, gangs are collecting protection money under a "services rendered" mantle. Is that okay? Is it unethical to ally with a company that converts Brazilian rain forests into agricultural land if your policy is strongly environmentally friendly? And what about allowing acidic effluent from your joint-venture plant to be dumped into a river?

In most cases, ethics are a matter of your compass and your conscience. The real answer is to form alliances with partners who share your values and reject alliances with potential partners whose values you distrust or disagreed with.

Language

The most visible difference between parents of a multinational joint-venture alliance is language. The standard practice is to use the language of the country in which you are doing business for day-to-day business activities, and to communicate with the parent companies in their languages. Managers need at least two languages. If you add all the countries in which the enterprise is engaged, quite a few languages will be spoken around the enterprise and used for contracts, reports, studies, and so on.

I bring language up because the relationship enterprise has the potential to become a Tower of Babel. You can imagine the number of languages and the problems in communications in a network of alliances from several countries. A simple e-mail to inform all principals could be written in five or more languages with the potential for misinterpretation at every lingual intersection. What to do?

ABB (Asea Brown Boveri) has an interesting solution. Percy Barnevik was the CEO when ABB was formed by a merger of Asea of Sweden and Brown Boveri of Switzerland. He and his team had global ambitions and developed a strategy and organization to consolidate national power companies into a global corporation. The story is fascinating. Barnevik decided that a common language was necessary or communications would become a major obstacle to the nine global businesses ABB was pursuing. He decided that *all* intercompany communications would be in English, that all management committee and board meetings would be in English, that the language in the headquarters offices in Sweden and Switzerland would be English. He concluded that it would be a lot easier, more practical, and more effective to train everyone in English than to have hordes of translators throughout the world converting memos back and forth among many languages.

Relationship enterprises should seriously consider ABB's example. Interestingly, the predominant language of our one global communications vehicle, the Internet, is English. Air-traffic controllers in major airports everywhere use English.

People and Operating Choices in the Joint Venture

A major factor in setting the direction of a joint-venture alliance is *choosing the top team and the systems and business processes.* Whose people get which jobs? Whose systems get used? Whose business processes are adopted? What should be wholly new or different from the practices of the parents?

There are no easy rules in making these decisions. Experience with many of these situations tells me that the parents should first define the mission and determine the key values or principles. The parents should then choose the leadership of the alliance. (We will consider leadership qualifications and tasks in a subsequent chapter.) The parents and the alliance leadership should choose the top team together. This new team should develop the strategy for the venture with approval by the parents. It is important that the strategy be developed by the leadership of the venture to ensure ownership, commitment, and feasibility. No doubt there will be plenty of interaction with the parents on objectives and goals, performance measures and milestones, and the reward system. But it must be the venture's plan.

The next set of decisions—organization, whose systems (from one parent or wholly new), what business practices, policies on everything—should be made by the venture, in counsel with the parents. But the parents should not have veto rights, except on issues of principle defined ahead of time. If things get too far out of hand, the parents can remove the leaders, but they should not dictate how they run the business.

Although the idea of whole new systems, operating practices, and policies sounds appealing, cost, time to implement, and the risks of the untested are serious considerations for the new management team; often, some compromises are desirable to speed the venture along and reduce risks. The flip side of the argument is that management can take advantage of the unique moment to get it right from the start.

I argue for neither side, but recommend that these issues be analyzed and discussed openly and that the choices be made consciously, based on a full set of facts.

MANAGING ALLIANCES AMONG SEPARATE ORGANIZATIONS

The second type of strategic alliance, in which the people remain in their parent organization, is tougher than the separate joint venture in many respects. In these alliances, companies typically contribute capabilities, rather than assets and people, to the alliance. An example is Mazda's designing small cars for Ford and Ford's designing larger cars for Mazda. Another example is Intel's designing microprocessors that are the platform for Microsoft's operating software for personal computers. Intel and Microsoft are joined in planning and designing chips and microprocessors that Intel can produce at a low cost and very high quality and that will run new Microsoft software. Consider also the design, development, and manufacture of the Boeing 777; five partners formed an alliance that produced the plane. In all three cases—an automobile, an operating system for a PC, and the creation of an airplane—the employees stayed with their parent organizations. Success in the marketplace depended on multiple companies working as one.

How do you make this happen? Booz·Allen research suggests that the best companies have six important features:

1. A written (and agreed-upon) statement of mission, objectives, and milestones and a performance-measurement system
2. An understanding and agreement about who does what, when, the cost, and how profits are to be divided
3. A first-rate communications system
4. An understanding of how knowledge will be managed and who will own what
5. An understanding of the partners' various cultures
6. Agreed-upon organization, business processes, methods for dispute resolution, governance, and other issues of managing the alliance . . . and a dissolution provision.

Let's address each in turn.

Statement of Mission, Objectives, and Performance Measurement

First, you need a no-nonsense agreement among the partners on what you are trying to achieve. For example: "We will be designing an aircraft that meets five key objectives for range, speed, fuel economy, passenger capacity, and avionics within a development budget of X dollars and a cost per plane of Y dollars."

In many cases, the product of the alliance cannot be so clearly specified. Consider the case of Intel's microprocessor. The mission and goal of the Intel/Microsoft alliance is to develop and produce the best PC operating system on the market. The requirement for objectives and milestones exists, but cannot be stated as explicitly as those for an airplane, a car, an engine, or a pharmaceutical. Milestones are built around the development of electronics and software, and there is substantial interaction as new ideas are tested and modified back and forth.

An alliance between a manufacturer and a distributor has another set of objectives, typically designed around product reliability, customer service, cost, and speed. W.W. Grainger distributes a wide range of products for electrical manufacturers. With each manufacturer, Grainger has an agreement for each key area against which the performance of both partners will be measured.

Division of Responsibility, Costs, and Profits

Who does what is usually determined well before an alliance is formed. The reason partners form the alliance in the first place is to gain the benefit of the other's capabilities. The capability a partner brings to the table dictates what that partner should do in the alliance.

But it's not quite that simple. The capabilities of the various partners rarely fit together nicely. Gaps or overlaps lead to confusion if not managed properly. Hence it is necessary to be explicit about who does what, and to ensure that the activity stream is continuous from beginning to end with no gaps or overlaps.

To accomplish this, you need to agree on what performance standards should apply. This may seem obvious, but ask Airbus about common performance standards. Cost overruns and misunderstandings have plagued Airbus. Each company operates independently and chooses suppliers with an eye toward national employment. If Airbus managed itself as a single enterprise, it could substantially reduce costs and development time and be a significantly stronger competitor to Boeing and its partners.

In an Arthur Andersen audit, twenty or thirty independent audit firms must apply the same principles of accounting, and just as important, the same level of rigor, objectivity, detail, and integrity. Arthur Andersen invests heavily to achieve that consistency, putting virtually all professionals through extensive formal training at various points in their careers.

Once you've decided who does what, and agreed on performance standards, most costs are clearly assigned—most, but not those elusive and potentially large indirect or overhead costs, that each partner incurs in supporting the alliance. There are countless ways to measure and allocate these costs, none of them right or wrong. The partners need to agree on which indirect and overhead charges will be allocated to the alliance and must establish a budget and mechanism for allocating these costs. This issue is typically much simpler in a joint-venture alliance in which the alliance can be separated from the parents. But in an alliance that is embedded in the partners' businesses, there is plenty of room for misunderstanding and mischief.

How should you value prior investment? What if a partner, like Monsanto, brings years of experience and $10 billion of research in biotech to the party? What about the expertise a partner contributes? These issues need to be hammered out fairly and in advance.

The performance tracking and measuring system needs to inform the partners what's on or off centerline. What factors get tracked, how milestones are set, and how the system works are specific to the alliance. Rarely will a company's in-house performance-monitoring system suffice. This doesn't mean you have to spend millions to create a new tracking system, but it does mean all partners have to participate in setting the objectives for the system and determining how the system will collect and consolidate information. Because the actions of one partner frequently impact the others, it is not enough to add up the status of each partner to determine where the alliance stands against its overall objectives. A good tracking system is a good (and not necessarily large) investment.

The tracking system may not exist on someone's shelf. For the Boeing 777, the tracking system looks more like a project management system than a normal budget, but has elements of both. The common workstations feed central program control with times and costs against which all partners work, and constantly recomputes the status of the whole project. For Intel and Microsoft, the tracking system resembles multiple product development systems with substantial interaction and iterations as the two companies go back and forth with new ideas.

First-Rate Communications System

A third factor necessary for success is a first-rate interactive communications system. On the 777 project, the partners had fifty workstations designed to work seamlessly with one another. They understood that every subsystem affected the whole airplane and that that effect had to be understood at every level by every partner. Arthur Andersen auditors all over the world receive changes in accounting standards (and all the backup necessary to implement them) for almost every country in the world continually. These partners must be up-to-date on standards and work together. The

Mazda-designed small car manufactured at Ford has supplier plants worldwide; Ford and Mazda must be totally current on the capabilities and idiosyncrasies of every producer of every part.

Advances in telecommunications and information technology—e-mail, modems, the Internet, satellites, fiber optics, workstations—all make communication easier. The development cycle has been shortened substantially, and accomplishing major tasks through alliances has been made possible by new technologies. The demands on an effective communications system rise exponentially with the number of companies involved and the complexity of the alliances. The relationship enterprise will present a challenge in communications of a new order of magnitude. There will be multiple alliances, with multiple partners in multiple locations; there will be multiple tracking systems; there will be multiple organizational units and many individuals with responsibility for decisions and actions and results. If a communications system is to be effective, it must be simple. Sounds tough, but those are the requirements, and the enterprises that get it right will have an important competitive advantage.

Knowledge Management

One of the hottest topics of the next decade is knowledge management. In thinking about how to tap into the knowledge that exists in the four corners of his own company (forget the complications of alliances) and utilize it effectively elsewhere, Didier Pineau-Valencienne, chairman of Schneider S.A. of France, once said, "I have thirty plants which produce the same type of products. How can I get all thirty to adopt the best practice that exists in the system in each phase of the process?" Such an achievement would double productivity, reduce costs dramatically, and improve quality in any company. It's not easy in your own company. Imagine how hard it is in alliances.

Knowledge management is a topic of such magnitude and complexity that it deserves an entire book. Here we will review just a few points that are relevant to the relationship enterprise.

For the relationship enterprise, knowledge is power. Virtually all the understandings that we have been discussing as requirements for creating and managing alliances and a relationship enterprise are founded on knowledge. Knowledge is an elusive goal. It's impossible (and impractical) to know everything, but competitively crucial to know certain things. Capabilities, technology, business practices, markets, competitors are all important and constantly changing. The key is to understand what you need to know in each important category and to set up a system to collect and use that knowledge. The system needs to include all partners in the relationship enterprise, and yet must protect the proprietary property of each member. The system must be timely and accurate, yet must not be overly burdensome or costly to maintain or it will sink like concrete overshoes. Executives at all levels must be able to get the information they need in the form they need without requiring a database the size of the Pentagon.

I have found that knowledge management is a process, not a computerized database. The best companies establish knowledge management as a strategic objective and set about deciding what they need and how best to get it. Frequently, most of the knowledge required exists somewhere in a form close enough to what the executive requires. Hence the challenge is collection and retrieval.

Some companies use master computerized systems to store data and allow users to retrieve it in the way most useful to them. SAP is one of the best examples for financial information.

Booz·Allen has a knowledge database system. It holds the important elements of the firm's research, cleansed (i.e., nonproprietary information only) versions of client reports, and publications, seminars, and speeches by Booz·Allen professionals. For example, an associate can ask for the most current thinking on approaches to credit rating for financial institutions and receive fifty or one hundred papers or reports the firm has generated on the topic. As a result, every professional anywhere in the world can approach a client with the best thinking of the firm.

Other companies knit together the systems and sources of information they have, augment it to meet the objectives of their knowledge-management strategy, and provide a process for retrieval, which can be anything from a manual describing where things are to a surfing navigator on a company's intranet.

The approach doesn't matter. Here's what does: partners must take knowledge management very seriously and invest in the process at the same level they invest in new machines and engineers.

Cross-Cultural Understanding

Earlier we discussed cultural issues from the perspective of a joint-venture alliance—that is, how to establish a separate organization from multiple parents. Here the issue is how to manage an alliance between two or more partners from different cultures without melding them. The roots of the issue are the same, but the two situations have unique challenges.

In an alliance of separate organizations, the cultural differences creep up on you when you least expect them. You know they exist, but you are not confronted with them in day-to-day activities. There is far greater risk that cultural issues will not receive adequate attention when people remain in their own organization where their own culture is constantly reinforced. In a joint venture, cultural issues are on the table and in your face every day.

Lord David Young, former Thatcher cabinet minister and then-chairman of Cable & Wireless, told me that the greatest impediment to a unified EC (European Community) was the difference in legal codes and the philosophy on which they were founded. The United Kingdom and Scandinavia operate under common law, and France, Germany, and southern Europe operate under the Napoleonic Code. In common law, the individual is permitted to do anything that is not specifically prohibited; under the Napoleonic Code, the law establishes individual obligation. In other words, the philosophy of the Napoleonic Code is the exact opposite of the philosophy of common law.

Yes means different things in many societies. A contract is the starting point for negotiations in Iran and Korea. Culture runs deep, and people in every country on earth wish to retain and defend their cultural values and even their language. For example, in France, decrees are periodically issued to prohibit pollution of the French language with words such as *weekend*. Gaelic is spoken in Ireland as a matter of tradition and pride, not for convenience, commerce, or communication.

Companies are products of their home culture. Although several companies based in non-English language countries use English, the global tongue of most firms is still the home country's language. For example, check the communications from Mercedes do Brasil to the home office in Stuttgart. Attitudes toward business practices are the home country's. Visit a Honda plant anywhere—Japanese management and labor practices prevail. Acceptable behavior finds its roots in the home country. Note the difference in the competitive practices of French and U.S. companies operating in the Middle East—the French expect their government intelligence organization to obtain competitive information, whereas the CIA and other U.S. government agencies are prohibited by law from spying on non-U.S. corporations or sharing commercial information with U.S. companies. How people think, what is important, their core beliefs all are founded in a homecountry culture. Global industry norms penetrate to some degree, but Toyota is still much more like Sony or Mitsubishi Bank than it is like Ford, VW, or Renault.

The actions companies take to achieve cultural awareness for alliances of separate organizations are the same actions they take for joint-venture alliances. The key is to understand that cultural differences are important, despite the lack of day-to-day contact. Performance will be best when partners truly understand one another's thinking, values, and national and religious norms.

Agreement on Organization, Processes, and Management Style

Finally, the partners need to agree on how the alliance will be managed. We have already discussed some elements of managing the alliance—communications, management of knowledge, tracking performance. Now we will discuss organization, business processes, and management style.

Two elements are important to the organization of alliances that are not separate from their parent organizations: the overall structure that comprises all the resources committed to the alliance wherever they are housed, and the structure for the alliance within each parent. I will touch on both.

Overall Alliance Structure

There are principles, not rules, that should be followed in organizing an alliance. Rules don't apply, because no two alliances are exactly alike.

- Someone has to be in charge. No matter how warm the relationship among the parents, when the dust settles and the alliance goes to work, there has to be a leader. The role of the leader will be discussed in Chapter 8.

- A governance structure should be created to ensure that all partners are aware of and have input into the key decisions of the alliance. Note that I used "governance" and not "management," because the partners must delegate management to the alliance leader. They should hold the leader responsible, but should not do the leader's job.

- The responsibilities and deliverables (what, when, where, at what cost, what quality, and to what specs) of each partner must be clear, clear, clear. The partners must map out every task against the overall strategy to ensure there are no gaps and that everything meshes.

- The business processes that wire the alliance together will be as simple or as complex as needed to coordinate activities of the partners. Designing an A300 Airbus requires extraordinary coordination—the plane must fly every time it takes off. A distribution alliance, such as that of Pepsi and Lipton Tea, needs less coordination, and a relatively simple demand-and-supply system should do the trick.

Alliance Structure within Each Partner

The organization of the alliance within each of the sponsoring companies is equally important. The first question is whether to segregate those involved in the alliance in a separate unit or to get the alliance work done through the current organization. The preferred solution is to create a separate unit, which enables focus, performance measurement, clear responsibility, and isolation of costs. But this is not always feasible. The product development system may not be effective if a slice is carved out. Matrices are tough to chop up. Scale and efficiency are often important in activities and would be lost if a piece were separated. The same person or small unit may be needed to work on both the alliance and the company's other businesses. The less competent workers in the organization could be assigned to the alliance.

If a separate unit devoted to the alliance is not appropriate, you must ensure that the proper resources and attention are devoted to the alliance. It cannot be one of ten things for which a unit manager is responsible. It cannot be so dispersed throughout the organization that focus and communications become major problems. In such cases, the best companies take the following measures:

- Name a full-time alliance executive with overall responsibility for coordinating all individuals and units working on the alliance.
- Clearly identify individuals and groups with alliance responsibility.
- Ensure that all individuals involved understand their roles, responsibilities, and objectives.
- Tie compensation and progress in the company to individuals' performance and to the performance of the alliance.

The biggest pitfalls are perceiving work on the alliance as extracurricular to the mainstream or as temporary duty, assigning available staff rather than the right staff, and assuming that coordination is not necessary because employees should know their jobs and do them.

Special attention needs to be paid to designing and installing business processes that pull together all the activities into a coordinated whole. Do not underestimate how hard this is when resources are scattered among several organizational units that have other things to do.

A good example is the design and development of an automobile. Multiple vehicles go through the system at the same time. Several functional organizations and multiple suppliers are involved. A program-development system controls the involvement of these scattered organizations. For example, for brakes alone, the 2001 Ford Taurus program coordinates design work in five or six Ford departments with suppliers. Multiply this by all the subsystems and you have a very complex undertaking—and consumers all expect the car to work perfectly, meaning that all those subsystems must mesh flawlessly when the driver steps on the gas.

The requirement for an alliance is exactly the same. Each element of work needs to be coordinated with all others, and the product must be on time, on cost, on spec, and on quality—*and* it has to mesh flawlessly with the work of other alliance partners.

THE RELATIONSHIP ENTERPRISE:
MORE THAN THE SUM OF ITS ALLIANCES

Everything we have discussed about strategic alliances is magnified tenfold in the relationship enterprise. By its nature, the relationship enterprise contains many alliances of different types, sizes, and purposes. The network is held together by a common mission and trust. Clearly, the creation and management of a relationship enterprise require a new way of thinking.

Few senior executives will be so bold as to think they already know how to manage and lead a relationship enterprise. The task is a cross between being a CEO and being the secretary general of the United Nations. The relationship enterprise must be knitted together with a common mission, a shared vision, common goals, and a level of trust that permits the members of the enterprise to share their deepest secrets in one area and compete ruthlessly against one another in another. The bond of mutual self-interest must be forged by reality—of markets, of economics and of capabilities.

As we have already discussed, a relationship enterprise should be created from a perspective ten to twenty years in the future. What will the principal markets and technologies be? Where must you have presence, and what capabilities will be crucial for the leaders? What will the competitive environment be? The economics? The role of government and international oversight bodies? The geopolitical context? Most important, how can this playing field be changed or leveled to your advantage? What partners do you need to be a major force in the world of 2010–2015?

Having pictured the future and imagined your dream team, you should determine what capabilities you need to put it together and make it work. This chapter discussed the wiring: common mission, goals, and strategy; shared values; an understanding and respect for cultural differences; an ability to bridge gaps to work together effectively; agreement on responsibilities, performance standards, and the capabilities each partner brings to the enterprise; and a communications system that enables many independent companies to act as one.

All these things are required and important, but they are not enough. The jobs of the CEO and the top management team change in a relationship enterprise. The concept of strategy evolves from corporate or business strategy to enterprise strategy. The level of thinking and analysis ratchets up several notches. The things that Henry Kissinger worries about become the concerns of the CEO. Political risk has always been on the CEO's agenda, but it now reaches a level only recorded in mystery novels. How to change the playing field? How to move governments to action? How to assure peace? How to work with partners who are arch competitors?

Working with an alliance toward a single goal is complicated. Moving a network of alliances in a common direction is far more complex. We will deal with that challenge for managers in the next chapter, for CEOs in Chapter 8, and for directors in Chapter 9.

To conclude this important chapter, a note of caution and of encouragement. The track record on managing alliances has not been stellar, yet it is improving. But once business leaders believe that something is truly important, they are far better than any other professionals at getting things done well.

The New Role of Managers:
Skills Required

In defining the new role of managers, it is useful to step back and think about the evolution of their roles. For centuries, the principal role of the manager was boss. The boss decided what everyone would do, held all the cards when it came time to reward and punish, and was viewed by everyone as the person in charge. The boss's desk was where the buck stopped; this held for the owner of the business down to the foreman on the shop floor.

This form of management still exists and has its advantages. It is efficient, clean, understandable. It fits with the Western macho attitude. We honor such attributes as decisiveness, toughness, strength, and resolve. A person without these qualities is soft and weak. Most owners of small or medium-sized companies still operate under the principle of "It's my sandbox and I'll decide who plays what games." In situations in which one person can keep everything in her head or at her fingertips, this system can work just fine. When relying on the skills or capabilities of others for crucial decisions, however, the solution changes. Unfortunately, a number of CEOs of large public companies operate under the boss philosophy, as do managers of the plant, the sales force, and the accounting department.

For the past fifty years, social scientists and business academics have been trying to change that model. In the late 1950s, Douglas McGregor told us about theory X and Theory Y managers. Theory X is command and control. The assumption is that subordinates are lazy, unmotivated, and maybe even dumb so you have to direct their every move and use the whip when they get out of line. Theory Y assumes the opposite, that subordinates are naturally motivated and smart and, given the proper encouragement, will perform very well. Bob Shapiro of Monsanto believes that treating employees like mature adults will result in them acting like mature adults. The Theory Y system is reward based whereas the Theory X system is fear and punishment based. Research strongly supports a participative style of leadership, yet only in the 1990s is the needle beginning to move toward Theory Y, and it is doing so slowly.

I believe that a shock is coming that will send the needle hurtling. First, a participative or collegial style is important today, because the best people have options and will go elsewhere if they don't get adequate responsibility or aren't treated with respect. Second, as we move from wholly owned divisions and subsidiaries to alliances and then to relationship enterprises, the need to gain cooperation and motivate without the tools of authority, compensation, and career dependence becomes paramount. We don't have a generation to prepare people to be effective in this new environment. Executives forging new alliances know it. But even they are underestimating the requirements of the relationship enterprise for multicultural, multilingual, politically sensitive, diplomatically skilled executives who can think strategically at the global level.

RELATIONSHIP ENTERPRISE IN THE AUTOMOTIVE INDUSTRY IN 2010

To illustrate the skills required, let's imagine a relationship enterprise in the automotive industry circa 2010 (even though I believe it will happen sooner). The structure of the imaginary relationship enterprise that we will call Zeus Motors looks like this: there are four large original equipment manufacturers (Modern Motors [U.S.], Toyota, BMW, and Fiat); five smaller OEMs (Porsche, Mazda, Volvo, First Auto Works [China], and Kia); forty small, medium, and large suppliers; and ten other members (financial, distribution, telecommunications, software companies).

The primary mission of the relationship enterprise is to dominate the automotive industry worldwide. The enterprise does all the things we discussed in Chapter 4: it has common platforms and engine families, cross manufacturing through suballiances, and common distribution in many countries. Countless cross alliances support, supply, manufacture, market, and maintain the products of other enterprise partners.

To create a good feel for what managers do in the world of relationship enterprises, we will build a scenario around the experiences of four hypothetical individuals in the following roles:

1. Enterprise vice president, small-vehicle platforms. Head of an alliance in which the members remain in their parent organizations; e.g., manager of small-vehicle platforms for Zeus happens to be with Toyota
2. Alliance manager, small-vehicle platforms. Head of alliance activities within one of the partners; e.g., manager of small-vehicle platforms for Fiat, which is a partner in Zeus for small vehicles
3. Human resources manager, joint venture. Manager for a joint venture in China between three members of Zeus
4. Alliance program manager, small supplier. Program manager from a member that is a small supplier; e.g., product manager for fasteners and forged parts at MacLean Fogg, a $200 million auto-parts manufacturer in 1998 that grew to $600 million in 2010 with Zeus

Enterprise Vice President, Small-Vehicle Platforms

Our enterprise vice president Yoshio Teikei, is a senior manager at Toyota. His job for the enterprise is to oversee, coordinate, and ensure success in the development (from R&D through product engineering and sourcing) of a small-vehicle platform from which the alliance partners will build compact and subcompact cars. He has only a small staff of six because the work is done by the partners (including his own company, Toyota) and suppliers. Two of the OEM partners, Toyota and Fiat, have deep experience in designing and building small cars; the other two OEM partners, Modern Motors and BMW, have huge markets and huge customer bases to which they can sell small cars. Yoshio's job is to draw on the capabilities of all and ensure that the result meets the market requirements of all the partners and of the other markets (e.g., China, India, Indonesia, Russia) that Zeus has targeted.

With next to no staff, and with work being done by organizations over which he has no real control, Yoshio must satisfy consumers across the world. He remembers how difficult it was for Ford in the 1960s through the 1990s to coordinate product development within a single company to get a world car. Yoshio must accomplish his task through multiple independent corporations, each with its own historic set of suppliers.

Yoshio understands the prize. A single platform from which many models will be built can save Zeus billions of dollars (and hundreds of billions of yen). Success will enable Zeus to build a plant in Indonesia and bring that country into the automotive world of the twenty-first century by offering a car at about 60 percent of the cost of current entries. That market could jump from 1 million cars per year to 5 million almost overnight. The impact would be similar to the impact of Henry Ford's assembly line and $5-a-day pay that allowed workers to buy Model Ts one hundred years earlier.

And that's just Indonesia. Think about China, India, Pakistan, Sri Lanka, Russia, Ukraine, Belorussia. Yoshio is pumped up, but perplexed. The task he faces is more formidable than anything he has done.

Yoshio is a graduate of Tokyo University, the best technical school in Japan, with a degree in electronic engineering. He earned his MIM (masters in international management) at Thunderbird in Glendale, Arizona (although many of his classes were taken in Tokyo through a long-distance learning program). He started work with Toyota in Australia, and over the next fifteen years moved to Brazil, Japan, and England. At the age of forty, he took a leave of absence from Toyota to join a UN delegation on environmental management based in Switzerland. For five years he worked with governments and activist groups all over the world, trying to implement the World Environmental Treaty, which was signed in 2002. His toughest task was to bring along the United States, Japan, and Germany, by far the world's largest polluters. Yoshio did an outstanding job. He was brought back to Tokyo by Toyota to head its development team for small cars, and after five years he was named enterprise V.P.

Yoshio's first move was to establish the enterprise mission for the small-vehicle platform. He gathered the heads of product development from each of the OEM partners and the five suppliers most important for the platform. Rather than summon them to Tokyo, he held the meeting on neutral turf, in Paris—a nice touch since that was where the World Environmental Treaty had been signed.

They spent two days together discussing the mission and the capabilities each brought to the task. They each agreed to assign one person to Yoshio's staff to provide inside knowledge of their company and to coordinate their company's work on the alliance. They adjourned after agreeing that their next task was to develop an overall game plan, timetable, budget, and management system. Yoshio's new staff was to develop a first cut in each of these areas and present it to the Paris Group, as they now called themselves. Yoshio contacted his favorite senior partner from Booz·Allen to join his team, and they went to work.

Preparing the overall game plan and budget, parceling out the work, and establishing schedules were fairly easy tasks, since everyone involved had been down that road a hundred times. How to manage the alliance was an elephant of a different color. Yoshio set down three principles that would guide the alliance in getting the job done:

- **Training is free.** Yoshio recognized that all the companies had experience working with alliances, but none had undertaken a cooperative venture of this magnitude. The payback on training was days and weeks, not months and years. He laid out a program for developing within each partner's organization an understanding of the mission, how it would be accomplished together, and how each partner would operate.
- **Communications are to be accurate, timely, relevant, open, and two-way.** To enable open communications, a system was established for three topics: technical, administrative and performance tracking, and issues of concern that needed attention and resolution. The technical system was designed around common workstations for all partners. The administrative and performance

tracking system was Internet- and intranet-based and handled everything from meeting schedules and personnel swaps to variances from budgets and time milestones. Straight Talk (the name given the system aimed at issues of concern) was an intranet facility that allowed any issues to be raised to a narrow or broad audience to suggest changes, offer ideas for discussion, or raise problems before they became evident through performance tracking. It also allowed people to ask for help—for ideas, resources, people, information, or virtually anything.

- **We are in this together.** The success of every partner was dependent on developing a platform within the agreed budget and on which each could build cars successful in their markets. In other words, they'd swim or sink together. A great job by one partner at the expense of another would not achieve the overall goal. All had to be motivated to help the other partners.

  To support this requirement, Yoshio designed a compensation system for the key people in the alliance that rewarded them based on alliance performance. Hence the alliance participants in Modern Motors, BMW, Toyota, and Fiat were no longer part of their home company's incentive compensation program. They continued to get salary and benefits at Modern Motors, BMW, Toyota, and Fiat, but their annual bonus and long-term compensation were now determined by the alliance's performance. Yoshio had to call on all his diplomatic skills to get that change approved and probably would have failed had the Paris Group not been totally committed to the mission.

In a short time, Yoshio had won the partners' commitment to the mission, aligned the objectives and incentives of all the key players, established a transparent and effective communications and tracking system, identified the capabilities and training requirements, created a program to handle them, and established his core leadership team, the Paris Group.

The results far exceeded the parents' (and the Wall Street analysts') expectations, but the team members knew how they would do better next time. Although the program was six months late, Yoshio is confident that he has learned enough to beat the time by twelve months on the next program. The partners got 80 percent of what they needed to build their small-car lines off the new platform; and they are confident that they can hit 95 percent or better next time. The program was on budget, which was a first for every partner.

Alliance Manager, Small-Vehicle Platforms

On the other side of the world, Maria Barolla was assigned to manage Fiat's participation in the alliance. Maria was an engineer who started her career in the palatial product development and styling center outside Turino. After ten years of rapid progress in product planning, she was invited by Renato Ruggiero, a former trade minister who was leading Fiat's expansion internationally, to work on a Russian joint venture. Three years later, Ruggiero was named head of the newly formed WTO (World Trade Organization) and he asked Maria to join him. For the next six years, Maria traipsed around the globe handling trade disputes. She returned to Fiat in charge of small-car product development. When the new relationship enterprise was being established, the CEO of Fiat asked Maria to help think through Fiat's role and how the whole thing would work. Two years later, Maria was named head of the Fiat piece of the small-vehicle alliance. She accompanied her boss, Francesco Borghesi, to the Paris Group meeting.

Maria participated with Yoshio in all the planning and in setting the three principles for managing the alliance. She had learned in the WTO that cooperative effort is far more powerful than lone rangers.

Maria asked Fiat's CEO to convene a meeting with the key managers from product planning, engineering, manufacturing, human resources, purchasing, quality, and information technology. They used Umberto Agnelli's (one of the principal shareholders in Fiat) villa in the mountains above Torino for three days. The fresh tomato soup was spectacular. The CEO attended.

Maria spent the first four hours describing the mission, the management philosophy, and Fiat's role in the alliance. Over the next day and a half, they talked about how Fiat could best perform its role in the alliance. They agreed on the organizational structure for the alliance and the individuals who would be assigned to it. On day three, the CEO left and the others were joined by Yoshio and the small-vehicle alliance heads from Modern Motors, Toyota, BMW, and three of the most important suppliers, ITT Industries, Nippon Denso, and

GEC of the United Kingdom. They spent the day discussing how they would work together and what support could be provided among the partners and gaining an understanding that this was a truly cooperative venture.

Maria recognized that she had to draw heavily on Fiat's common pool of engineers, product planners, and stylists to get her project done. She set up a matrix with her alliance team as project leaders and coordinators and with virtual teams of engineers, product planners, and purchasing personnel. She used Fiat's program-control system for tracking performance and progress. She figured out how to meet all the data requirements for the enterprise systems without re-creating systems that already worked well within Fiat. Each team head established contact with his counterpart in the other alliance partners. Maria worked out a training schedule for all her alliance team members and retained part-time coaches, Italians who were experts in U.S., Japanese, and German cultures.

Maria's toughest task was coordinating with the other OEM partners. All the OEM teams were accustomed to having control over their vehicle-development programs. In this case, none had overall control, yet the product of the alliance effort had to be one integrated platform that could be used by all the OEMs. Interactions at first were very difficult. All the cultural, language, and control obstacles were present and stood in the way of smooth progress. The three systems—technical, administrative and performance, and Straight Talk—were functioning fine technically, but weren't solving Maria's need for closer interactions with the other alliance teams.

The top managers in each company understood and were committed to the mission of the alliance, but managers at the levels below were not. They had not been a part of the discussions and quietly but surely continued working as they had in the past. After all, they knew best how to design a platform. The cooperative spirit that the leaders wanted was overwhelmed by the competitive spirit that was deeply engrained in everyone in Toyota, Fiat, BMW and Modern Motors. Suppliers were completely confused because conflicting orders and specifications came from the four companies. The OEMs redesigned the work they received from others, both to fit the designs they had developed and to fit their concept of how the car should be designed.

Communications were spun according to the letter, but not the spirit, of the alliance. Each company used Straight Talk to convince the others of the correctness of its views and designs rather than working out differences openly.

Maria prevailed on Yoshio to convene the Paris Group for a detailed review of progress and a frank discussion of the working relationships. At issue: everyone signed on to the objectives of the program and was truly trying to cooperate, but down deep, each alliance partner was tilting its part of the project toward the requirements of its own market and product planners. The U.S. team appeared to be designing a Belle 1320 replacement, the Germans a BMW 325 replacement, the Japanese a Corolla replacement, and the Italians a Fiat 500 replacement. The supplier partners all down the line were confused. Instead of one solid small-vehicle platform, the teams were heading toward a polyglot of compromises that would be a fiasco.

The Paris Group reaffirmed the mission and at Maria's suggestion (a tactic she had found effective at the WTO), partners swapped managers—for example, BMW sent a manager to each of the other seven major partners (three OEMs and four suppliers)—to infuse the perspectives of all the partners into the program of each. Prior to joining the other organization, these managers worked together under Maria's leadership for two weeks to develop a training program for all people who would be involved in the design of the new platform. The program did not attempt to change the way in which engineers worked; rather, it attempted to enable them to understand that the alliance fully intended to dominate the automotive industry globally and what their role was in the game. The program was designed to instill purpose and pride in their work and to do so by building on the national and company pride that was causing the dysfunctional behavior rather than by replacing it. The program laid out how all the pieces from the partner companies would fit together. It was so successful that Yoshio decided to use it with every alliance program.

The Paris Group also agreed to meet by video conference every Monday, and to meet in Paris every month for the first year. As an incentive for attendance, Yoshio arranged to rotate dinners through Paris's three-star restaurants. It worked.

Maria became the Paris Group's conscience as partners drifted off course. The Japanese were reluctant to confront anyone; the Germans just wanted to be let alone; the Italians wanted to argue about everything; and the Americans always *knew* they were right. Maria remembered working out the agricultural agreement between the EU, the United States, and Japan in 2002. Nothing, she had thought, could match that in polarized perspectives, animosity, political sensitivity, or intransigence. At times, she felt the small-vehicle platform was even worse. In 2002, down deep, every country knew its agricultural program was flawed and that it should be changed; but the contrary was true in this case because down deep, every auto company believed that it knew best how to design a car. Maria appealed to the common mission, to the participants' stated commitments, to their pride, to their mothers. In the end, she realized that the only effective leverage was their self-interest and began restating every issue, every position, and every dispute to each partner in terms of that partner's own self-interest. It worked.

Human Resources Manager, Joint Venture

Now we move away from the overall alliance and focus on a joint venture between three of the alliance partners and the city of Shanghai. The year is 2015. The venture will build small vehicles in China for the Chinese market. The small-vehicle program that Yoshio and Maria led is now three years old and has been the basis for all small vehicles built by the enterprise partners.

Modern Motors, Fiat, and Toyota formed the Chinese joint venture to build three plants—engines, stamping, and assembly—and to establish a supply chain for all the other parts and subassemblies necessary to build the cars. Zeus sanctioned the venture and enlisted the cooperation of all members to supply the plants what they needed either directly (e.g., build a plant in China or export to China) or indirectly (e.g., arrange for one of their partners to supply the parts). Zeus has already established an alliance distribution and marketing company to sell both products manufactured by the Chinese joint venture and imports from the OEM partners into China. BMW decided not to participate in the manufacturing joint venture because it did not want to enter the small-car market in China. BMW was positioning itself as a top-line company in China by exporting its new 900 series.

Ian Dornoch, a Scottish psychologist, has been assigned the job of human relations manager for the joint venture. An academic in his early years, Ian rose to be dean of the department of industrial psychology at the London School of Business (LBS). He was an active member of LBS's Robert Bauman Center for Leadership, and has written two books on cross-cultural organizations. Eventually, the lure of a higher standard of living caused him to join the corporate world, specifically, Royal Dutch Shell. Ian developed training programs for Shell personnel from many countries who were assigned to Shell's Chinese ventures. Ian had a subspecialty, more of an avocation, in Chinese language, culture, and arts.

During the last two years, Ian has lived in Shanghai, spending half his time as an employee of Shell running training programs and half as a consultant to other non-Chinese companies, advising them on how to set up, staff, and manage a business in China with the Chinese. Yoshio painted a fascinating career picture for Ian with his first assignment as human resources manager for the manufacturing venture in Shanghai, and convinced Ian to join the enterprise. The icing on the offer was a personal membership in the new, very prestigious Country Club of Shanghai, with its golf course ranked in *Golf Digest*'s top ten in the world. Remember, Ian is a Scot, with a love of golf and single malt running through his blood.

Ian spent the entire first month learning. He spent a week in each headquarters—in Chicago, Torino, Italy, and Tokyo. He read all the mission statements, scanned six months of traffic on Straight Talk, and reviewed all alliances and projects that Zeus had undertaken in the past three years. He interviewed the CEOs and all the alliance managers, such as Maria. He diligently attempted to get every perspective, to understand what worked in the alliance, what didn't, and why. He met several of the engineers and managers who were to be assigned to the China venture. He gained a solid grasp of how success would be defined in China. He got as many views as possible on how people thought the Chinese venture should be organized, staffed, and operated. He spent three days with AIG's (the global insurance giant, American International Group) recently retired chairman, Hank Greenberg, and several members of the Shanghai mayor's International Business Leader's Advisory Council, which Hank helped establish in the late 1980s.

Ian returned to China for two weeks to develop his game plan. He asked the CEOs of the venture partners to convene a meeting of the heads of manufacturing, engine, stamping, and assembly. He selected Shanghai, where the plant was to be located, for the meeting. The city of Shanghai appointed Jaing Ho Wang as its representative on the joint venture.

Ian knew that his idea for organizing, staffing, and managing the venture was quite different from anything the three partners had done or even seen. He risked being considered an unfettered lunatic if he dropped the solution on them cold. He knew how cautious the Japanese were, how argumentative the Italians, and how sure of themselves the Americans were, so he had to determine just how far he had to bring the partners along. Two weeks in advance of the meeting, he sent the attendees two things: a book on the cultural and religious history of China (each written by a China expert from the individual's home country) and a questionnaire. The questionnaire, which was artfully based on his experiences with Shell and his other clients in China, was designed (subtly) to answer four questions:

- How important is the success of this joint venture to your company, and which of your principles would you give up in return for its success?
- What organizational structure and business processes do you believe should be employed in China? Have you found them to be successful elsewhere, and why do you believe that they will work in the China venture?
- Which of your people do you wish to assign to China?
- Describe the cultural challenges that the venture will face in China.

Ian was looking for the members of the enterprise to give him a free hand and to trust what he did.

When the group assembled in Shanghai, Ian had already analyzed the responses to his questionnaire. He hoped they had read their books. His mission was to get the right people assigned, to set everyone's expectations appropriately, and to get their buy-in to the way he thought the venture should be run.

Ian spent the first half day on the mission, objectives, and the cultural challenges for the venture. He used as much from the questionnaire as possible. It must have sounded to the attendees at times as though Ian had learned about their organizations or cultures from their questionnaires. He packaged his point of view skillfully through their words. In effect, he wasn't trying to convince them of something foreign; rather, he was telling them they were right, they had correctly grasped the situation. Of course, he was using their thinking in a way that shaped his conclusion.

By the end of the morning, the challenge had been laid out well, and everyone agreed with it—though I suspect that no one would have signed up for that description of the challenge walking into the room at 8:00 A.M.

In the afternoon, Ian prepared a war game (the strategic simulation described in Chapter 3) in which attendees were assigned to the venture and to competitors, foreign suppliers, and other local manufacturers. He brought in several Chinese professionals—entrepreneurs, politicians, and managers from the partner in Shanghai—to play the market, the government (regulators), the local Communist Party, the distribution chain, the Chinese plant workers, and a few managers on the venture team. Each move represented six months; there were five moves, which carried the meeting into the wee hours and through the following day. No one cared, because everyone was totally wrapped up in the game.

The Chinese were prepared to be very Chinese to make the cultural point clear. The government was involved with everything, throwing sand in the planning gears, making importing components a major hassle. The workers wanted to control the plant and got the support of the local party. Chinese competitors appealed to the government for favored treatment for themselves and higher taxes for the joint ventures. The Chinese consumers, on the other hand, loved the product.

As Ian predicted, the venture went through pure hell in its three years of the game. Machinery for the plant was hung up in customs for a year. Several pieces were prohibited from entry, and the joint venture had to contract for local manufacture. Imported components were delayed by three to six months on average. The joint venture had to make a special deal with the local party to compensate them for instructing the plant workers to take the training courses and direction from the joint-venture managers. The distribution company (a separate Zeus joint venture) had huge problems obtaining import permits, obtaining sales and service sites, contracting with the military-run transportation company, and hiring and training a sales staff. Turnover for both joint ventures in the first year was horrendous. But the lessons were emblazoned on the minds of the attendees from Italy, Japan, and the United States.

The following morning, Ian restated the conclusions from the first morning—but this time, the venture partners really understood. That afternoon, he set up six teams (each team was a mixture of people from the venture partners and the Shanghai partner) to discuss and decide how the venture should be organized, who from their companies should be assigned to what jobs, and what special steps should be taken to ensure the success of the venture. The teams worked through dinner, and the team leaders (selected by each team) convened after dinner.

The following morning, the team reports were made, and even Ian was surprised at how far they had come. Their conclusion: Ian and the Shanghai partner would choose virtually all the managers from China, and the partners would assign coaches and support teams. On their arrival four days earlier, they had believed that all managers should be expatriates who would run the plant and show the Chinese how to build cars. The business processes would be developed by the Chinese managers and their coaches, but the Chinese managers would have the final decisions. The group agreed on a set of principles that would guide the choices of managers, coaches, support teams, and business processes. All coaches and support teams would spend their first two weeks in China in a specially designed cultural training program. All Chinese managers would spend two months in the plants of Zeus partners in Japan, Italy, and the United States.

The venture was eight months late in producing its first car; there were a few failures in staffing and coaches; the language problem was more difficult than assumed. But the quality was world-class; the vehicle cost was on target; the market launch was a great success; the first year's production exceeded expectations by 30 percent.

Alliance Program Manager, Small Supplier

Zeus has sixty partners ranging in size from over $100 billion to under $100 million in revenues. MacLean Fogg is an eighty-year-old

THE NEW ROLE OF MANAGERS: SKILLS REQUIRED

company serving auto manufacturers. In the late 1990s, Barry MacLean, the CEO, decided that the company had to serve its customers wherever they were in the world. He launched a program of acquisitions and alliances.

When he learned that Modern Motors was moving from bilateral alliances toward a network and then into the enterprise, Barry contacted the CEO of Modern Motors and they discussed how MacLean Fogg could become an enterprise partner. The requirements were rough, and MacLean had to make some difficult choices. Two of his largest customers, GM and Chrysler, which accounted for 40 percent of his sales, had to be dropped. Three other customers, Honda, Renault, and Nissan, also had to be dropped. They agreed that MacLean Fogg could continue to serve the U.S. aftermarket through its NAPA (National Automotive Parts Association) affiliation, but only if all Zeus demands were met satisfactorily.

In a moment, MacLean Fogg's direction, strategy, and future were changed completely. MacLean Fogg would have a new slate of customers, would become truly global, and would be a full member of an enterprise that would participate in charting the course for sixty of the most important participants in the auto industry. Barry was named to the twenty-five-person council that would approve the strategy and method of operation for Zeus. He was catapulted from his secure enclave in Libertyville, Illinois, to the world stage in his industry. He loved it.

Barry appointed Joe Schultz as his alliance manager. Joe's job was to ensure that MacLean Fogg was involved in the design and engineering of all Zeus vehicles that contained MacLean Fogg products, "to ensure that MacLean Fogg products were lowest cost, highest quality and reliability, functionally perfect, and available wherever and whenever Zeus partners needed them," as Barry described it.

Joe's background was good, but not perfect, for the task. He was an engineer by training, by experience, and by personality. He had participated in and later led MacLean Fogg's alliance program. The closest he had come to cultural adaptation was marrying Lucinda Alvarez, a Mexican beauty who taught their children Spanish. Joe's Spanish worked well in Mexican restaurants. His Marine Corps training taught him that obstacles were no excuse for missing your objective.

Barry chose Joe because Joe knew the company inside and out. He had had a role in the design of every product, had helped set up every alliance, and had Barry's complete trust. Joe got things done. He was totally reliable and his word was gold. He was inquisitive to a fault and would leave nothing to chance.

Joe dove into his work with the passion of a missionary. He set out on three tasks: understand the Zeus enterprise partners and their requirements for his products; establish communications links with the partners; and determine what changes were necessary within MacLean Fogg to succeed in their new mission. Barry began working on phase-out plans with those customers that he would not be servicing in the future. Together, Barry and Joe developed a set of performance measures and milestones to track the company's progress through the transition. Barry and his board understood the danger of allowing cash flow to decline during this critical period.

Joe spent the first month on the road, meeting with product planners, engineers, and manufacturing managers in the Zeus companies that used MacLean Fogg products. MacLean Fogg was to be one of two suppliers of fasteners and forged parts for the undercarriage. Although competition might develop, the total purchase by Zeus of the components involved was three times the combined volume of the two suppliers. The task was to crank up, not to bash, the competition. Whichever company was able to meet demand quickest would have the majority of the market. To ensure security of supply, however, most Zeus plants used both suppliers, although the suppliers' shares of any one plant could be dramatically different.

The policy on two suppliers for most components was set by the Zeus council to protect against strikes, government actions, destruction of a supplier plant (tornadoes, bombs, arsonists, or accidents), transportation problems, and the host of other potential interruptions that could occur. The policy was not intended to pit the two suppliers against each other in a price battle. To the contrary, Zeus expected—no, demanded—a high level of cooperation between suppliers of the same products. If one supplier couldn't deliver crankshafts on time, the other was expected to respond with help immediately. If one had an engineering problem it couldn't solve, the other sent its experts in to help. Most important, Zeus recognized that two minds were better than one and that no company had a monopoly on good ideas.

Joe met with the operating managers from several of the alliance companies to gain an understanding of their requirements and, not incidentally, their support. Joe brought along the product plans that the Zeus council had sent him and a folder of literature on each company. He also brought a booklet that Maria had developed on cultural issues facing Enterprise partners. The meeting went well, but confirmed in Joe's mind how far MacLean Fogg had to go to meet Zeus' requirements. Partnership was not going to be easy.

Joe was briefed on the Zeus system, obtained the software, and got three systems managers from partner companies to spend two weeks in Libertyville installing the systems and training his people. Joe spotted three changes that would increase the value of the system to MacLean Fogg. First, he added the company's performance measures to the system so that there was coincidence between Zeus and company measures. Second, he added a feedback system on parts performance from each company in the chain that used his products, and from dealers and customers to get a firsthand understanding of how his products performed and were perceived. Finally, he added a module with projections for the next twelve months by component and by user. The systems managers thought the first two were excellent additions and were embarrassed that the system had not already included the projected requirements.

By the end of the two-week training period, the system was running, the additions were being developed, and MacLean Fogg staff was up to speed on the Zeus communications system. Joe submitted a request to Barry and the board for five new workstations to be linked into the product planning and engineering system for Zeus.

Joe's first move to prepare MacLean Fogg for its new world was to run the Zeus training program, not only for the development staff, but for all employees. He then set up focus groups of employees from different departments to discuss the challenges and opportunities presented by their membership in Zeus. At the conclusion of the training and focus groups, he collected and edited the notes from all the meetings, drawing together common questions, concerns, suggestions, and complaints, and circulated the edited notes to all employees. Each department sent a representative to a meeting called by Barry to chart the firm's future in Zeus.

In the meantime, Joe pulled together a team of people from development, engineering, and manufacturing to study and decide on necessary organizational adjustments. This core team also began developing a strategy for tripling production and expanding delivery capability globally.

Some years later, Joe would comment that he was lucky to have taken these actions, but he wished he could rerun the calendar to change many other things. Life within Zeus was exciting, demanding, and difficult. Joe found that he spent over half his time discussing and negotiating with Zeus partners, a quarter of his time with dealers and consumers in twenty countries, and only a quarter of his time managing his direct reports at MacLean Fogg. Joe had been promoted to president in recognition of his achievements and of the fact that Zeus dominated MacLean Fogg's business. The NAPA aftermarket business remained flat, while total company revenues tripled in five years. The four members of the core team that planned the transition were now top executives in the company.

A NEW SYSTEM OF EDUCATION AND TRAINING

How will these new managerial marvels be created? Business schools in Europe and the United States are beginning to understand these requirements and are modifying their programs. The educational infrastructure is coming, but not soon enough. We need to retool an entire generation of managers and professionals over the next ten years.

We should look to three familiar sources for this training, but each source will have to reorder its priorities, change its curriculum, and deliver in wholly new ways.

- **Academia.** MBA schools have been the traditional source of business training through masters and executive programs.
- **Company programs.** Formal training and on-the-job coaching have been traditional vehicles for training managers as they advance in their careers.
- **The individual.** The ultimate responsibility for a successful career rests with the individual. If you were training to be a great golfer

(e.g., Tiger Woods), you would read and study about the best, you would practice eight hours a day, you would get the best coach you could find and afford. Why should business be different?

Academia

Like a spreading brushfire, business schools are rushing to change their curricula to include global management issues. In my view, that's not enough. Every course should be designed from a global perspective, with cases on cross-border alliances, cross-cultural issues, and global markets and competition. Today's students in the United States must understand how Japanese and Indian managers think, not just to compete with them, but also to partner with them.

A few schools, such as Northwestern's Kellogg School of Management and Thunderbird, the American Graduate School of International Management in Glendale, Arizona, have devoted themselves to this cause exclusively at both the graduate and executive levels. Thunderbird has campuses and affiliates in Japan, China, France, Russia, and Mexico and distance learning (Internet-based courses with brand-name lecturers) to cover the rest of the world and for busy executives who can't sit still for several weeks. Thunderbird pioneered international business education with a focus on business, languages, and area studies, including the economic, political, and cultural differences of Europe, Eastern Europe, the Middle East, Russia, Africa, Asia, and Latin America.

Northwestern's Kellogg School of Management pioneered team training, weaning students away from the sharklike predator model that was the norm for new MBAs. Its robust executive program offers specific training designed around individual company requirements. Kellogg has alliances across the world that provide the cultural and business understanding tomorrow's leaders require.

The leaders—INSEAD, Harvard, IMEDE, Northwestern, and Thunderbird—have students from over forty countries at any one time. Future managers need to return to learning about civilization, behavioral psychology, diplomacy, economic systems, and the great thinkers of history—both Eastern and Western. The next wave of business education will marry these approaches and add political science and geopolitics.

Company Programs

Specific Company Offerings

Many companies are investing in internal development programs to bring managers up to the level of understanding needed to be effective in alliances. Motorola University has multiple course offerings on cultural awareness and alliance training.

BellSouth and Nortel have built an alliance training engine to ensure that their alliances run smoothly. Exhibit 7-1 shows the key elements of the program and what each is doing.

BellSouth recognized the phenomenal growth of alliances in the telecommunications industry. After trying a number of different training approaches, it decided to put 150 senior managers through an alliance workshop for two days. BellSouth learned some intriguing lessons from this experience: (1) behavioral learning doesn't happen through books—people learn from each other; (2) seminar content must be specific to the company and industry; (3) well-structured processes work.

Exhibit 7-1 ❖ **BUILDING THE ALLIANCE ENGINE**

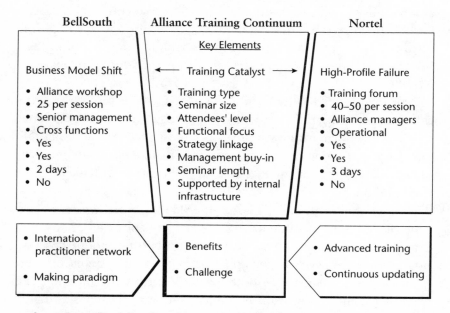

BellSouth	Alliance Training Continuum	Nortel
	Key Elements	
Business Model Shift	← Training Catalyst →	High-Profile Failure
• Alliance workshop	• Training type	• Training forum
• 25 per session	• Seminar size	• 40–50 per session
• Senior management	• Attendees' level	• Alliance managers
• Cross functions	• Functional focus	• Operational
• Yes	• Strategy linkage	• Yes
• Yes	• Management buy-in	• Yes
• 2 days	• Seminar length	• 3 days
• No	• Supported by internal infrastructure	• No
• International practitioner network	• Benefits	• Advanced training
• Making paradigm	• Challenge	• Continuous updating

Source: Booz·Allen & Hamilton, *Survey on Institutionalizing Alliance Capabilities, 1997.*

After a failed alliance, Nortel also decided that training should become part of its alliance program. Nortel's program was built on three legs: organizational planning, three-day workshops, and networking. Like most companies, BellSouth and Nortel are also learning by doing, disregarding what doesn't work and embracing what does.

Hewlett-Packard has always recognized that alliances are an important element in its value-creation strategy. Hewlett-Packard formed scores of alliances through the late 1980s and early 1990s. Senior management, however, assumed that managers were getting up to speed by attending seminars taught by academics and business schools. No one at the corporate level was really thinking about technology leakage, exit mechanisms, governance issues, or equity commitments.

This all changed in the early 1990s when a survey of HP managers overwhelmingly ranked strategic alliances as the number one area in which managers wanted more training—a shock to corporate executives who thought everything was fine. Managers indicated that external seminars, while interesting, were not HP specific, and offered no best practices or specifics to follow.

Exhibit 7-2 illustrates some of the actions HP has taken since that fateful day when managers spoke out. Today HP best-practice development is internally and externally driven. Internally, an in-house best-practice program consisting of training sessions, case histories, tool kits, and checklists is used. This material is reinforced by assessments by partners, comparison of external best practices of other successful companies with those of HP, and outside case studies. In short, HP has adopted a disciplined approach to best-practice development and sees it as a success differentiator against other companies.

As they prepare for the brave new world of alliances, wise executives will bring skills into their companies that they would not have considered before. For example, they will be looking for individuals with diplomatic backgrounds and training in business or law. They will seek individuals of one nationality who spent formative years in another culture.

Schlumberger has been a model for years. Some years ago, Schlumberger was setting up an office in Brazil. It planned to transfer 200

Exhibit 7-2 ❖ **HEWLETT-PACKARD ALLIANCE BEST-PRACTICE DEVELOPMENT**

- HP best-practice development is internally and externally driven
- Field interviews with successful U.S. and non-U.S. alliance companies
- Comparisons of HP best practices with practices of other successful alliance companies
- Internal case studies and experiences of HP alliance managers and postmortem
- Disciplined approach to capturing best-practice information, leading to manual and best-practice seminars

Source: Booz·Allen & Hamilton *Survey on Institutionalizing Alliance Capabilities,* 1997.

engineers to launch the operation. Brazilian government officials said they would approve the office, only if Schlumberger hired 180 Brazilian engineers. Schlumberger agreed to hire the engineers, but none would start working in Brazil. Schlumberger is truly global. Professional engineers and managers are deployed on a global basis. A career normally includes several countries. Schlumberger retains experts in cultural change to work with executives and rewards achievement in dealing effectively with alliance partners.

Selecting and Training of Managers

It is not good enough to assign your best and brightest to alliances (though you should). Managers must be skilled in dealing without command-and-control tools and with groups from different cultures. Never underestimate the training required, even for your most talented and most successful young managers.

Selecting the right kind of manager for a particular mission is critical. The idea that a good manager will be right for any situation is simply not true. For example, when the alliance objective is to create a new market, the alliance operating manager should exhibit entrepreneurial characteristics. For an alliance whose objective is tough cost containment and rigorous execution, choosing someone who is control oriented and measurement driven is likely to be the right formula. Switching the two could be disastrous. Many companies select the best talent available, using such yardsticks as promotable, smart, good with people, knows the industry, has the confidence of top management. Although these are desirable characteristics, they are not enough. The individual should be matched to the strategy.

The Individual

What should you do as an aspiring young manager? Be prepared! Get an MBA or attend an executive program that focuses on international management at a leading school that specializes in that area. Be careful, because not all leading schools are on track yet. Accept an assignment to live outside your home country and be part of a team managing a strategic alliance. Put yourself in the line of fire—the fire that will light the twenty-first century.

Read everything you can on managing in an intercultural environment, on participative management, on values-based leadership, on the culture of the region in which your company is most interested. Make yourself valuable in those areas crucial to the success of alliances, such as communications systems, managing across cultural boundaries, thinking out of the box on strategic and interpersonal issues. This is what Yoshio, Maria, and Ian did.

Both companies and individuals have important roles in preparing for the age of collaboration. Companies need to be thoughtful about how to create an environment that will spawn managers and executives with the skills required by relationship enterprises and need to present opportunities for development of these managers. Individuals need to take control of their own development. Both companies and individuals need to be smart about spending development dollars and time.

CONCLUSION

— ❖ —

A different perspective on leadership is required when you are part of a relationship enterprise. Without the advantages of control in the traditional sense (hire-fire, compensation, career advancement), a leader must lead. A leader must determine where the group needs to go and provide the means and incentives for the group to get there. Eventually, the people down the line will determine a venture's success or failure, so they must embrace and own the mission, the vision, the goals, and the course of action necessary to achieve success.

One of my favorite stories making this point is from *Moments of Truth* by Jan Carlzon, the CEO of SAS.

There is no better way to sum up my experience than with the story of two stone cutters who were chipping square blocks out of granite. A visitor to the quarry asked what they were doing. The first cutter, looking rather sour, grumbled, "I'm cutting this damn stone into a block." The second, who looked pleased with his work, replied proudly, "I'm on this team that is building a cathedral."

Leadership in the Relationship Enterprise: The New Role of the CEO

There are at least a thousand books in print offering advice for CEOs. Focus on the CEO's role as leader of a company. I do not intend to add to that pile of literature. Instead, the comments here are directed to the CEO in the role of head of a relationship enterprise—and eventually in the role of head of the trillion-dollar enterprise.

In the age of the relationship enterprise, the CEO has two distinct functions: captain of his ship, and leader of a flotilla of independent vessels from several countries, with missions and objectives of their own that are quite separate from their mission as a member of the flotilla. In the business world, the second task is about as easy as corralling and training a group of raccoons.

How do you lead a relationship enterprise? The political world offers better analogues than does today's business world. Imagine the task faced by an incoming prime minister in Italy: pulling together leaders of various factions to form a coalition government to run the country in the face of strikes, inflation, and a loss to the French in the World Cup. Each faction has its constituency and power base. Separately, they can only cause problems. Together, they have the power to govern.

Of course, for the incoming prime minister, the game is not won simply by putting the coalition together. Creating and implementing an agenda for the government requires extraordinary negotiating and interpersonal skills. It requires a deep understanding of the perspectives and strengths of each faction (both allies and opposition) and sympathy for the aspirations and agendas of each partner. Through that morass, the prime minister must navigate the ship of state to a safe and prosperous harbor. This is exactly the task of the leader of a relationship enterprise.

How are decisions made in the political process? In strange and mysterious ways. Have you ever witnessed the final night before a bill is presented to the U.S. Congress, the U.K. House of Commons, the French Assembly, or the Japanese Diet? It's truly ugly! How are decisions made at the United Nations to send troops to Bosnia or Somalia, to place embargoes on Iran or South Africa, or to select a secretary general? The process is not for the squeamish. Politics is the "art of the possible" according to the character of Juan Perón in Andrew Lloyd Webber's *Evita*. The great skill of the diplomat or political leader is to bring together competing forces to work toward a common goal. That is also the great skill required of the leader of a relationship enterprise. The big difference is that leaders of relationship enterprises must have both political and business leadership skills because they need to fill those two distinct roles (see Exhibit 8-1).

Exhibit 8-1 ❖ TOP CAPABILITIES OF LEADERS	
Political Leaders	**Business Leaders**
Visionary	Visionary
Compromiser and consensus builder	Has Values and conviction
Flexible and resolute	Decisive
Coalition builder	Motivator
Charismatic	Confident
Understands electorate and constituencies	Understands the business and its people
Expert in the political process	Driven to succeed
Superb public communicator	Superb private communicator

Examples of individuals who have both sets of capabilities are hard to identify. Leaders of the major Japanese *keiretsu,* such as Minoru Makihara of Mitsubishi, come to mind. In the United States, Bob Galvin of Motorola has these characteristics. With the exception of Margaret Thatcher, few Western political leaders pass the test. How, then, will these roles be filled?

The answer in the short term is that someone will seize the opportunity and either grow successfully into the job or fall on his face. Longer term, companies and countries need to develop the skills required in the next generation of leaders.

In the past, future leaders have sought international assignments to prepare themselves for the top job in global companies. Leaders for the twenty-first century should add experience in government and diplomacy. It is hard for career business executives to appreciate the skills involved in politics and government without experiencing them. The common approach in the business world is to belittle government bureaucrats. Yet in many cases, the talents of these bureaucrats, although different from those of the profit-centered commercial executive, are no less sophisticated and well developed. Ushering a new program through a government department in the face of entrenched opposition (our usual image of the bureaucrat), taking the program to Congress for funding, and then executing the program through the red tape of ten federal and fifty state agencies takes real skill, determination, and commitment. In no case can the bureaucrat order someone to approve the program. Why is that situation different from working in a multiparent alliance? It's not.

A wake-up call is ringing for CEOs. If you wish to lead in the twenty-first century, you need a new set of skills. How successfully you develop them will be a major factor in determining your role as leader or follower in the age of relationship enterprises.

THE LEADER OF THE RELATIONSHIP ENTERPRISE

Let's return to our relationship enterprise in the automotive business. Again, it is 2010. Omar Assad has just been named chairman and co-CEO of Modern Motors Company. Omar has spent the last three years putting together the relationship enterprise. He and a few colleagues were set up as a special task force by

Modern Motors (undoubtedly just after they had read *The Trillion-Dollar Enterprise*) to create a relationship enterprise whose objective was to dominate the automotive industry globally in the twenty-first century. Omar retained two advisors: Renato Ruggiero, the former head of the World Trade Organization, and a senior partner from a prestigious management and technology consulting firm.

Omar has been with Modern Motors for fifteen years. He was born in Egypt. His father was a successful merchant and his mother was a professor. He was educated in Europe through Oxford and did his graduate work in political science and business at Harvard. He worked on the EU commission in its early years and became the Egyptian ambassador to the United Nations at age thirty-three. He was highly respected, and at 35, was being talked about in the back rooms as a future candidate for secretary general. A few years later, coincidentally, Bob Anderson (then a promising executive in Europe with Modern Motors and later its CEO) was on a conference panel with Omar. Anderson liked him and convinced Omar to join the business world and Modern Motors Company.

Omar spent his first three years learning the business in a succession of jobs in manufacturing, engineering, product development, and finance. His next three years were spent leading product development for Modern Motors Europe, attempting to create a world car. Anderson then assigned Omar to the task force that totally reorganized Modern Motors into a global company. For the next six years, Omar held several top management jobs in product development and marketing. During that time, he led the alliance-development team, which concluded nearly one hundred major alliances. Then Omar was assigned the task of creating the relationship enterprise, code name Zeus.

Omar and his small team created the concept of the four auto manufacturers (OEMs) at the center of a web of alliances. The team did considerable research in selecting the companies it felt would make the strongest contribution to the enterprise. The question went well beyond "Who would be a good alliance partner?" to "With whom should we ally to dominate our industry?" Partners were selected three levels down: level 1, OEMs; level 2, major suppliers, distributors in major countries, financial partners; and level 3, suppliers to the level 2 suppliers and smaller companies dealing directly with the OEMs.

When Omar was elected chairman and co-CEO, Modern Motors also elected a president and co-CEO. Omar's job was to lead the relationship enterprise. The president was to lead Modern Motors, the traditional CEO role. All partners agreed on Omar's role in the relationship enterprise.

Omar established an enterprise council with the CEOs of twenty-five of the partners in Zeus. The other thirty-five companies in Zeus were represented on the broader operations council. There were an additional thirty companies with associate status; these were either small companies or larger companies not focused principally on the automotive industry.

The enterprise council met monthly. It approved the mission, membership, and broad strategy for the enterprise. For example, the council decided how Zeus would enter China and agreed with Omar's recommendation that Ian Dornoch would set up the manufacturing venture. The council also signed off on the small-vehicle development program under Yoshio Teikei's leadership.

The most important and difficult task for Omar was to gain agreement among the four OEMs—Modern Motors, Toyota, Fiat, and BMW—to drop their own engine families and vehicle platforms for ten common engine families and six common vehicle platforms to be designed cooperatively and used by each company. Omar and Renato made the rounds to each company at least ten times before a joint task force was formed to hammer out the details. The prize was huge, but so was Middle Eastern peace. Also like peace in the Middle East, the task was daunting and took all the diplomatic skill these two could muster. A breakthrough occurred when Fiat finally agreed to let a Japanese engineer, Yoshio Teikei, lead the small-car development program as the pilot for common vehicle platform for Zeus. Fiat did not go away empty-handed. In time-honored diplomatic tradition, it traded agreement for Fiat leadership of the 1000cc engine family and a promise for a major EC manufacturing facility for the new enterprise small car near Torino. The car would have distinguishing characteristics for each of the venture partners. This sounds like Kissinger's shuttle diplomacy between Egypt and Israel—and it was.

Omar's primary job in those three years leading up to the launch of Zeus was to drive agreement on the platform and engine rationalization. In retrospect, he thinks the UN negotiations were grammar school stuff by comparison. To his advantage, he had a bag full of big favors to dole out: leadership of programs, new plants, supply contracts, allocation of everything from styling and engineering to R&D and systems development. The industry would never be the same.

To ensure that everyone concurred with the allocations, Omar took the major ones to the enterprise council. He prepared the council early on by taking them through the strategy and economics of the rationalization program and by reviewing the packages of activities that would be assigned to individual companies and countries. Rather than building a large staff at the enterprise level, virtually all coordination was assigned to the partners; for example, Yoshio Teikei of Toyota had the coordination responsibility for the small-car platform for all of Zeus.

At the enterprise level, Omar and Renato had a small staff. In Omar's view, nothing should be done by the enterprise without the full involvement of the partners, and the most effective involvement was to do the work. Consequently, at any point in time, there were fifteen or twenty joint task forces. The role of the enterprise staff was to keep track of everything that was going on in the task forces, to coordinate council meetings, and to produce a monthly report to all the members, including associate members. The report was more like a newsletter than a board report. It covered as many of the joint activities of Zeus partners as the staff could uncover. Not all alliances and activities among Zeus partners involved Omar and his staff. Countless supply, shared-services, shared-staff, and smaller joint-venture agreements occurred among Zeus partners. The companies found that working relationships became easier, because communications links were already established and bonds of trust existed.

Enterprise task forces were set up to undertake a wide range of projects. One of the first task forces developed the specs for the engineering workstations to be used on all Zeus product development programs. The council had agreed that a common language and common hardware and software standards would be used on all programs. Each company could design its workstations in any way it wanted as long as the enterprise requirements were met. Another task force took on the job of developing a supply-chain information system for Zeus that would enable all members to order, track, invoice, and communicate intercompany transactions. Similarly, other task forces were set up to ease employee loans and transfers among companies, to develop standardized e-mail and other communication vehicles, and to seek out and qualify new members. Each time a new Zeus-wide program was seriously considered (e.g., research on emission-free engines), a task force was formed. A big challenge was to ensure that task forces were disbanded when their work was done.

PRINCIPLES OF LEADERSHIP

Through these examples I have attempted to demonstrate that traditional command-and-control techniques cannot work in alliances, and certainly not in relationship enterprises. The job of any leader is to ensure that the organization is successful. This is the leader's job in all types of organizations and for any agreed-on definition of success. Success for a museum is different from success for a symphony orchestra, or the FBI, or a division of General Electric. Nevertheless, each organization has a set of criteria (and measures) that defines success, and that is what the leader must ensure. The leader's success should be judged by the organization's success; if the organization fails, the leader has failed.

Describing what leaders do (to succeed) is difficult. My favorite description of what leaders do flows from the following definition of the leader's principal responsibilities:

- To ensure that the organization has a vision and values, which are understood and embraced throughout the organization.
- To ensure that the organization has a viable strategy and goals for fulfilling the vision, and mechanisms to adjust the strategy as conditions change.
- To ensure that the organization has the people, funds, systems, information, communication, training, and capabilities necessary to execute the strategy.
- To ensure that the incentive systems are in place, aligned with the vision and strategy, and executed with fairness.

Note that I used the word *ensure* rather than *do*. Leaders are responsible for ensuring that the right things get done, not for doing them themselves. As a matter of fact, doing them themselves may be counterproductive, because buy-in and execution become more difficult. This gets to what leaders actually do. Here is my list:

- Select leaders and create the conditions for other leaders to be developed and emerge
- Create the conditions for all members of the organization to contribute to the top of their potential toward meeting the organization's vision and strategy
- Create the conditions for decisions at all levels to be made in the best interests of the organization, its vision, and its goals

Again, note that the action of the leader is to create the conditions, not to make all the decisions. Decision making has been the standard by which we have measured leaders in the past. I would argue that decision making is the wrong criterion by which to measure a leader, certainly a leader of a relationship enterprise. There are few decisions that the CEO of a huge company is better positioned to make than are others in the company. If the people closest to the customer or closest to the factory floor are not well suited to make decisions about customers or production, it is because they don't have the information they need, they don't understand the vision and strategy of the organization adequately, their incentives aren't appropriately aligned with that vision and strategy, or they have no business being in that job in the first place.

In my model, the responsibility for ensuring that the person on the line has the right training, information, incentives, and understanding of the organization's vision is the leader's. But, you might ask, how can the CEO ensure that the factory-line supervisor has all those things? Answer: the CEO's job is to create the conditions for other leaders to emerge. Those people will be the ones who ensure that the supervisor has all she needs to make the correct decisions.

This position on leadership makes a big assumption. In his book *Vanguard Management*, Jim O'Toole, an expert on leadership and now a director of Booz·Allen's Center for Leadership, reports on his research on Motorola's assumptions about employee behavior and attitudes. The following list summarizes Motorola's assumptions:

- Employees' behavior is a consequence of how they are treated.
- Employees are intelligent, curious, and responsible.
- Employees need a rational work world in which they know what is expected of them and why.
- Employees need to know how their jobs relate to the jobs of others and to company goals.
- There is only one class of employees, not a creative management group and a group of others who carry out orders.
- There is no one best way to manage.
- No one knows how to do his or her job better than the person on the job.
- Employees want to have pride in their work.
- The responsibility of every manager is to draw out the ideas and abilities of workers in a shared effort of addressing business problems and opportunities.

In contrast, O'Toole takes a look at the management attitudes of what he calls the Old Guard. The parenthetical comments are mine, to remind us that the Old Guard is not dead yet, but lives in practice, if not in our speeches.

- Workers are paid to do, not to think (the founding principle of the assembly line).
- Workers have little to contribute in terms of ideas that will improve productivity (there are fifty to sixty job classifications in U.S. auto plants, compared with two or three in Japan).
- The sole reason people work is to make money (many managers have this infectious view of workers).
- Workers are all alike (the unions have helped institutionalize this belief).
- There is one best way to manage workers (my way).
- The function of managers is to manage; the function of workers is to carry out orders. (Ever read the job descriptions of your supervisors and workers?)

- Employees do not want to accept responsibility for the quantity or quality of their own work. (The typical manager's reaction when something down the line fails: "If I want something done well, I've got to do it myself.")
- Capital and management are the major sources of increased productivity (just look at your company's investments in productivity—new machines, reduction of employees; rarely do we see worker training, worker focus groups, reorganizing decisions to the worker level).
- Worker participation, profit sharing, stock ownership, and the like are softheaded at best and socialistic at worst (no one will admit that he believes this, but count the companies who let employees down the line share in their company's success—it won't take long).
- Given any opportunity, workers will goof off; the role of the supervisor is that of law enforcement—to keep workers in line (only the bravest companies eliminate quality inspectors, time cards for hourly workers, and office hours for salaried employees).

My only quarrel with my colleague is that a number of senior managers today behave like the Old Guard, even though they make pompous statements at annual meetings about the importance of "our most valuable assets."

I want to be clear, however, that I am not suggesting that leaders should be softheaded or socialistic, nor should they revert to being conveners of meetings or master coordinators. The job of the leader requires great inner strength and confidence, extraordinary knowledge and understanding of the people and business of the organization, the ability to make very tough decisions about people, compensation, and organization, and the ability to chart the vision and strategy of the enterprise. The leader's job is *to ensure,* and that takes a lot of skillful, tough work. The leader has the ultimate responsibility for the success of the organization and the performance of its people. The leader can't duck that. He can't tell the board, "My people failed."

We need a different set of skills to lead in the world of the relationship enterprise. Leaders must be no less tough, knowledgeable, demanding, or confident than they are already. However, they must

Exhibit 8-2 ❖ **LEADERSHIP VERSUS MANAGEMENT**

Strategic Leadership	Traditional Management
Creates need for change	Focuses on content of work
Provides vision	
Establishes values	Establishes metrics
Recruits disciples	Implements changes
Communicates	Appoints subordinates
Sets and enforces limits	Trains workers
Energizes	Executes vision
Provides resources	Fixes accountability and monitors
Creates conditions for change	
	Solves problems
Empowers	Motivates
Removes obstacles	Enables
Rewards	Rewards
About what and why	About how to

be more skillful in ensuring without ordering, in gaining cooperation, in motivating people in other organizations, in raising their own, as well as others', vision to an enterprise level well beyond the traditional limits of "my company," and in understanding how to create more value by building and sharing than by owning and controlling.

The leadership task is about what and why; the traditional view of management is about how to. There is nothing wrong with traditional management; it will undoubtedly continue to be the dominant approach of most managers. Finely honed, it can be very effective. Just don't confuse it with leadership. Exhibit 8-2 makes the distinction.

LEADERSHIP EVALUATION

Leadership should be evaluated based on the performance of the organization. The quality of leadership can be measured by the behavior of followers. The following exchange makes the point nicely:

Q. How do you know if you have successful leadership?
A. When everyone in the organization behaves in a way that is consistent with the corporate vision.

Symptoms of Failure

There are three symptoms of failure in leadership for which you should be on the alert:

1. Not working
2. Doing the wrong thing
3. Working to rule

Not Working

When Calvin Coolidge was asked how many people in the government worked for him, he responded, "About half." If the people in the organization are not motivated, or are not working to their full potential, it is the leader's responsibility. As Bob Shapiro, CEO of Monsanto, put it: "The leader must articulate a vision which is practical, achievable, and exciting and which gives a meaning and purpose to work. Employees need to believe they are spending their efforts, careers and lives on something meaningful and valuable." Remember the story about the stone cutter? A true leader shares the vision (of the cathedral) that inspires others to build it.

Doing the Wrong Thing

Jan Carlzon noted in his book, *Moments of Truth,* that employees don't do things wrong intentionally. Rather, they do things wrong because they don't understand the objective of their job or they don't have the right and necessary information. "If they understood the company's objectives as I do," noted Carlzon, "if they had the information necessary to make the right decisions and if their incentives were properly aligned with the company's objectives, they would make the same decision (or a better one) that I would. Hence, if they do the wrong thing, it's my fault for not ensuring that the employee is appropriately prepared to make the right decision."

Working to Rule

Employees who believe that the way to succeed is to do exactly what they are told do exactly what they are told. How would you like to write the script for any employee in your company that correctly predicts every situation she will face and define how she should respond. Ridiculous? Many supervisors convey that message. Assembly workers in most U.S. plants dare not stray from their instructions. Personnel managers too often go by the book rather than by common sense. Jan Carlzon observed that the SAS ticket and customer-service agents were strictly following the rules rather than listening to customer concerns and using common sense, which resulted in poor customer service and very angry passengers. We all have had ample experience with that. On a grander scale, many companies are organized in silos, and managers within the manufacturing silo are discouraged from offering helpful suggestions (or in many cases, even talking) to those within the distribution silo.

One of the favorite ploys of the Airline Pilots Union (ALPA) is to have the pilots work to rule. The result is chaos in the skies. FAA rules limit the number of hours a pilot can work per day, specify time intervals between takeoffs and landings on a runway, mandate the thoroughness of preflight checks, and so on. When pilots follow these and the many other rules to the letter (rather than to the spirit, which is the pilots' usual approach), airports become clogged, planes are delayed, fuel is wasted, passengers are inconvenienced—and safety is not enhanced one bit. The purpose of this ploy is to gain negotiating leverage with the airline.

WHAT GREAT LEADERS DO

One of the most difficult questions to answer is, What do great leaders actually *do* to achieve extraordinary results in their organizations? For example:

- What does Lew Platt, CEO of Hewlett-Packard, actually *do* as leader that regularly causes lower-level division managers to create new products and work processes that continually best the competition?

- What does Herb Kelleher, CEO of Southwest Airlines, actually *do* that motivates his frontline employees to "make flying fun" for their passengers?
- What do the leaders of Toyota in Tokyo actually *do* that motivates their hourly workers in the United States to take the initiative to stop the assembly line to fix quality problems?
- What does the secretary general of the United Nations actually *do* to get independent nations to act together on a program that is good for world order, but not necessarily a priority for those nations?
- What do political leaders in a democratic society actually *do* to enact new laws, initiate new programs, and raise or lower taxes in the face of opposing interest groups?

What do leaders do? Leaders create vision and values; leaders create conditions for constructive change; leaders reward appropriate behaviors. Leaders also create disciples who encourage others to lead change, who build capabilities, and who translate vision into tangible behaviors. Jim O'Toole calls this the double diamond for leadership (see Exhibit 8-3).

The basic principle is cascading leadership. Leaders create disciples for their vision, who create more leaders, who create more leaders. At the front line—in the plant, with the customer or client, at the design or engineering workstation—the people are building cathedrals rather than chipping rocks.

In our examples, Omar Assad was the enterprise leader who, together with the leaders of the partner companies, fashioned the vision for the enterprise. He created disciples such as Yoshio Teikei, who created more leaders, such as Maria Barolla and Ian Dornoch. The engineers who actually designed the small-vehicle platform for the enterprise were the cathedral builders.

Great leaders throughout history have understood the need to create leaders within their organizations. Rather than weakening their own power, this practice enhances it. Moses had Job; Jesus had his apostles; Eisenhower had Montgomery, Bradley, and Patton. In each case, the follower-leaders created more leaders under them. At times, we confuse creating leaders in an organization with

Exhibit 8-3 ❖ BOOZ·ALLEN STRATEGIC LEADERSHIP FRAMEWORK

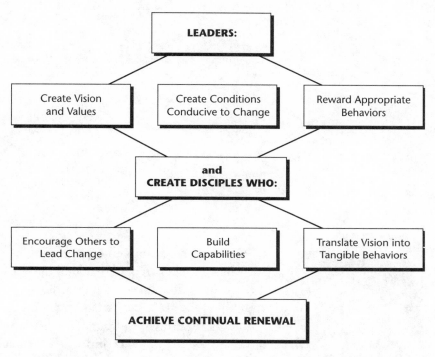

Source: Booz-Allen & Hamilton analysis; presented to Booz-Allen advisory board, June 1997.

succession. Leaders are necessary to accomplish all the organization's tasks. Orderly and successful succession is a by-product, not the primary purpose, of creating leaders.

Cascading leadership is an essential ingredient in the relationship enterprise. Leaders transcend company and organizational boundaries. Leaders create visions that are right for the enterprise and create leaders who can carry out the vision.

The New Role of
Directors and Governance

How will the relationship enterprise be governed? The members are independent, mostly publicly traded companies, with boards of directors watching out for their individual shareholders' interests. Although there may be some cross-equity ownership in the relationship enterprise, the predominant interest of shareholders will be in the stock they own of one company. Ceding sovereignty in core areas to a network of alliances—however compelling strategically—is scary to a director whose seat is voted by shareholders of her company, who is subject to the laws and regulations of the home country, and who is a target for the local media and outspoken critics of her stewardship of the company she was elected to govern.

Yet it is equally clear that the relationship enterprise cannot operate without the full cooperation and trust of its members. Effective governance of the enterprise is imperative. What to do?

Rather than plunking an answer on the table cold, I believe some context is required. Our situation is a moment in history, not an isolated event. To understand the forces at play and the options available, let us look back on the history of corporate governance as a framework for understanding what lies ahead.

THE FOUR STAGES OF CORPORATE EVOLUTION

Governance has evolved over four periods.

- **The Age of Dynasties.** This age ran from the beginning of time through the Great Depression. During this period, the interests of owners and managers were almost perfectly aligned.

- **The Age of Hired Kings.** Born with the U.S. Securities Act of 1933, this age died sometime in the early 1970s. It was a time when equity ownership became dispersed, and professional CEOs, who often owned little or no stock in their companies, achieved extraordinary power, often without the consent of shareholders. During these four decades, the link between owner and manager was ruptured.

- **The Reformation.** This period, circa 1973 to today, has been characterized by the rise of institutions as majority owners and by the struggle to reconnect ownership and management.

- **The Future.** We don't know whether this will be a renaissance, in which owner and manager interests again become realigned, or whether it will become an age of reconstruction, which grapples with new realities of competition, alliances, and global businesses, all of which demand new forms of governance.

Let's spend a minute discussing how we got to where we are today.

The Age of Dynasties

The first period of governance, the Age of Dynasties, lasted for centuries and ended with the Great Depression. This period was characterized by a close alignment of owner and management interests, which isn't surprising, since the owners either were the managers or had direct control over the managers they hired. This period saw the evolution of the family enterprise. Business everywhere was a family or state affair. The Medicis, the shoguns, and the barons all owned and controlled their businesses.

Ownership mutated into its current representative form with the advent of the public equity markets. For the Western world, that occurred sometime in the eighteenth century. Public equity markets introduced stakeholders (owners of company stock or debt) who, though outside the family's inner circle, still wanted to be represented when corporate decisions were made. Stock markets became important in the United States, Europe, and the Commonwealth countries during the last one hundred years of this period. In contrast, in Asia a family style of ownership and governance was maintained. While stock markets were developing in the West, Japan saw the evolution of the powerful *zaibatsu,* and the taipans, rulers of the great Asian trading companies, were coming to power in Hong Kong.

Late in the dynasty period, the principal characteristic of boards of publicly held companies was that their members had a vested interest in the corporation. In addition to being directors, they were owners, managers, financiers, and/or suppliers. There was a clear alignment of owner and manager interests. General Motors in the 1920s is a good example. Its thirty-one directors included seventeen GM executives, several of whom were owners of companies that had merged to create GM; five bankers, all of whom were financing the company; five suppliers; and four Du Ponts (including Pierre, the chairman of General Motors), who were large owners. Similar situations existed elsewhere. For example, German banks dominated the boards of the companies they financed.

Economic development was well served during the Age of Dynasties. The results were good, even great. Family enterprises grew, and the private-enterprise system provided the capital for the Industrial Revolution. But the two distinct classes of shareholders caused an inherent inequity. Insiders exploited their preferred position; outsiders played roulette.

No one worried much about insider trading, CEO compensation, conflicts of interest, or the independence of directors. There was no real reason to worry. Shareholders, or their surrogates, sat on the board. If things got off track, the insider owners did their best to correct them, taking care to make sure their interests were fully protected. Outside, or public, shareholders were left in the cold.

The system broke with the stock-market crash of 1929.

The Age of Hired Kings

The second period of corporate governance, the Age of Hired Kings, began with the U.S. Securities Act of 1933 and lasted for forty years, into the early 1970s. Companies grew rapidly during this time, and their requirements for capital drove many of them to public equity markets. In the process, family owner-entrepreneurs were replaced by professional managers—hired kings. These new leaders gradually replaced stakeholders on their boards with professional managers—usually other hired kings.

During this time, ownership of many of the largest U.S. and European companies became dispersed. In 1950, only 6 percent of publicly traded equities in the United States were in institutional hands. Consequently, barring large blocks of family-held stock, there were no concentrations of shareholders to exercise influence on the board or on management. The link between the shareholders and the board was effectively broken. The board could decide unilaterally how it should govern, and whose interests the company would serve. In many cases, boards rose above self-interest and indifference; but in many cases, they did not.

Adolph Berle, the great economic observer of the 1930s and 1940s, foresaw the split between owners and managers in his landmark studies. Berle believed that the interests of the owners and managers had to be aligned. The Berle-Means hypothesis predicted the conflict that would eventually emerge as shareholders became unable to influence management.

On the other side of the world, the Japanese shifted from *zaibatsu* to *keiretsu* after World War II, with almost no change in the governance process. Family was replaced by professional managers, as in the West; ownership remained concentrated within the *keiretsu*, particularly with the *keiretsu's* bank. The board continued to be made up of insiders. The real governance power was held by a small group of elders, mostly the former CEOs of the largest companies.

In China, the powerful families were pushed out by the Communist government, but they retained their family form of business in Taiwan, Hong Kong, and Southeast Asia. In the Philippines today, for example, ethnic Chinese make up 2 percent of the population, but control 55 percent of private business. The numbers and power of the overseas Chinese in Indonesia, Thailand, and Vietnam are similar. There are probably more billionaires per capita in Hong Kong than anywhere else in the world. The power in these enterprises is closely held by major owners and their nominees. The enterprises themselves look remarkably like the relationship enterprise—a network of independent companies linked by alliances. In many cases, these networks focus on a single mission (e.g., rebuilding the infrastructure in China) and hence operate as relationship enterprises.

By the early 1970s, the time we mark as the end of the Age of Hired Kings, boards in the United States were populated with friends of the CEO, who had little or no equity stake in the company, and with company executives, who, of course, had little incentive to disagree with the boss. One might say that CEOs reached the pinnacle of power during the Age of Hired Kings. They had almost absolute control of boards that not only had little ownership stake, but served at their pleasure. Even if a shareholder wished to complain, there was no effective way to do so, unless the shareholder personally owned a large block of stock. The prevailing attitude was that shareholders should vote by buying or selling the stock, not by trying to change the behavior or direction of the top managers of the company. The most serious problem was that there was no effective mechanism to hold management accountable. CEOs had friendly boards, and often even sat on each other's boards, holding such influential positions as chair of the compensation or audit committees. So who was there to blow the whistle? And whistle-blowing in the boardroom was viewed as very bad form.

Nevertheless, the economic growth of the 1950s and 1960s gave owners little to complain about. Stock markets in Europe and North America flourished as public investors became the major owners of industries and financial institutions. The total market value of U.S. equities grew sixfold, from $143 billion in 1950 to $860 billion in 1970, with almost no inflation. So it is fair to note that the Age of Hired Kings was also the time when U.S. corporations led the United States to become the strongest economy the world has ever known. The unfettered power of the CEO had its benefits. The Age of Hired Kings concluded, though not abruptly, in the early 1970s, as new powers arose.

The Reformation

The third age of governance, the Reformation, saw the emergence of the institutional shareholder as a voice and force in the business arena in the Western world. During the 1970s and 1980s, institutional holdings of U.S. equities rose dramatically, from 19 percent in 1970 to 50 percent in 1990. By 2000, they could reach 60 percent.

As their holdings grew in size, institutions also grew in courage. They took to the media, the courts, and the halls of government in an attempt to gain a voice. As noted, up to this point stockholders had expressed their opinions by buying or selling, rarely by attempting to influence the company.

The government supported the institutions' efforts, laying down legal requirements for institutions to vote their shares. Shareholder rights' groups were spawned and attacked through proxies and at annual meetings. A crescendo was reached in the late 1980s and early 1990s, when worldwide attention was focused on such issues as greenmail, CEO compensation, poison pills, and shareholder rights. Corporate governance had become front-page news.

What was really happening was the reconsolidation of ownership. The driver was performance. At stake were power and accountability. Berle's thesis was right; when there is a split in owners' and managers' interests, the situation is inherently unstable, and a struggle ensues.

During the Reformation there has been a rush of new powers for shareholders in an attempt to rebalance the interests of stockholders and boards of directors. The courts and the SEC have made clear that boards must be more responsive to shareholders, both in communicating and in considering what is in their best interests. It is now far easier for shareholders to bring matters up for a vote. And as Judge William Allen of the Delaware Chancery Court, who has been considered the dean of governance jurisprudence in the United States, said, "Boards must truly consider what offers are in the best interests of the shareholders, or risk having their decisions overturned in court."

To underscore that corporate governance has become a political issue as well, President Clinton was successful in getting Congress to pass a tax penalty on CEO compensation over $1 million—

clearly an attack on the power of boards. There is no such ceiling on Barbra Streisand, Michael Jordan, or Tiger Woods.

While the Reformation has been clumsy, and the steps taken risky, the two principal mechanisms for ensuring that boards are the de facto representatives of shareholders—independence from the CEO and increased shareholder communications—are becoming commonplace. Yet two other important problems remain. Boards have only blunt tools with which to correct serious management problems. And many boards have not yet made an adequate effort to understand the companies they are governing. As a result, few have had the courage to act except in a crisis.

The Future

In light of all the turmoil and the advent of the trillion-dollar enterprise, we want to know how corporations will be governed in the future. Studies show that four powerful forces will drive change in the coming years.

The First Force for Change: Quest for Performance

The first and probably most important force is the quest for performance. In an attempt to improve performance, shareholders have shifted their pressure to the board, and, quite frankly, that is where shareholder pressure should be applied. Board members are the elected representatives of the shareholders.

In part because of the huge holdings of institutions and in part because of increased competitiveness within the global economy, almost every board now is asking how its company can do better and how it can avoid the calamities that have confronted previous industry leaders. In the United States, IBM, GM, American Express, Westinghouse, Kodak, Kmart, and Apple went through serious upheavals because they lost their way in their industries. In Japan, the scandals of the mid-1990s (DKB and Nomura, for example) have led to questions about the insular and ineffective governance process. Throughout Europe there are debates about governance in the face of falling competitiveness and government ownership.

The lists of the top one hundred corporations in virtually every major country were dramatically different in 1933, 1973, and today—the end points of the first three ages of corporate governance. They will be different again in 2030. Boards are concluding that it is not enough to fire the CEO after a crisis. The board's responsibility for the long-term health and success of the enterprise demands a more active role for the board.

Boards are also grappling with ways to measure and predict performance that go beyond the traditional financial parameters of earnings per share, return on equity, or total returns to shareholders. There is a growing recognition of the importance of nonfinancial performance. Customer and employee satisfaction and adequate provision for management succession are being raised as legitimate performance measures for CEOs. As indicated in the previous chapter, the leader should be judged by the performance of the organization; how the organization performs with its customers and employees and how it prepares for the future are certainly relevant.

Performance in a global economy will require alliances, networks of alliances, and eventually relationship enterprises. As companies move down that road, boards will be confronted with the complex and conflicting roles played by independent companies amid a network of alliances.

The Second Force for Change: Shareholders' Demand for Board Independence and Accountability

Changes in the boardroom during the Reformation came slowly between the 1970s and 1990s, but the cumulative impact of those changes has been dramatic. Booz·Allen and the Conference Board conducted a survey a few years ago of 546 U.S. publicly traded companies, which was supplemented by over one hundred interviews of CEOs and directors. The findings, which have been updated recently, showed that boards are becoming significantly more independent. Specifically:

- **Board composition.** Over 90 percent of the companies have a majority of outsiders on their boards, and over 60 percent have no more than two insiders. Over 60 percent of the companies have no directors who have business connections with the company. This situation is in stark contrast with the situation in the Age of Hired Kings, when inside directors and conflicted outsiders were common.

- **Audit committees.** Today virtually all companies have audit committees, compared with less than half twenty-five years ago.

- **Outside consultants.** More than 90 percent have compensation committees, and half hire compensation consultants directly, a practice initiated during the past twenty-five years. The use of outside consultants by boards in other areas is expanding rapidly.

- **CEO appraisals.** Today formal appraisals of the CEO by the board are conducted by over half the companies, and that number is growing. The practice was nonexistent—even unthinkable—in 1973.

All these actions strengthen the board's role as representative of shareholder interests. Leading-edge companies, and there are a good number, are taking the initiative to swing the pendulum toward greater independence of their boards. They have seen the potential danger in waiting and the value of moving ahead.

Over the past five years, boards have shown their increasing assertiveness in key ways. For example, one of ten boards has asked a CEO to resign or retire early. More than a third changed management's recommendations on the CEO's compensation; most of those revisions were downward.

On the best boards, directors are working hard to understand the business. Some directors are using company money to fund independent staff for analytical support, others retain consultants, legal counsel, and investment banks to appraise the state of the company or to assist in major decisions. Typically, this level of support occurs only when a company is in crisis, as with Borden, Paramount, GM, and other celebrated cases. Observers such as top board lawyer Marty Lipton urge boards to hire independent counsel, consultants, and bankers to ensure that they carry out their fiduciary duty. How, asks Lipton, can a board judge management's recommendations independently if all the board's input comes from top management?

But once the board has the information, it is incumbent upon its members to speak out to prevent a crisis. This requires a delicate balance for directors; they don't want to micromanage, yet at the same time they can't let things get out of hand. A chief justice in Australia captured the dilemma well when he drew a distinction between the board's responsibilities, as governed by law, and the director's obligation to improve corporate performance through judgment and best practice.

We cannot underestimate how important this movement toward board independence and accountability has become. From a positive perspective, it realigns the interests of the shareholders and management.

But there is also a dark side. As shareholder groups win battles in the courts, in the media, and through proxies, they may be tempted to reach beyond what many people may consider constructive. Institutional investors could, for example, attempt to select or put their nominees on boards—a clear potential conflict of interest because the investment objectives of a pension-fund or mutual-fund institution are not necessarily consistent with the long-term strategic interests of the company. Similarly, institutions are not well positioned or well enough informed to influence executive selection, strategy, or acquisition decisions (beyond those requiring shareholder approval). Their appropriate role is to let the company know their concerns, to communicate with the CEO and increasingly with directors. After all, the directors are shareholder-elected representatives.

The Third Force for Change:
Global Capital Will Demand Representation

The changes in capital markets of this century in Europe and North America are spreading through Asia and Latin America. As family businesses reach out for capital, their new shareholders demand a voice. The conflicting forces of a strong family tradition in Asia and the Western attitude that control accompanies capital will cause major friction.

China is already entering the commercial capital markets in Europe and the United States, and Russia will follow. At an accelerating pace, the West is investing in rising and maturing stock exchanges throughout the world as it seeks market positions and greater return on capital. Major new enterprises in developing economies (created through privatization), are entering the world's capital markets.

These forces will change Asian and Latin American governance practices. Whether Asians adopt the Western model, which is many cultural miles apart from Asia, is an open question. The recent economic collapse in Asia puts a spotlight on both government and the leaders of industry for their failure to provide honest, objective stewardship. There will be change, but unfortunately it will take time.

As companies tap capital sources outside their home countries, the demand for a voice at the board level will grow louder. I envision boards shifting from almost exclusively national enclaves to multinational in their composition.

The Fourth Force for Change: Governance without Ownership— Alliances and the Relationship Enterprise

At last we come to the punch line. Given boards' history and the other forces for change on boards, what will be necessary to provide fair and adequate governance in the age of collaboration and relationship enterprises?

I suggest four important governance actions that companies should consider as they move toward relationship enterprises.

1. **Include nonnationals on the board.** Historically boards have been insular in their membership. Less than 10 percent of the boards in any country have nonnational membership. Boards are typically dominated by individuals who live within a hundred miles of the company, for reasons that are easy to understand. Desirable board candidates (CEOs are at the top of everyone's list) are busy and don't want to spend time crossing several time zones for four-hour board meetings six to twelve times a year. In addition, chairs and heads of nominating committees know the people locally and are comfortable with them. Although we are moving away from boards as old boys' clubs, they still consist primarily of members of the same community, who know one another and frequently socialize together.

The time has come to change the mold. Every chair of a large global company knows that nonnational board members are desirable. Gradually, boards are adding them. Two of the boards on which I serve—Household International and Security Capital

Group—have added Europeans in the last few years. Both companies have major investments and operations in Europe. The contributions of these new board members are outstanding. I am sure that Pete Peterson (founder and chair of Blackstone, a Wall Street investment bank, former U.S. secretary of commerce, CEO of Bell & Howell and Lehman Brothers, author and chairman of the Council on Foreign Relations) provides real value on the Sony board, which is causing other Japanese companies to reconsider their nationals-only practice. The age of collaboration, the relationship enterprise, and the trillion-dollar enterprise all place new urgency on having nonnational board members.

Changes in board operations are necessary to accommodate nonnational (particularly transoceanic) board members. Committees on which nonnationals serve should be scheduled around board meetings. If necessary, the number of board meetings can be reduced, perhaps to four per year, and their length can be increased. A full day allows much more time for discussion and debate. If you must have monthly meetings, you'd better find someone who has children or grandchildren in your headquarters city. Understand that once in a while, the nonnational director will attend by conference call—video conferencing is even better—but choose someone who can be physically present most of the time. Many European and Asian executives travel frequently to the United States for other business purposes and vice versa. Finally, one meeting per year should be held in the home country of your nonnational board member. Remember, one of the reasons for choosing that member should be your economic, market, or business interest in her homeland.

Probably the most important incentive to nonnationals is the value they attach to the experience. Pick someone for whom the association has a high value, such as someone from a similar (but not competitive) industry, or who has an interest in understanding the home country of the company or in networking with top individuals (the other directors).

An alternative to having nonnationals on the board is having an international advisory board. An advisory board typically meets twice a year for one day. The agenda focuses on issues of importance on which the management desires outside perspectives. Unlike a board of directors, advisory board members are not legally required to approve, review, or discuss anything; their agenda is free from obligation. They have no liability, little homework, and no committee obligations. As a result, advisory boards can attract busy, high-level executives who would not be available for regular board service. Advisory boards provide an excellent network for busy CEOs—where else could a German CEO get the attention and advice of top U.S., Japanese, and Brazilian executives?

Booz·Allen set up an international advisory board in 1990. The current membership is shown in Exhibit 9-1. Henry Kissinger chairs the board; former directors include Renato Ruggiero, director general of the World Trade Organization, Robert Galvin, former CEO of Motorola, Richard Rosenberg, former chairman and CEO of Bank of America, and Drew Lewis, former CEO of Union Pacific and secretary of transportation under President Reagan.

Booz·Allen's board meets every nine months, rotating among Booz·Allen offices around the world. The board acts as a laboratory for management ideas for the twenty-first century. At the meetings, proprietary research, trends in management and business, and the business and geopolitical situation in various parts of the world are actively discussed and debated. The board gives frank, objective, no-holds-barred counsel. As a partner of Booz·Allen, I have found the firm's advisory board to be invaluable. Our advisory board launched the concept of the trillion-dollar enterprise.

2. **Create an enterprise board.** If the relationship enterprise is to act as one company on major strategic issues and the cooperation is essential beyond the agreements on individual alliances of the members, then some mechanism should be established for governing the enterprise. This mechanism cannot replace or mitigate the legal responsibilities of the boards of the independent companies. Rather, it should have three broad responsibilities:

- To be a sounding board and advisor on major strategic moves for the enterprise, such as country focus, membership, very large enterprise investments.
- To oversee the mechanisms that bond the enterprise together—values, culture, communications linkages, transfer and cross training of people, and common systems.

Exhibit 9-1 ❖ BOOZ•ALLEN ADVISORY BOARD, 1998

Dr. Henry A. Kissinger
Kissinger Associates
New York, New York

Robert P. Bauman
Chairman of the Board
BTR, Plc
London, England

Oscar P. Bernardes
Chief Executive Officer
Bunge International Limited
São Paulo, Brazil

Jürgen Dormann
Chairman & CEO
Hoechst AG
Frankfurt, Germany

H. Laurance Fuller
Chairman & CEO
Amoco Corporation
Chicago, Illinois

Yotaro Kobayashi
Chairman & CEO
Fuji Xerox Company, Limited
Tokyo, Japan

Yoh Kurosawa
President & CEO
The Industrial Bank of Japan,
Limited
Tokyo, Japan

Ann McLaughlin
Chairman
Aspen Institute
Washington, D.C.

Mark Moody-Stuart
Chairman
Committee of Managing Directors
Royal Dutch Shell Group of
Companies
London, England

Yoshio Okawara
President
Institute for International Policy
Studies
Tokyo, Japan

Didier Pineau-Valencienne
President, Directeur General
& CEO
Schneider SA
Paris, France

John B. Prescott
Former Chief Executive Officer
Broken Hill Proprietary Company
Limited
Melbourne, Australia

Robert B. Shapiro
Chairman & CEO
Monsanto
St. Louis, Missouri

Ratan Tata
Chairman & CEO
Tata Group
Bombay, India

Dr. Peter Wallenberg
Investor AB
Stockholm, Sweden

The Rt. Hon. Lord Young of
Graffham P.C.
Chairman, Young Associates Ltd.
Former Cabinet Minister,
Thatcher Government
London, England

- To approve policies that span member companies, such as positions on government affairs and international trade.

Although size and membership of such a body are tough to design in general terms, some rules should be followed. Members should come from outside the enterprise and should be selected by a joint nominating committee of enterprise board members. As partner CEOs are members of the enterprise, their presence would make the enterprise board analogous to a corporate operating committee. The only insider should be the chair of the enterprise. The board should be of workable size, with ten to fifteen members.

The enterprise board should not be a legal board subject to the laws of the various security and exchange commissions throughout the world. We don't want that! We have enough regulation. The enterprise board should be positioned between a regular board and an international advisory council; it has some powers, but is predominantly advisory in capacity. It should provide a platform for discussing cross-enterprise issues, and it should focus on the enterprise rather than on the roles, ambitions, and performances of the individual companies that make up the enterprise. An enterprise board allows the enterprise to think, plan, and act like a single entity.

Let me raise one huge caution flag, though. The enterprise board cannot, in fact or in perception, violate any antitrust or other laws governing the competitive arrangements among its member companies. The enterprise board cannot override the decisions of any of the partner-company boards, although it can recommend or counsel a member board to change a decision. The enterprise board cannot assume any of the legal responsibilities of member boards. Member companies' board operations are governed by the laws and regulatory authorities of their home countries. They represent shareholders of the company and are responsible to those shareholders for stewardship of the company. Company boards cannot and should not cede their powers to anyone. They can, however, listen and take suggestions from an enterprise board.

The reach of the enterprise board can be extended by creating committees and task forces to study major enterprise issues or a policy on ethics. Greater involvement of partner executives and directors can be achieved through such activities.

3. **Establish cross-directorships.** Having a director of one enterprise company sit on the board of another member company is very desirable, for obvious reasons. The closer members become, the more mechanisms that link them together, the more trust that is developed, the more likely they will act together on important issues. The caution here is also obvious. Directors may not serve on boards of competing companies or of companies that present any other conflict of interest (e.g., as supplier, financier, major customer).

4. **Build real understanding.** Boards of the enterprise's member companies should routinely be informed about the activities, plans, and strategies of the enterprise. Some presentations should be made by members of other enterprise companies. Routine communications on enterprise issues—similar to board communications—should occur between board meetings. But that is not enough.

— ❖ —

Partnership in a relationship enterprise makes a much greater requirement of board members to understand what drives the long-term success and profitability of their company. The relationship enterprise involves substantial collaboration and sharing among companies; sometimes membership in the enterprise means allowing other partners to do things previously considered the core of the director's own company. The automotive example, in which companies share the development of the small-vehicle platform, makes that point.

As a result, directors must develop a deep understanding of their own companies as well as of the economic impact of alliances on their companies. They must understand the legal implications of the alliance network and the implied obligations and guarantees of membership in the relationship enterprise.

Finally, directors need to understand the mission, vision, and strategy of the relationship enterprise of which their company is a partner. They need to understand its competitive position and its likelihood of success. Directors must be comfortable with the values and ethics of the enterprise and its members, for "by your associates will you be judged." Directors need to be able to support the leadership of the enterprise and be satisfied with provisions for succession. In fact, directors of the partner companies must approve entry into the relationship enterprise. They need to understand that the success of their company is tied to the success of the relationship enterprise of which they are a partner.

If the basic hypothesis of the trillion-dollar enterprise is correct—that global business is heading inevitably in the direction of the relationship enterprise and the rules of competition are changing—then it is in the individual company's best interest to participate in the network of alliances. Boards should encourage their managements to prepare for and participate in the age of collaboration. Boards should encourage their management to take seriously the requirements for leadership in this new age and should take the initiative to lead rather than follow.

I see no conflict of interest, from a director's point of view, with a company's participating in a relationship enterprise. Boards should exercise caution to ensure that potential conflicts don't become real and that all laws and regulations are carefully followed. But these are not reasons for inaction. Boards have the responsibility to ensure the long-term health and success of their corporations. Actions to prepare for the new age are wholly consistent with that responsibility—they may even be mandatory.

The Trillion-Dollar
Enterprise—Good or Bad?

From a macroeconomic perspective, the trillion-dollar enterprise is wonderful if it increases productivity, expands markets into new locations, accelerates the development and implementation of new technologies, increases consumer choice, reduces prices, reduces regulation, and creates new markets that create new jobs.

If, on the other hand, the trillion-dollar enterprise becomes a modern version of monopolistic cartels, inhibits competitive forces, corrupts governments, bullies competitors and suppliers, lowers productivity, restricts trade, circumvents laws, and slows the development of new technologies, new markets, and new jobs, then it should be killed before it is born.

The trillion-dollar enterprise will present challenges in virtually every area of public policy. Over the next twenty years, as a result of the rise of relationship enterprises, regulations will be revised, tax policy will change, public spending will shift, national economic priorities will be debated and altered, new laws will be enacted, and political parties will rise and fall. Remember, one of the objectives of the trillion-dollar enterprise is to change the landscape in its favor, though it will be cloaked in the platitude of leveling the playing field. Such force will create change.

Chapter 10 presents two scenarios for the future to demonstrate how the trillion-dollar enterprise could impact history. My intention is to start the debate by showing the forces at work in both scenarios, good and bad. The final chapter explores the policy questions and options facing governments. The trillion-dollar enterprise is coming, and we must channel it for the good of nations. We must define the world in which it will grow and impact us all so that that impact will be positive.

Dark Side or Bright Side:
Which Way Will We Choose?

In this chapter we will view the future in two scenarios, both beginning in the year 2000 and both assuming that relationship enterprises become the dominant structure of industry in the twenty-first century. The Dark Side case takes us down a path on which enterprises use their power to amass more power and to control markets and countries; they view the global economy as theirs to manage. The individuals involved are not Darth Vaders, who wish to rule the world by evil means, rather, they are powerful, capable business executives, who truly believe that economic development is the means to higher living standards and fewer wars and that economic development should take priority over petty national and individual self-interests. Their goal is noble, and their vehicle is honorable, but their means are not.

The Bright Side takes us down a path that most of us could find comfortable and constructive. Power is not intrinsically bad and can be used effectively to achieve noble goals without trampling rights, traditions, and the beliefs of individuals or nations.

THE DARK SIDE

Fast-forward to the year 2025. The relationship enterprise has become common in most global industries. Several have achieved trillion-dollar status.

Club 2000 of the Dark Side

The Club 2000 was established at the turn of the century as a social organization to allow the leaders of the world's largest corporations to network. Over time, the membership shifted to leaders of large relationship enterprises. Now, in 2025, the club's fifty members meet twice a year in secluded resorts around the world. To qualify as the site of a meeting, the resort must be secure for anything short of a Martian invasion, have a runway suitable for supersonic jets, boast outstanding recreational facilities, and be closed to other guests for the three-day recreational outing as well for the preceding week to accommodate elaborate security and other preparatory arrangements. Cost is no object. Marcel Montreaux, the most celebrated chef in France, is a regular in the kitchen; the current Masters and British Open champions play golf with the guests; spouses are lavishly catered to during the day while the members engage in networking discussions. Dinner speakers include heads of state and heads of international organizations; no one rejects an invitation.

All the recreation and speeches are, however, diversionary trappings for the real purpose of the organization and its semi-annual recreational outings. This group of fifty business leaders wields more power than any nation on earth. They meet to decide how the world's economic playing field should be shaped. They determine the flow of trade, the kind of rules and laws that will govern international business. They reward and punish nations for their cooperation or lack of it.

Before we tune in on the meeting in 2025 on an island off the coast of Brazil, let's review what has happened in a few industries between 2000 and 2025. Remember, it doesn't have to be this way, but it could be.

By 2010, relationship enterprises were well established in the automotive, airline, and telecommunications industries. Each enterprise had formed some kind of council or committee to coordinate the activities of its member companies. Initially, these committees focused on strategy for the enterprise, new members, and, most important, execution. Members learned quickly that unless they could work together effectively, the whole concept of consolidation through networks of alliances would fall apart. From 2000 to 2010, failures outnumbered successes as these networks struggled to operate as single entities in their industries and marketplaces. Execution became the primary concern. Now let's turn to what relationship enterprises did in some specific industries.

Auto Industry: Colossus of the Dark Side

Colossus Unlimited, one of the three relationship enterprises in the auto industry, was having difficulty with work stoppages in France at its major engine plant. The unions demanded a shorter workweek, elimination of incentive pay, and new work rules. To get management attention, they held one-hour work stoppages each day, which disrupted shipments and caused serious problems in assembly plants all over the world.

Colossus executives called on the French minister of industry and labor. They carefully explained that, although Colossus wanted France to be an important manufacturing location for the enterprise, it was displeased with both the demands and the behavior of the union. They also explained that the enterprise had plans to add a components plant in a depressed area east of Paris and to expand the engine plant in the southwest, an industrial area with high unemployment,—a total investment of $4 billion. An alternative plan would place the component plant in the Czech Republic and expand the engine plant in Brazil, which would then replace the plant in France within five years.

Colossus not only wanted union demands and behavior reversed, but also wanted to liberalize work rules substantially and to gain the freedom to fire unproductive employees without hassles. The extraordinary French social-benefit payments would be replaced by a one-time payment equivalent to the severance packages offered in the United States and Brazil. The choice belonged to France. The union leaders were not even consulted by Colossus.

The president of France called an emergency meeting of the cabinet. The impact on unemployment, social unrest, and the balance of payments was too horrible to contemplate, particularly in an election year. Within an hour, the cabinet consulted with the leadership of the Assembly; that evening, union leaders were called to the Elysée Palace; and the following day, the Assembly passed a bill to establish a special fund for terminated Colossus employees. Five militant unionists were fired by the union leadership, replaced by hand-picked, cooperative individuals who met all night with the union leaders and two government representatives to craft a document that met every Colossus demand.

On the third day, an article in *Le Figaro* announced a major new investment by Colossus in France and a settlement between the union and Colossus. A brief paragraph noted that union-company disputes had been settled amicably and that a new labor-management committee had been established to ensure smooth labor relations in the future. Not mentioned was a donation to the president's political party of 20 million francs.

Aviation Industry: Wings of the Dark Side

Wings was one of four relationship enterprises in the global aviation industry. The enterprises were formed in the 1998–2008 decade. They consolidated schedules, frequent-flyer programs, marketing, and pricing. In each country, the national enterprise member staffed reservations, sales offices, ticket counters, baggage handling, and customer service activities on behalf of all the members.

Two major breakthroughs with the unions were achieved during this period. First, pilot training was consolidated in one organization, although most actual training was still done in-country. Second, a separate maintenance organization was established to serve all the members' fleets. The transition to a common aircraft configuration had been going on for several years, so maintenance practices could be standardized.

The leaders of Wings recognized that costs could be reduced dramatically if they could schedule crews—pilots and flight attendants—centrally, cross-utilizing them on aircraft of other members. The systemwide savings would exceed $3 billion and could be accomplished without reducing employment. Growth would absorb the increase in productivity. They had tried for years to persuade the unions to agree on central scheduling, but were greeted with a brick wall. They had to take another approach.

The Wings executive council met in 2008 and decided to implement centralized scheduling for four of the members. These companies were willing to agree in return for premium wages, employment guarantees, and added flying. With central scheduling, flying could be given to any member that had the rights to fly the route. The four enterprises had worked hard during the previous decade to achieve a fairly high level of flexibility in substituting one member for another on international routes; though national routes remained as protected as ever for each nation's airlines.

Wings' leadership laid out a plan that reduced international flying by half for the members whose unions were most strongly opposed—the airlines in the United States, Germany, and Japan. The leaders of those companies agreed to the plan because of a creative profit-sharing scheme that enabled them to maintain their profitability even though the flying was being done by other member airlines.

The unions threatened to strike, but the Wings leadership had created a web of contingencies in anticipation of that response. It had negotiated agreements with the governments of Germany, the United Kingdom, and Japan to halt the strikes and had forged an agreement with two of the other three airline relationship enterprises to suspend all flights to the United States if U.S. pilots went on strike against Wings. Wings was the point on an industry-wide plan to implement centralized crew scheduling. The industry understood that by reducing costs, it could substantially increase traffic. The U.S. secretary of transportation and president were briefed on the plan and its consequences for the U.S. economy.

A strike began against the U.S. member of Wings on September 1, 2008, after three interventions by the president. All international flights to and from the United States were suspended. By September 5, the pressure on the union from the media and the public became intense. A well-orchestrated public relations campaign describing the life and income of international pilots and flight attendants (the only groups affected) cut the union's cause deeply. By September 10, the unions relented. On September 15, a large, undisclosed donation was made to the president's political party, which was in the middle of a heated battle for both the White House and the Senate.

The unions granted centralized scheduling with severe initial restrictions and increases in compensation. Over the ensuing seventeen years, these restrictions were dismantled one by one. By 2023 the entire industry was operating under flexible, centralized scheduling and Wings' pilots were totally interchangeable and 40 percent more productive.

Telecommunications Industry: GlobalLink of the Dark Side

The telecommunications industry continued the extraordinary growth of the 1990s into the next decade. The collapse of several Asian economies in the late 1990s was a distant memory by 2005, when growth throughout Asia averaged 10 percent. The demand for telecommunication services was exploding. Two giant relationship enterprises and three smaller regional enterprises ruled the telecommunications world.

The largest of the enterprises, GlobalLink, had already exceeded a trillion dollars in revenues by 2010. GlobalLink was governed at the top by a council of fifteen: twelve were CEOs of the largest member firms and the other three were outside experts—a telecommunications technologist, a public relations executive, and a geopolitical analyst. GlobalLink's problem in 2010 was a reluctant Chinese government. Telecommunications in China were controlled by state-owned ChinaCom. Although ChinaCom had an alliance with GlobalLink, the relationship was clearly at arm's length and too frequently uncooperative, even combative. The particular issue of the moment was unlimited usage of certain wideband frequencies by GlobalLink members. GlobalLink's satellite system, with the lowest cost and broadest range in the world, required these frequencies to serve China as it did most other countries. The government of China wished to reserve those frequencies for ChinaCom. The stakes were very high on both sides.

GlobalLink argued that ChinaCom did not have the capability to deliver the services that the Chinese population was demanding and that the government could not afford the tens of billions of dollars of investment required, let alone the decade it would take to implement a do-it-yourself program.

The Chinese government argued that GlobalLink should make its resources (the satellite systems and the worldwide distribution system) available to ChinaCom, which would manage (and control) the local frequencies. That request might sound reasonable, except that GlobalLink had gained access to the targeted frequencies everywhere else, and its entire system was designed to make the capabilities of all of its members available everywhere on earth. This feature distinguished it from all other telecommunications providers and made GlobalLink the telecommunications enterprise of choice among global corporations and relationship enterprises. One of the most important of its services was total security. Control over the targeted frequencies by ChinaCom could compromise the security system for any traffic routed through China's airspace.

After three years, negotiations were at an impasse. The Global Link council met to discuss its options. It concluded that further negotiations were fruitless and that it had to force the Chinese government to agree to its terms. The council devised a five-point plan, which would be disclosed in full to the Chinese government but would be implemented one point at a time.

First, GlobalLink would offer China a $10 billion satellite-construction contract, in effect putting China into the satellite business. A joint-venture company would be established in China, owned by GlobalLink members and the Chinese government. GlobalLink partners would provide technology, special equipment, and training. The project would take five years and would leave behind a world-class manufacturing infrastructure. The Chinese government had eight weeks to decide whether to accept the plan, after which the offer would be withdrawn, and the satellites would be built in other nations. If it accepted the proposal, China would agree to all GlobalLink's demands and sell a part ownership of ChinaCom to GlobalLink members.

In stage two, GlobalLink would offer to build and operate forty satellite relay and switching stations in the poor provinces of Shanxi in central China and Gansu and Xinjiang in the northwest to provide low-cost telecommunication services to those remote areas. It would sell 10 million handsets at cost to the small businesses and homes in these provinces to jump-start the use of telecommunications.

If the government agreed to GlobalLink's terms in stage one, China would receive this deal also. If it did not agree in the first eight weeks, the satellite deal would dissolve, but the relay and switching station deal would remain open for an additional eight weeks. The terms were the same.

If China still refused, GlobalLink would shift to hardball. China would have four weeks to agree to GlobalLink's terms or have all contacts with GlobalLink and its partners severed. To ensure that ChinaCom did not simply shift to one of the other relationship enterprises, GlobalLink had closed that door by negotiating agreements with those enterprises making cooperation with GlobalLink in their best interests. The Chinese telecommunications industry would be set back twenty years, and its economic growth and world position would be seriously damaged.

The final step would be tantamount to a hostile declaration of war. No one at GlobalLink believed that the situation would degenerate to this point, but GlobalLink leadership wanted to let China know how seriously its reluctance to cooperate was regarded.

Since the turn of the century, a number of renegades had caused serious problems with global telecommunications. They were a new form of organized crime, extorting companies for protection of their global telecommunications, selling intercepted messages to the highest bidders, acting as a huge spy network. They had the capability to intercept, scramble, and totally disrupt satellite transmissions. These pirates of the airwaves arose from the dismantled technology community in the former Soviet military and disaffected (and opportunistic) employees of NASA, the National Security Agency, the CIA, Israel's Mossad, and the communications spy organizations of Japan, France, and the United Kingdom.

GlobalLink had developed proprietary security software that protected satellite transmissions from pirate invasion. It leased this software to other telecommunications companies. GlobalLink's final action would be to lift all protection from transmissions into and out of China, effectively cutting all commercial traffic, and potentially all traffic, to China. Every element of commerce, from simple orders to international money flows, went through the world satellite system. No one could risk the damage the pirates could cause; their demands would be infinitely higher than those of GlobalLink and far more intrusive. To ensure the cooperation of the other telecommunications enterprises, security software leases would be terminated immediately for any company or enterprise that went to China's or ChinaCom's rescue.

GlobalLink executives met with the premier, the vice premier for the economy, and the head of the Chinese military. The issue was well out of the reach of the head of ChinaCom. Up to that point, nothing so bold had been attempted by a relationship enterprise. The record of coercion was well documented, so the Chinese leaders knew that GlobalLink was serious and could deliver on its promises, both good and bad.

During the first four weeks of step one, the Chinese hit the diplomatic road and tried to get the governments of the United States, Japan, Germany, and the United Kingdom to pressure GlobalLink to withdraw its demands and drop its threats. Global Link had already prepared for this action. Business leaders in all these countries supported GlobalLink's proposal because their communications to China had been consistently intercepted and given to the government and competitors; no proprietary information could be transmitted because intellectual property rights were flaunted. Consequently, the government officials of these countries encouraged China to accept GlobalLink's generous offer—it was good for everyone.

China relented. The following four weeks were spent agreeing on the details of GlobalLink's demands and investment offer.

Influence: Club 2000 of the Dark Side

Back to the Club 2000 recreational outing on the island of Busios off the coast of Brazil in 2025. A small steering committee put together an agenda based on suggestions from the members and research by a group of economic, political, and security analysts and scientists. The agenda included four items:

- The upcoming elections in Japan
- Oil pricing and capacity
- Social legislation in the European Community
- Currency stabilization

Each item was handled professionally. A briefing book sent out in advance described the issue, including its implications for world commerce and for Club 2000 members, and suggested alternatives that the group might adopt, along with possible outcomes of each. The purpose of the meeting was discussion and decision. One member led the discussion of each topic. All meetings were conducted in English, although simultaneous interpreters were available. An outsider would have been impressed with the level of understanding each member of Club 2000 had of each item on the agenda. An outsider would have been stunned by the unemotional, analytical, dispassionate approach to meddling in country politics, changing the rules of international commerce, and influencing relations among nations.

At the Busios meeting, members decided whom to support in the Japanese elections and what commitments to extract in return for that support. They agreed on a program of shifting orders for oil to bring Algerian and Venezuelan prices into line. The program included low-interest loans to other oil-producing states to expand capacity. Within one year, they could stop external sales of oil from Algeria and Venezuela.

Next, they developed a plan to modify the social legislation in the European Community to bring it fully in line with other major regions of the world. The plan included a basket of actions, such as political donations, promises of investment, potential public exposure of politicians' dark sides, a media blitz, and various forms of coercion. On the last day, members of the club tackled their toughest challenge—stabilization of world currencies.

In 1997 and 1998, Asia underwent a very difficult period of currency destabilization. Several countries suffered major setbacks in their economic progression toward full players in the world economy. The currency virus spread across Latin America, Russia, and Eastern Europe. Only the United States and the European Community retained stable currencies during those years. World trade suffered wide gyrations as nations scrambled for exports to cover their depleted reserves and pay their international debts. The IMF (International Monetary Fund) intervened, but the OECD (Organization for Economic Cooperation and Development) nations would not come up with the $200 billion that the IMF ultimately requested. The price tag turned out to be much higher.

Major changes in the world currency system were made in the following years. A new organization was established as a joint venture between the (IMF) and the WTO (World Trade Organization): the World Currency Board (WCB). The task of the WCB was to monitor all major international financial obligations and transactions and to ensure that banks remained solvent and that currencies were appropriately valued. The WCB rated banks and currencies much as Standard & Poor and Moody's rate company debt. A low rating on a currency caused major concern within a country and heightened trading of its currency on world markets. Most countries adopted policies requiring their banks to maintain minimum WCB ratings or face disciplinary action.

For fifteen years, the system worked. But over the past twelve months, members of Club 2000 had noticed warning signals of instability in India, Indonesia, Thailand, Japan, Ukraine, and Russia. They were concerned about a repeat of the 1997–1998 crisis on a much greater scale. The WCB ratings on those currencies had fallen into the danger (weak) zone. Several of their most important banks were moving toward a liquidity crisis if foreign banks refused to roll over paper.

At the meeting, they discussed options for heading off a severe problem. Their view was simple: stable currencies were good for business and therefore for the world and should be maintained at any cost. A small task force had worked out a few options, which were the basis for the discussion. At the end of the day, they agreed on the following program.

- In each affected country, one major bank would be put into bankruptcy, one major bank would be merged into a foreign bank (they had lined up the acquirer and very tough terms), and one bank would receive an infusion of government and local private capital backed by the IMF—totaling $200 billion for six countries.
- The central banks of these countries would be autonomous and would maintain a special relationship with the WCB for a minimum of two years. During that time the WCB would monitor internal operations closely and approve interest rates, currency exchange rates, and monetary policy in advance of actions within

the country. In three of the six countries major devaluations were required immediately.

- Each Club 2000 member would maintain production in the six countries and double exports and halve imports. The result would be a sharp reduction of goods available on the local markets and a rapid buildup of foreign reserves to pay back old debts.
- Prices on critical imported raw materials—oil, iron ore, grain—would be reduced by 25 percent for twelve months.
- Several government officials would be replaced with individuals selected by Club 2000.

The plan fundamentally usurped the sovereign rights of six nations. It instructed the IMF and the WCB in their roles, with little consultation in advance, although the heads of those two organizations were invited to attend the discussion at the Club 2000 meeting. Finally, the plan required several nations to subsidize exports from the six countries. The representatives of those countries were not diplomats, ministers, or economists, but leaders of relationship enterprises that had headquarters or operations in the countries. You can imagine the protests from governments around the world as their balances of trade were trashed by Club 2000 in the interests of international order. In effect, the bailout was paid for by the countries that lost exports and took more imports, that reduced the price of their exports, and that were adversely affected by the devaluations. Club 2000 members paid nothing. In case any country thought about refusing to comply with the plan, the sanctions were so onerous, so immediate, and so certain as to make protests brief and ineffective.

The Club 2000 meeting was extended by one day, and three top government officials of each of the six countries were summoned to Busios. Protests lasted all morning. By noon, each chief of state had acquiesced. By late afternoon, the press releases were agreed on and sent. Meetings with the press were set in the six countries the next day. Concurrent press conferences were held in Geneva and Washington with the heads of the WCB and the IMF. To the uninformed observer (which included almost everyone who didn't attend the conference on Busios), it seemed that the heads of the WCB and the IMF had successfully negotiated agreements with each of the countries to avert a potential global currency crisis. The bankruptcies and mergers took place over the next month, with all the appearance of having been decided by the countries and individual banks involved.

— ❖ —

Whether you are a sophisticated observer of the international scene or a lover of spy novels, these scenarios may sound outlandish. We all hope that they are, but who wants to risk such a future?

Throughout history, accumulation of great power has frequently led to the exercise of that power in ways that all thinking people find deplorable. And the trillion-dollar enterprise certainly represents accumulation of great power.

THE BRIGHT SIDE

We are still in 2025 and about to join the Club 2000 conference on the island off the coast of Brazil. The scenario of the past twenty-five years has been quite different from that presented in the Dark Side case. Again, let's look at Club 2000 and what has happened in the automotive, aviation, and telecommunications industries.

Club 2000 of the Bright Side

Club 2000 was established at the turn of the century with all the trappings described in the Dark Side case, but with a dramatically different purpose and operating format. The media, although barred from most sessions, were omnipresent. Any TV station or publication that wasn't there really didn't matter. Imagine a sports publication's not sending a representative to the World Cup championship—same idea. No one refused an invitation to speak, and unsolicited offers to speak would fill a room. The world knew the agenda in advance, and hundreds of articles appeared before the meeting speculating on what Club 2000 members thought about everything from grand geopolitical alliances to the price of a Big Mac in Sierra Leone.

Initially a social networking organization, Club 2000 evolved into a serious forum for debate and for advising countries and world organizations, rather than a political force for intimidation, coercion, and control. Conference attendees typically included fifteen or twenty heads of state and world organizations—the WTO, WCB, IMF, and World Bank, for example—and heads of selected regional organizations—the EC, AFTA (Americas Free Trade Association, which included all the Americas), and ASEA (the Association of South East Asian states). Representatives of states and organizations that would be affected by items on the agenda were invited, but only one person from each state or organization was allowed in the meeting—the head or a designee. In most cases, the top dog attended and brought a retinue for support that camped outside the conference room.

Before we tune in on the Club 2000 meeting, let's check out the annual meetings of Colossus, Wings, and GlobalLink, the three relationship enterprises we visited in the Dark Side case.

Auto Industry: Colossus of the Bright Side

The Colossus meeting in 2020 was held in Beijing at the new Qing Dynasty Hotel. All members of the Colossus council attended, as did representatives of several alliance members from China. The auto industry in China had gone through cycles of state ownership, privatization, and consolidation in the past twenty years and now had three major Chinese auto companies, one of which was a member of the Colossus enterprise. Three publicly owned Chinese component manufacturers were also members of Colossus, as were more than thirty smaller suppliers and two major distribution and service networks. In addition, there were a number of joint ventures among foreign Colossus members in China, which jump-started the industry in the early 2000s.

The ten-year progress report was delivered to the Colossus council by Igmar Lubov, the chairman of Colossus from Russia. The report was simultaneously delivered to news agencies in one hundred countries and to each major stock exchange in the world.

"In the past decade," reported Lubov, "Colossus expanded its membership by 210 companies, mostly smaller suppliers that filled a strategic gap in the enterprise in Africa and western Asia. We can now boast that Colossus is the first truly global automotive enterprise, with manufacturing and sales in 90 percent of the world's countries. Our products are available to 95 percent of the world's population. We have increased our market share of cars, trucks, and personal vehicles to 38 percent of the world market, well ahead of our nearest competitor, Automovnik Enterprise, which has just under 30 percent. Employment in our enterprise members reached 5 million this year, and sales reached $4 trillion, which represents a tripling of productivity in the past twenty years. Total direct and indirect employment of all our partners easily exceeds 200 million.

"We are proud that the prices of our products have declined in real terms every one of the past ten years and are 25 percent lower cumulatively. The cost of operation has dropped substantially as a result of our investments in technology and our successful platform and power-train consolidation program, which we began fifteen years ago. These reductions for the consumer have made automotive and personal transportation affordable everywhere and to most families in the world. In fact, our growth in Europe, the United States, and Japan has averaged about 1 percent in this century, while the rest of the world experienced growth in vehicle sales of 10 percent annually.

"Automobiles today use 25 percent as much petroleum on average as they did twenty-five years ago, thanks to extraordinary advances in alternative power, such as electric, solar, and atomic sources. Harmful emissions from autos are well within the safety range published by the UN's Environmental Protection Committee. Global warming is a threat of the past.

"Our partnerships with nations have benefited everyone— higher employment, better economic conditions, and hence better automotive markets. We have worked cooperatively with the World Bank, for example, to bring industry to countries like Albania, Somalia, Chad, Bangladesh, and Nepal, which had none. Even in more developed nations, we have put new plants in high unemployment areas—good politics and economics for the host countries and good business for Colossus and its partners.

"As part of our good citizenship programs, we have supported countless social and educational organizations in cities and towns where we have operations. Our primary focus is to assure an educated, motivated workforce, which we have achieved in areas with hard core poverty. Our Partnership for a Rising Living Standard has worked. We have found that our emphasis on ethics in business and government has had a broad and beneficial impact on people everywhere."

Aviation Industry: Wings of the Bright Side

At the Wings annual meeting earlier in 2025, the chair, Luis Villares of Brazil, gave a similar report on progress over the past ten years. Wings had succeeded in gaining pilot approval for central crew scheduling through an innovative profit-sharing scheme, which gave the pilots 25 percent of the productivity savings in bonuses. A joint Wings–pilot union group oversaw the program, so there were no arguments about the calculations of productivity and hence about the bonus pool. A joint Wings–pilot union committee decided on distribution of the bonuses.

Airline service tied the entire globe together, and thanks to the productivity improvements in every phase of airline operations brought about by the consolidation of the industry, air-travel prices had dropped to the $0.05 to $0.10 per mile range on average from much higher levels. Affordable travel resulted in large annual increases in travel. In the decade ending in 2025, the average annual increase in passenger miles was 8 percent globally.

At the encouragement of the airline industry, an international authority had been established to set safety standards and oversee compliance, supervise the global air-traffic control system, ensure fairness in competitive practices, resolve disputes, oversee industry and airport capacity development, and move all countries to some form of international open skies. The organization was funded by the industry and placed under the supervision of the WTO.

Telecommunications Industry: GlobalLink of the Bright Side

The annual meeting of GlobalLink was a celebration of a major alliance with CompLink, the largest computer and software relationship enterprise. Although the details hadn't been worked out, the vision of a strong relationship between the telecommunications and computer industries might at last be realized.

GlobalLink had established joint-venture partnerships in every country on earth and had a network of four thousand satellites circling the globe and over one hundred space probes monitoring activity throughout the universe. New telecommunications stations on the moon offered interesting promise, but rotational problems had yet to be solved.

GlobalLink had won approval of the wideband frequencies in China by bringing several Chinese partners into GlobalLink and naming two Chinese executives to the GlobalLink council. Working through three major Chinese entrepreneurs, GlobalLink built a telecommunications infrastructure in China in fifteen years that gave virtually every Chinese city, town, and village full access to modern telecommunications technology—and gave the world access to China. A security system worked out with the Chinese government protected the legitimate security interests of the country while providing companies and individuals the privacy and security they required in a highly competitive world.

Influence: Club 2000 of the Bright Side

Back to the Club 2000 conference. The agenda focused on economic development, cooperative activities among the enterprises, and the pace of deregulation in several countries. A day was spent on each topic.

On the first day, the meeting began with a one-hour briefing on the poverty pockets around the world. Progress had been made over the past decade and several countries and poor regions had experienced dramatic increases in per capita income and health care. One of the goals of Club 2000 was to bring its economic power to bear on poor regions to raise them to an acceptable standard of living. The club achieved this goal by setting aside 10 percent of the members' capital budgets for investments in areas with intractable poverty. These investments always included a major share for education and training.

The relationship enterprises had discovered that investing in a country such as Ethiopia had several benefits: cheap labor reduced costs; high-tech equipment protected quality; the hope of a better life drove ambitious people to work hard; and the increased income of the people created markets. The major difference from all past economic development efforts in poor countries—which up to then had never produced the hoped-for results—was that all the funds were private and control of the in-country investments were in joint-venture hands (i.e., a member of the enterprise and local companies). Governments played no direct role in allocating or supervising funds, only in clearing the field of regulations and other obstacles to economic development. In most countries, even education and training programs were run by nongovernment joint ventures.

The presentation concluded with a list of countries that had yet to achieve Club 2000's threshold standard of living. There were twenty target areas—countries and major regions within countries—on the list, compared with fifty a decade earlier. This represented quite an accomplishment, particularly since the threshold for real per capita income had been raised by 25 percent over the decade. These target areas still accounted for 30 percent of the world's population. Three areas were selected for serious discussion: Outer Mongolia, Bangladesh, and Central Africa.

During the afternoon, several projects were discussed for these countries. By the end of the day, there was agreement on ten specific programs across the target areas, with a major training component in each. More than one relationship enterprise was involved in every program. Representatives of the governments attended the session. A list of regulatory changes had been submitted to them in advance for approval from their governments. Without those changes, the projects would not go ahead. Since the media were also told about the potential investments, the countries had to agree with any reasonable request, or their own people would rise up in protest.

The second day was devoted to cooperative activities among enterprises. Great care was taken within Club 2000, as in virtually every relationship enterprise, to avoid even the hint of collusion. Hence cooperative activities never included competitive activities. Rather, the members focused on how they could work together to achieve common objectives—economic and social development were high on the list.

Every relationship enterprise depended on an educated, motivated, healthy, population wherever it produced or sold its goods and services. Hence education, training, and health care were areas open to cooperative activity. The issue on the table was how to prepare people with minimum education and no exposure to work within an organization to be productive employees on enterprise projects and businesses.

By the end of the day, Club 2000 members had signed on to a creative, ambitious, and promising program that they agreed to pilot in Bangladesh. There were 100 million retirees of Club 2000 member enterprises under the age of seventy. A major program was launched to engage at least 1 million of these as mentors, trainers, and coaches for workers in Bangladesh. The companies of the retirees would pick up all their expenses. The program could be the most ambitious and comprehensive effort ever to bring a population into a disciplined, capable workforce.

As not every retiree would be qualified or able, a significantly larger group had to be identified and screened, trained, and culturally prepared for Bangladesh. Similarly, a huge planning effort had to be undertaken to synchronize the development of labor with the availability of projects and work needing that labor. Club 2000 set up a task force under the guidance of the United Nations to handle this planning. We can only hope that the program is successful and can be made to work in the other nineteen countries and regions with hard-core poverty.

The final topic, deregulation, was the most difficult. Deregulation efforts had been going on for many years and were virtually universally supported by Club 2000 members, but financial muscle and the will of Club 2000 were not enough by themselves. Although progress seemed reasonable when viewed over decades, the process was aggravating and difficult. Club 2000 members understood that not all regulation was bad—the aviation industry even recommended formation of a world regulatory body—but many regulations were designed to protect vested interests and maintain a status quo that was rarely in a nation's long-term interest, much less in the interests of global commerce.

The world continued to labor with countries that fostered trade barriers masquerading as ethnic or national preference, temporary measures to allow national industries to get on their feet, or reasonable steps to protect the health and safety of their citizens. Local political forces with vested interests dominated the debate within countries. The countries at issue were China and Ukraine, which had enjoyed enormous growth in their economies over the past twenty-five years.

China's GNP had averaged 7 percent growth and was by far the largest in the world, although on a per capita basis it remained below that of most industrialized nations. China had become a major exporter of manufactured products, electronics, and software development. The problem was a restriction on imports of machinery and parts. To boost internal machinery production, the Chinese had placed requirements on imported machinery making their importation uneconomical.

The Chinese delegation argued persuasively that it had made more progress on deregulation than had any other country and that it was essential that China develop its own machinery industry. It pointed out that it had licensed technology from U.S. and European countries, so China did participate in the growth of the machinery industry through license fees. The WTO in turn argued that the Chinese were protecting their industry so they could charge high prices internally and dump machinery (with modern U.S. and European technology) on the world market at below manufactured cost.

Ukraine had experienced an average 6 percent growth, far exceeding the economic performance of the other former Soviet states, including the oil-rich Caspian countries. Along with the United States and Brazil, Ukraine had become the breadbasket to the world. Several major biotech and food-processing companies led by Monsanto had entered Ukraine in partnership with the government two decades earlier and had piloted revolutionary growing and processing techniques. The soil, weather, and political conditions were so favorable that these companies (which were allied in a relationship enterprise) stayed and poured billions in research and facilities into Ukraine. Ukraine now (2025) produced over 15 percent of the world's wheat, soy, corn, cotton, alfalfa, canola, rapeseed, and sunflower, plus export levels of a wide range of vegetables. Ukraine was the world's largest exporter of feed. Both food and feed products were designed around specialty traits that food processors and animal producers could specify with the precision of a chemistry laboratory.

The problem in Ukraine began in 2010. The Ukrainian government set up privately owned monopolies for food and feed processing. The arrangement was made to retire the country's president, Ivan Petrov, in a peaceful revolution. A law was passed to prohibit any additional processors in the country. The law was modeled after U.S. electric-utility regulations prior to 2005, when the United States deregulation was completed in the industry. The law provided for low prices on food and feed consumed in Ukraine, but allowed prices at world levels on exports. Until 2025, each local processor had been limited to processing 10 percent of total Ukrainian production, which gave it most of the local market and about 5 percent of Ukrainian exports. No one cared much. However, a bill was in the legislature to remove the 10 percent limitation, and the largest bank, which was owned by the Petrov family, was prepared to loan the Petrovs $10 billion to increase capacity fivefold. The result would be to give the Petrov's monopoly processing rights over half the exported agricultural products, or 8 percent of the world's supply of those products.

The Ukrainian delegation argued that Ukraine had every right to allow a local manufacturer, Petrov Processing, to expand. In fact, delegates pointed out, the original law limiting the amount of processing by Petrov to 10 percent of the agricultural output had just been declared unconstitutional by the Ukraine Supreme Court, and, therefore, there was nothing they could do to prevent Petrov from expanding.

The Ukrainian case was particularly difficult because of the power of the Petrovs. Former Ukrainian president and founder of Petrov Processing, Ivan Petrov, had died ten years earlier. His daughter, Olga Ivanovna Petrov, ran the company and the dynasty. She had rebuffed all offers to join relationship enterprises. Why should she? She had a solid position and a cash flow that rivaled that of many oil-rich kingdoms. Petrov was providing low-cost food to millions of poor Ukrainians, and its products on the world market were sold at world prices. Where was the harm?

Club 2000 members saw things differently. The Petrov family was not the Ukrainian government or state. Sovereignty was not the issue. Personal power and wealth were the issues. Giving one family control over 8 percent of the world's food processing was dangerous. Markets and countries could be held hostage. World prices could be affected significantly. Shortages and surpluses could be created by one family. The only analogue was the world's oil supply, which was watched carefully by most major countries. The delicate balance of power, although fragile, was maintained in oil.

Something had to be done in both the Chinese and the Ukrainian situations. After hearing all the arguments pro and con, Club 2000 declared an unusual executive session. Only primary delegates remained. An extraordinary discussion followed.

Surprisingly, the members were split. A small majority believed that free trade was the most important principle to uphold. The others argued that national sovereignty was the higher value. Even though it might be costly to commerce in the short run, the stability of nations was essential for long-term economic growth. In the end, a compromise was reached.

In the case of China, Club 2000 agreed to allow the restrictions on machinery to remain for ten years, during which two relationship enterprises would negotiate terms for the two major Chinese manufacturers to join their enterprises as full partners. They had previously been denied membership because of the trade practices. At the end of the ten-year grace period, imports of parts and whole machines would be allowed duty free. To give the Chinese the incentive to accept the deal, a carrot and stick were added. During the ten-year period, exports would be reduced by 10 percent per year by agreement among the relationship enterprises that purchased Chinese machinery. At the end of the ten-year period, when imports were to be allowed, all license fees would be forgiven. The Chinese instantly agreed.

In the case of Ukraine, Club 2000 believed that the Petrovs' interests had to be aligned with world interests and that there had to be leverage to assure that they operated responsibly in accordance with those interests. Although there was no evidence that the Petrovs had acted counter to world interests in trade, their power would be magnified manyfold by the proposed expansion.

After considerable debate on actions ranging from pleas for reasonableness to harsh sanctions, the conversation focused on secret meetings, recently discovered, between Olga Petrov and Paulo Morales, the Brazilian-born CEO of Monsanto. Paulo Morales, age fifty, had lost his wife in a tragic boating accident ten years earlier.

Monsanto was at the center of a life science relationship enterprise that included several biotech companies, major processors, international traders, food companies, and pharmaceutical firms. The relationship enterprise, named Apollo after the Greek god of prophecy and healing, was the world's largest agribusiness, food and pharmaceutical enterprise and was a key player in every major agricultural area in the world. Its technology had revolutionized agriculture. Productivity of farmland (tons of grain per acre per year) had doubled, and productivity of individual plants had increased manyfold. Plants were engineered to produce more oil or more protein or special minerals or other characteristics. Plants had become the primary source of plastics, and the plastics were biodegradable. Apollo was very important to Ukraine. And now Petrov Processing was becoming very important to Apollo.

Reluctantly, Morales briefed Club 2000 on the partnership with Petrov Processing, which was in the final stage of negotiation. If concluded, Petrov would become the most important processor in Apollo. Apollo would invest in a major plastic plant in Ukraine, which would make Ukraine one of the world's largest biodegradable plastic exporters.

One month later, Petrov Processing joined Apollo, and six months later, the engagement of Paulo Morales and Olga Petrov was announced.

— ❖ —

There can be no conclusion to this chapter that satisfies. We have seen two worlds that could evolve—both born of the same conditions at the end of the twentieth century, and assuming a similar structure of world industry. Both begin in a similar fashion. Nevertheless, these two ships chart very different courses and produce radically different worlds. Which shall it be, and how can we influence the outcome?

How We Can Influence the Outcome

The first task in initiating the debate on the trillion-dollar enterprise is to set out the areas in which influence is desirable and possible. If neither you nor the companies you will work with in your career will be affected by relationship enterprises, then you need not be concerned about influencing their development. This chapter is for the rest of us.

In some countries relationship enterprises will begin to develop earlier than in others. Governments that are early movers in dealing with relationship enterprises will set the course for the rest of the world.

TRILLION-DOLLAR ENTERPRISES: ADVANTAGES

Let us examine how trillion-dollar enterprises can help a nation and what could be done to encourage that help.

Investment and Jobs

Probably the biggest potential advantage of having relationship enterprise partners in your country is investment. The enterprises will have large investments, consolidated across companies, that will be far greater than the investments of any single partner. The challenge will be to attract that investment.

Direct investment in plants, equipment, and training is the lifeblood of every economy. The investment budgets of trillion-dollar enterprises will dwarf those of any current corporations. Thousands of jobs will follow their investments; training and developing people to perform valuable tasks will be integral to their method of operation. This makes sense when you look at investments from the perspective of the trillion-dollar enterprise. It wants to achieve the optimal economic scale (which normally means very large); it wants a highly skilled workforce (which means top-notch training and support of the educational community that is the pipeline of future talent); it wants supporting businesses (which can mean building a strong local supply base and efficient distribution system). The trillion-dollar enterprise wants favorable living conditions to attract talented managers and employees (which means support of cultural, civic and recreational institutions), and as a result will multiply local investments. All these factors—stirring economic activity, raising GNP, creating jobs, bringing social (and therefore political) stability, raising tax revenue—make a trillion-dollar enterprise a very desirable neighbor.

The levers available to countries to attract investments are well known and used often—tax incentives; government support of critical areas for investors, such as regulatory relief; special training; and preferred land arrangements. The problem with these sorts of inducements is that they are available to most nations, and the price of attracting good investors (and trillion-dollar enterprises will be among the best) will be bid up to levels at which most of the value created for the country will be given away.

Nations need to be much more creative in attracting foreign investments, particularly from sophisticated investors such as trillion-dollar enterprises. Rather than approaching the problem by reducing the front-end transaction costs for the investor, consider how your location can be the most profitable long term for the investor and build your case and your concessions around that perspective. At least you'll be unique.

Capabilities

To the extent that a trillion-dollar enterprise is active in your country, it creates world-class capabilities. The fundamental purpose of the relationship enterprise is to have advantaged market access and the best capabilities the world can generate in its industry. The most important competitive advantage a nation can have lies in its capabilities—the best place in the world to make wine, to make steel, to create biotech breakthroughs, to develop sophisticated software, to make textiles. Each nation attracts business because of its markets and its capabilities. If a nation has markets but no capabilities, it will not be able to import goods for very long. If it has capabilities but no market, the market will develop quickly as the country leverages its capabilities and builds an affluent populace and therefore a consumer base.

The moral of the story is simple: if a company or enterprise can help build your country's capabilities, go for it. Recognize that you are competing with other nations to attract the trillion-dollar enterprise. You need to determine the areas in which the trillion-dollar enterprise will be able to build world-class capabilities in your country or region. Making this determination requires a penetrating and objective evaluation of what your people and your country can and can't do better than anyone else.

Balance of Trade

The trillion-dollar enterprise's network generates substantial trade flows. Where it manufactures, it creates exports; where it sells and distributes, it creates imports. Clearly, its decisions on plant locations and target markets will have a major impact on balance of trade. I am on the side of such economists as Fred Bergsten, who voiced his opinion in his article "Globalizing Free Trade" in *Foreign Affairs* in 1996.

> Economic success in today's world requires countries to liberalize to attract mobile international investment, which goes far to determine the distribution of global production, jobs, profits, and technology. Success also requires countries to compete effectively in international markets rather than simply at home. A process of competitive liberalization, therefore, has driven the trend toward

free trade among a myriad of countries in all parts of the world with very different economic systems, at very different stages of development, and with very different prior philosophies.

Free trade is the oxygen that allows the trillion-dollar enterprise to breathe and grow. The enterprise consists of a series of world-class manufacturing, research, marketing, and distribution capabilities spread across the world in the most advantageous locations, each supporting the other in a giant supply chain. The enterprise is better equipped than the global corporation to leap over protectionist obstacles, but a global system turned inward and protectionist will eventually suffocate any global organization structure.

In summary, the trillion-dollar enterprise can bring substantial economic benefits to the countries of its partners. The enterprise can also raise a country's political stature in the world to the extent that the enterprise supports the country's political agenda in world forums.

TRILLION-DOLLAR ENTERPRISES: PROTECTION FROM THE DARK SIDE

Now let's look at the other side of the coin. What does your country need to protect itself from trillion-dollar enterprises? The Dark Side case in Chapter 10 offered just a few examples of how a trillion-dollar enterprise could coerce a country. There are many ways in which such an enterprise could intrude on the internal activities and well–being of a country. My list follows.

Jobs and Workers

Ethan Kapstein, Stassen Professor of International Peace at the University of Minnesota, observed in *Foreign Affairs* that "growing income inequality, job insecurity, and unemployment are widely seen as the flip side of globalization." He further noted that the social contract of the post–World War II industrialized world of "full employment and comprehensive social welfare" is being broken by fierce competition in the global economy and fiscally conservative governments. Masses of workers are being displaced; and the safety net and required retraining are inadequate to soften and smooth workers' transitions because balanced budgets come first. Kapstein argues, "Easing pressures on the 'losers' of the new open economy must now be the focus of economic policy if . . . globalization is to be sustained."

The trillion-dollar enterprise will certainly cause dislocation in the workforce as it redeploys investment and jobs from one country to another. The losing country is left to pick up the pieces—economic support and training for its displaced workers. The very economic policies necessary to attract the trillion-dollar enterprise—stable currency, low inflation, fiscal conservatism, low taxes, limited restrictions on employment practices—snap back harshly on the workers who lose their jobs. The converse is also true. "Any state that deviates from 'responsible' economic policies will be punished by currency markets and bond holders," says Kapstein. Hence the nation that protects its workers by providing comfortable safety nets and training and by regulating employment practices will be an unattractive suitor for international capital, and certainly unattractive to the trillion-dollar enterprise.

This is a Catch-22 for countries. Countries must be competitive, yet must protect their citizens. The solution is likely to be found, much as it is for corporations, in creative approaches to contingency planning and reserves for crises.

Balance of Trade

International trade is a two-edged sword: exports and imports. Virtually every government seeks higher exports, and all want positive balances of trade. Of course, arithmetic will not allow 165 nations to have positive balances of trade. The trillion-dollar enterprise will have a major impact on the balance of trade of many nations. It will also have a major impact on the volume of trade, as it parcels out segments of the value chain that come together in a product or service, creating substantial intra-enterprise trade before a final product is created. Exporting the final product then creates more trade.

I do not believe that reducing a nation's exposure to swings in trade balances by reducing trade is an appropriate response. I do think free trade wins in the long term and that short-term setbacks to a country should result in its preparing a better plan for the future.

Strong support for international organizations, such as the WTO, is important, because an impartial referee with clout can bring even giant enterprises into line. Creating new international organizations, for example, a world currency board or world aviation authority, is not a bad idea, either.

National Laws and Regulations

Each country has laws and regulations designed to meet its societal goals. The WTO and other international organizations are trying to make sure that laws and regulations are not designed or employed to restrict trade. Trillion-dollar enterprises may be considered a threat to a number of legal and regulatory areas not only because they might violate national rules, but also because they might use their leverage to change laws in their favor.

The areas of greatest concern are antitrust, currency transactions, environmental protection, labor, and securities. I am not suggesting that trillion-dollar enterprises and their partners will break the law. To the contrary, they are likely to adhere religiously to national laws, regulations, and customs. Remember that being at home in many countries is one of the fundamental reasons for the existence of trillion-dollar enterprises. Rather, I believe that there are some areas in which trillion-dollar enterprises could transgress national laws more easily than could multinational corporations. Appropriate policies will be discussed in the next section.

Sovereignty

Although the definition of *sovereignty* may vary among nations, part of everyone's definition is political and economic independence of a country. The issue of sovereignty has been central to the discussions on the European Community. Do you lose (some, all) sovereignty if you cease to have a national currency? If you cede central bank functions? If you submit to the Community's legislation? If you give up cherished social policies, fiscal policies, government ownership to meet group norms? Supporters of EC would say no emphatically. Opponents of EC would say yes just as emphatically.

The trillion-dollar enterprise can also threaten sovereignty. Opponents to trillion-dollar enterprises will argue that although a national company that is a partner in a trillion-dollar enterprise may legally belong to the country and its citizen shareholders, its soul will be owned by foreign interests. They will argue that these alliances violate antitrust laws in spirit, if not in fact. They will argue that key decisions impacting the nation (e.g., investments, trade flows, currency handling, job dislocations) will be made by others not legally established in the country. They will argue that the nation's interests will be subordinated to the enterprise's interests, and that national social and economic priorities will be trampled by the power of the giant. They will argue that their culture will be blended into obscurity by the influence of these global giants.

The Dark Side case showed how sovereignty could be trampled by the trillion-dollar enterprise. Protection and preservation of national sovereignty is a fundamental duty of government. The citizens of a country must define core sovereignty, and the government must understand what constitutes a threat to that sovereignty and put plans and laws in place to protect it.

PUBLIC POLICY

The trillion-dollar enterprise raises important public policy questions, some of which have already been mentioned. My intent here is to present policy issues from a global economic and political perspective, rather than from a national perspective. I will set the questions and framework for debate rather than attempt to provide answers for our national and international leaders. I have structured the discussion around four policy areas.

Antitrust

Antitrust laws are built around ownership and collusion. Antitrust laws are national—you have to violate a particular nation's laws to be guilty. In most countries, antitrust laws exist to guarantee free competition and to avoid concentrations of power that may result in monopolistic behavior. Other laws exist to prevent competitors from restraining trade through price fixing or carving up the market.

Alliances present a real challenge to the intent and power of antitrust laws. The trillion-dollar enterprise raises the challenge to a very serious level. Our first task is to define antitrust in the global economy. How and where is it relevant?

Is a network of companies bonded together into a trillion-dollar enterprise, and going to market as a single enterprise, a restraint of trade? Is joint R&D, product development, engineering, manufacturing, and distribution, as described in Chapter 8, restraint of trade, collusion, or an antitrust violation? Should competitors, such as Deutsche Telekom, France Telecom, and Sprint, be able to form an alliance and agree on the price of their combined service? Should American Airlines, British Airways, Japan Air Lines, and six other partners jointly set price, schedules, and service levels across the globe and even on competing routes? Is the trillion-dollar enterprise simply an elaborate scheme to circumvent antitrust laws and enable global price fixing?

All these events are happening, and with the trillion-dollar enterprise, they will accelerate. Today we have no mechanism to ensure the competitive freedom of the global economy. Should a current organization (e.g., WTO, or IMF) have responsibility? Should we create a new global antitrust cop? Or, should we adopt a laissez-faire approach and let countries fend for themselves?

Consolidation of Economic Power

Even if we can solve the antitrust problem to the satisfaction of most world communities, we cannot ignore the immense economic power that a trillion-dollar enterprise will have. The Dark Side scenario illustrated the threat of this power to individual countries. Just imagine a world with four auto enterprises, three telecommunications enterprises, four airline enterprises, two aerospace enterprises, and five media enterprises controlling more than half their respective industries worldwide. Today we worry about the power of a $100 billion multinational corporation. We are faced with a tenfold increase in size and an even greater increase in power.

Economic concentration has been an eternal concern of economists. Suddenly a new formula has been developed that avoids many of the disadvantages of size (e.g., bureaucratic, slow to move, indecisive, inefficient, risk averse, uncreative, not entrepreneurial). The trillion-dollar enterprise captures the best capabilities of its partners and does not tamper with the entrepreneurial spirit, creative genes, or low-cost mentality. At its best, it will be swift to move and capable of action far beyond any corporation alone.

If the trillion-dollar enterprise reaches its potential, it will have enormous economic power. It will be able to create new industries within countries; shuffle billions of dollars and multiple currencies around the world daily; shift trade balances; meaningfully raise or lower the GNP of a country; influence laws, regulations, and customs to its benefit; and become the focal point of national and international economic and political policy. We can easily imagine the enterprises accelerating the shift to three international currencies— ECU (European currency unit), U.S. dollar, and possibly the yen— with all other currencies pegged to one or a basket of the three.

Consolidation of economic power will enable major dislocations of workers and greenmail of countries into agreeing to actions favorable to the enterprise, such as reducing competition, raising price levels, and raising or lowering currency values.

Over the past twenty to thirty years, the nations of the world and their international organizations have figured out more or less how to control large, multinational corporations and how to manage large and growing trade and capital flows. They have learned how to deal with trade imbalances, hyperinflation, and currency failure, and are learning how to handle financial derivatives, reckless traders, and bandit nations. But they've never thought about an enterprise with the size, reach, and power of the trillion-dollar enterprise. They've never considered the possibility that global industries could be controlled by two or three entities. It's time they did.

Emerging Nations

Trillion-dollar enterprises will probably have their greatest impact on emerging nations. Although it's unlikely that these enterprises will dramatically raise or damage the standard of living in the United States, they have the power to be a savior or a devil to emerging nations. They can build an industry in a country; they can develop natural resources and create great wealth for a nation; they can build capabilities in a country that will enable it to compete as it never could; they can raise a nation's level of education and standard of living. On the other hand, trillion-dollar enterprises can exploit workers through low wages and poor conditions, deriving great economic benefits for themselves and sharing little. These enterprises can exploit rather than develop a nation's natural resources, driving very tough negotiations in which the leverage is all on one side because the emerging nation's options are limited. They can violate the environment in a nation that has no laws or little will to save its environment at the cost of losing jobs that these enterprises can create. Trillion-dollar enterprises can trample the culture, ignore regulations, mistreat workers, and violate laws with the impunity of a bully, in return for jobs and hope of a better life for the nation's citizens. This scenario is not unreasonable; we have seen this behavior in the twentieth century.

Who will protect the emerging nations? We have organizations such as the WTO that help them join the world trading community. We have the IMF, the World Bank, and regional development banks (e.g., InterAmerican Development Bank, Asian Development ment Bank) to stabilize economies and finance their growth. We have the United Nations to protect their national security and the World Health Organization to prevent epidemics. But we have no one to protect them from a powerful economic bully. Do we need some organization to take on this task? Or should we trust in the goodness of humankind to do the right thing in the developing world even if it has the power to behave otherwise? It is crucial that these questions be addressed directly rather than by default.

Universal Capitalism

The trillion-dollar enterprise is a capitalist invention. It is the ultimate capitalist tool. It presumes that the global economy is capitalist, and it has the power to move noncapitalist economies toward capitalism.

Those in the world who believe that capitalism is the right economic system should applaud the trillion-dollar enterprise. Those who support other systems should oppose its development with all their strength. I suppose the acceptance or imposition of capitalism is an odd issue to raise. After the fall of communism in the Soviet Union, the liberation of Eastern Europe, and the slide to the capitalist road in China, who would disagree that capitalism is the best and only economic system that nations should pursue? Remember that for all its merits, capitalism is only a few hundred years old, and one could argue that capitalism in its current form (free competition, free market forces, free trade) has evolved since World

War II, even though it was born in *Wealth of Nations* by Adam Smith in the eighteenth century.

Government intervention continues on a major scale in some countries. Socialism puts serious restrictions on capitalism. The social contract in many nations of full employment and a good safety net requires boundaries on free capitalism. We are now faced with an entity that, left alone, could return us to the unfettered capitalism that spawned the robber barons and corporate moguls of the late nineteenth and early twentieth centuries in the United States and Europe and the *zaibatsu* of Japan.

I believe deeply that capitalism is the right economic system. I also believe in the economic freedom of sovereign nations, which may take them in directions different from capitalism. The concern, therefore, is the freedom of nations to choose, and the potential of the trillion-dollar enterprise to force that choice.

IN SEARCH OF AN ANSWER

There is no clear answer to the question, Is the trillion-dollar enterprise good or bad for the world? Like all other complex policy questions, it depends. One thing is clear: governments, economists, and international organizations should begin debating how to deal with these enterprises, and the sooner, the better.

We cannot predict the future. The best we can do is observe trends and forces in a historical context and imagine where they will take us. In observing the political and economic forces on corporations and industries and the benefits of consolidation, I have concluded that a world of large enterprises will emerge. This new world may look like the one I have described, or it may be different. We can be certain, however, that consolidation will continue as the economic stage moves from national to regional to global. We can be certain that collaboration will be a major and potentially the dominant vehicle for consolidation as we move into the twenty-first century. We can be certain that alliances will continue to evolve (as they have in the past twenty years) toward deeper, more strategically central collaborations of corporations as they strive to become global leaders in their industries. In my view this evolution will lead to networks of companies bonded together by series of alliances that eventually will see the power in joint action as a single entity. Hence I see the evolution toward the relationship enterprises and their ultimate offspring, the trillion-dollar enterprise, as inevitable.

Whether or not you agree with my conclusion, you should see that the road is leading in that direction. Consequently, you should be prepared—whether you are an aspiring young professional, a senior executive of a global corporation, or a political leader.

I believe that the creation of relationship enterprises and their successors, trillion-dollar enterprises, is hopeful and positive for the world economy and for the standard of living for most of the world's population. If the world's population growth slows to 1 percent in the twenty-first century, there will be almost three times as many people living on earth in 2100 as there are today. The vast majority of those additional people will be living outside today's industrial nations—Europe, North America, and a few Asian countries. In raw numbers, we will have 10 billion more people in the developing world to feed and house and clothe and who need jobs and health care and pensions—and who consume Cokes and Walkmen and cars and computers.

I am optimistic that human creativity and ingenuity will carry us across the twenty-first century successfully. Biotech will enable us to feed the additional 10 billion people and ensure a healthier and longer life. Electronics will enable us to educate, communicate, and advance the productivity of the masses. Other technologies will save our environment, extend our natural resources, provide our energy, and make life easier and more fun. Just as happened in the twentieth century.

The trillion-dollar enterprise is coming, and there is an important place for it in the world economy of the twenty-first century. There is so much to do to prepare for it. The power of the trillion-dollar enterprise must be harnessed to create a better life.

Notes

Unattributed quotes and references are based on the author's interviews and nonproprietary information from client engagements. Substantial information has been drawn from Booz·Allen research projects. Citations are noted for published information. Some information has not previously been published.

Booz·Allen has granted permission to use its research data and nonproprietary client information. The conclusions drawn, however, are the author's.

Chapter 1

page 7: Martin Feldstein, professor of economics, Harvard University, and president of the National Bureau of Economic Research; former chairman, Council of Economic Advisors for President Reagan, *New York Times*, 1996.

page 8: Irving Kristol, *New York Times*, 1997, Op Ed. Also refer to Martin Feldstein and Charles Horioka, "Domestic Savings and International Capital Flows," The W.A. Mackintosh Lecture at Queens University, *Economic Journal*, June 1980.

page 15: Christian de Duve, *Vital Dust* (New York: HarperCollins Publishers, Basic Books, 1995), p. 274. Dr. de Duve is a Nobel laureate in biochemistry who has devoted the past twenty years to research and thought on the origins and evolution of life. An evening with Dr. de Duve is an extraordinary and enriching experience.

page 19: Dani Rodrik, "Sense and Nonsense in the Globalization Debate," *Foreign Affairs,* July/August 1997. Also see Dani Rodrik, "Has Globalization Gone Too Far?" Institute for International Economics, Washington, D.C., March 1997.

page 19: Timothy Lassiter, *Balanced Sourcing* (San Francisco: Jossey-Bass, Inc., October 1998).

page 22: Carlos Fuentes, "Another French Chance to Make Idealism Work," *Herald Tribune,* 18 June 1997.

page 22: Tom Friedman, "Foreign Affairs: Politics in the Age of NAFTA," *New York Times,* 7 April, 1996.

page 22–23: Michael Sandel, *Democracy's Discovery* (Cambridge: Harvard University Press, April 1996).

page 23: William Greider, *One World, Ready or Not: The Manic Logic of Global Capitalism* (New York: Simon & Schuster, 1997).

page 24–25: James Hoge, editor's note, *Foreign Affairs,* Summer 1995.

Chapter 2

Note: Data on alliances were drawn heavily from research by Dr. Peter Pekar, visiting associate professor at London School of Economics and senior advisor to Booz·Allen & Hamilton, and John Harbison, senior vice president of Booz·Allen & Hamilton and director of the Center on Mergers, Acquisitions, and Alliances. Much of the research has been published by Booz·Allen in a series of copyrighted *Viewpoints:* "A Practical Guide to Alliances: Leapfrogging the Learning Curve," 1993; "Cross Border Alliances in the Age of Collaboration," 1997; and "Institutional Alliance Skills: Secrets of Repeatable Success," 1997.

Students of strategic alliances should read the recently published *Smart Alliances* (San Francisco: Jossey-Bass, Inc., November 1998) by John R. Harbison and Peter Pekar, Jr.

page 49: M. Y. Yoshimo and U. S. Rangan, *Strategic Alliances: An Entrepreneurial Approach to Globalization* (Boston: Harvard Business School Press, 1995), p. 103.

Chapter 3

page 54: Motorola's satellite investments, which include Iridium, a sixty-six-satellite voice system and a larger data and voice system, have been publicly announced several times by Motorola and have been widely published in the financial and telecommunications press.

page 64: Corning's published reports, including its annual 10K, include sales and investments in joint ventures.
page 69: The history of Mitsui was drawn in large part from John O. Roberts, *Mitsui: Three Centuries of Japanese Business* (New York and Tokyo: John Weatherkill 1973).

Chapter 4
page 86: *Automotive News,* published by Crains, reports market shares in the United States on a weekly basis.
page 87: Ford publishes its ownership of various subsidiaries and joint ventures in its annual 10K.
page 88: "Toyota and GM are each other's largest customer," from private discussions with top executives of Toyota and GM. Subsequent checking with GM resulted in the less expansive version of their relationship used in the book.

Chapter 5
page 105–107: Best practices were derived from the studies conducted in 1993, 1995, and 1997. See the notes for Chapter 2 for the publications from which most of the data have been drawn.
page 111–112 The survey on alliance capabilities was reported in a Booz·Allen *Viewpoint:* "Cross Border Alliances in the Age of Collaboration." Details on the best practices of all one hundred subtasks are proprietary to Booz·Allen and are used exclusively on client engagements.

Chapter 6
page 126: James O'Toole, *Leading Change: Overcoming the Ideology of Comfort and the Tyranny of Custom* (San Francisco: Jossey-Bass Publications, 1995). Also see James O'Toole, *Leading Change: The Argument for Values-Based Leadership* (New York: Ballantine Books, 1996).
page 127: Example for "Creative Plan to Bridge Management Style of Partners" was taken from a client engagement in 1997.

Chapter 7
page 163: The HP case was obtained by Booz·Allen interviews and analysis.
page 166: Jan Carlzon, *Moments of Truth* (New York: HarperCollins Publishers, 1989), p 135.

Chapter 8

Note: The leadership concepts discussed in this chapter are derived heavily from research and lectures by Jim O'Toole. These concepts are the foundation of Booz·Allen's leadership and training programs for partners.

page 174–James O'Toole, *Vanguard Management* (Garden City, NY: 175:   Doubleday, 1985).

page 178: Bob Shapiro's comment on leadership was made to the Booz·Allen advisory board in July 1997.

page 178: Jan Carlzon, *Moments of Truth,* (New York: Harper-Collins Publishers, 1989).

Chapter 9

page 184: Alfred P. Sloan, *My Years at General Motors,* (Doubleday, 1963).

page 185, Carolyn Brancato, Conference Board, Governance Research 186, 187: Report. Ms. Brancato has conducted several research projects on corporate governance and the impact of the rising share of public equities held by institutions such as mutual funds and pension funds.

Note: Several of the concepts used in the book were derived from Ms. Brancato's conference board projects, in which I was a participant.

The governance conferences sponsored by Kellogg Graduate School of Management, Booz·Allen, and Spenser Stuart were a rich field of ideas from which I drew heavily.

page 185–The *New York Times* ran a series on the power of the Chi 186:   nese in Southeast Asia in 1997. Several other countries, such as Thailand, Indonesia, and Vietnam, had similarly few overseas Chinese controlling large shares of private business.

page 187: Judge William Allen has made this statement at several conferences. He told the author that this is his belief.

page 189: Carolyn Brancato, "New Corporate Performance Measures: A Research Report," Conference Board, New York, 1995.

Chapter 11

page 226–Fred Bergsten, "Globalizing Free Trade," *Foreign Affairs,* 227:   May/June 1996, p. 105.

page 227–Ethan B. Kapstein, "Workers and the World Economy," 228:   *Foreign Affairs,* May/June 1996, p. 17.

Author's Note

The Trillion-Dollar Enterprise was in development for six years. The concept was framed at a Booz·Allen Advisory Board meeting in Paris in October 1992 and has been shaped and built and verified by events of the ensuing years. The forces of globalization and nationalism have intensified and the desire for size and potential market dominance through consolidation have played out continually through the mega-mergers and explosion of alliances over the six-year period. The book is not a technical treatise for practitioners, but rather it presents a stage on which the managers, professionals and leaders of the future will act out the first part of the twenty-first century.

My sons, Stephen and Scott, chided me from their Wall Street bases that I should move to publication more quickly because the concepts in *The Trillion-Dollar Enterprise* were materializing in the news. In my view, the timing of the publication is good—enough evidence is at hand to confirm the forces and trends that I believe will lead to relationship enterprises and their giant offspring, the *Trillion-Dollar Enterprise*. Some industries—like telecommunications, commercial aviation, and public accounting—are already close to or actually operating as relationship enterprises. *Keiretsu* have been firmly established for a long time. The leap from concept to reality is no longer as daunting as it was when

I first presented the *Trillion-Dollar Enterprise* publicly at the World Economic Forum in Davos in February of 1993.

The Trillion-Dollar Enterprise was written because I believe the message is important. At a personal level, I wished to leave something valuable to a broader audience than the clients I have served over the past thirty-two years. My profession is privileged to be exposed to many companies in many industries and in many countries. This has given me the good fortune to work with some of the most talented business executives in fifteen countries and almost every industry on issues of critical importance. At Booz·Allen, I have been challenged continually for all these years by extraordinarily bright and knowledgeable people. The lessons learned have been countless and the book draws heavily on these experiences and lessons.

The best creative work is done by teams and collaborators. This was clearly the case with the *Trillion-Dollar Enterprise*. The conclusions, of course, are mine.

My partners at Booz·Allen were key to every aspect of the book. John Harbison and Peter Pekar allowed me inside their comprehensive research on alliances at the same time they were writing their fine book, *Smart Alliances,* which is certainly recommended reading to all interested in building relationship enterprises.

Jim O'Toole fathered the concept of values-based leadership which I believe is crucial to successful management and leadership in the relationship enterprise. Jim's ideas are the backbone of Chapter 8. Jim also guided me to several other valuable books and examples used in *The Trillion-Dollar Enterprise.*

Many other partners provided examples from their client experience and perspectives on their industries, allowing me the luxury of building the case for *The Trillion-Dollar Enterprise* on real-life, inside experiences. Paul Anderson, Tom Hansson, Charlie Beever, Bruce Pasternack, Etienne Deffarges, John Treat, Marty Hyman, and Dan Lewis were particularly generous.

The Booz·Allen Advisory Board gets full credit for hatching the core idea for *The Trillion-Dollar Enterprise* in Paris in 1992, particularly Larry Fuller of Amoco. Bob Galvin of Motorola coached me at several points during the writing journey. Bob is one of the most extraordinary management thinkers of our time. Many of his ideas are in the book. Several other advisory board members provided valuable insights—Bob Shapiro of Monsanto; Bob Bauman, now of RBT; Didier Pineau-Valencienne of Schneider; John Prescott of BHP; and David Young, formerly of Cable & Wireless.

Dr. Henry Kissinger and Renato Ruggiero, head of the World Trade Organization, played particularly important roles. As we traveled through China together, I noticed that Henry was writing his book, *Diplomacy,* in long hand (which I have also done). He gave me encouragement and ideas at several points. The geopolitical slant of the book was inspired by him. Renato honored me by reading a full draft of *The Trillion-Dollar Enterprise,* despite his back-breaking schedule, and by giving me a thoughtful critique. All of his ideas were incorporated.

Several busy executives took the time to read the draft manuscript and to make constructive suggestions. Alex Trotman and Ed Hagenlocker of Ford, Jack Smith of GM, and Bob Lutz of Chrysler provided valuable input on the automotive sections. John Edwardson of United, John Richman, formerly of Kraft, Doug Ford and Richard Flury of Amoco provided ideas, understanding, and examples from their industries. Don Perkins, member of multiple boards, and Carolyn Brancato of the Conference Board have been my lighthouse on governance. Jim Kackley, Managing Partner–Finance and Administration of Anderson Worldwide guided me through the creation of one of the most successful relationship enterprises, Anderson Worldwide. My good friend, Don Clark of Household International, kept me away from the edge of fantasy with good humor and carefully directed jibes to be practical.

Nobel Laureate Christian de Duve raised my sights during a weekend we spent together and through his extraordinary book, *Vital Dust.* The *Economist* deserves a special thanks for having the foresight (bravery) to include a full-page article in February of 1993 on the *Trillion-Dollar Enterprise* as it was presented in Davos. Their confidence in the idea inspired me to push forward with the research to build the idea into a book.

The great team of publishers, editors, and proofreaders at Perseus Books had extraordinary patience and professionalism in guiding a first-time author from very rough drafts to a polished, professional conclusion. Special thanks to Nick Philipson, Eric

Rickstad, Lynne Reed, Carolyn Savarese, Elizabeth Carduff, and Hope Steele. Bob Dilenschneider of the Dilenschneider Group encouraged me to press on, and introduced me to my fine agent, Reid Boates, who worked harder for me than he ever expected. Paul Brown helped craft my speech in Davos and lent valuable support to making the drafts of the book readable and interesting. Thanks to you all for turning me into an author.

Dr. Roy Herberger, President of Thunderbird–The American Graduate School of International Management, and Dean Don Jacobs, head of Northwestern Kellogg School of Management, have been my mentors in considering the changes required in graduate business education. My involvement as Chairman of the Board at Thunderbird has shown me the extraordinary possibility that graduate education can offer in molding managers of the future.

Indispensable to the effort was my executive assistant, Vicki Anderson, who wondered deep into the tenth or twentieth draft if the book would ever be completed. Current events kept driving new examples. Vicki was a full partner in the effort as I drew heavily upon her Phi Betta Kappa in English and her good spirit to assure we got the job done.

Finally, my wife, Mitzi, deserves the most credit for the completion of *The Trillion-Dollar Enterprise*. At all stages, she served as my sounding board, my editor, and my inspiration to keep plugging away at the book. Little did we know what a monumental effort writing a book can be—forget about vacations! And my children, Lynn, Stephen, and Scott, freely gave their uncensored editorial comments, which were always welcomed and valued.

Index